A Livable Planet

A Livable Planet

Human Rights in the Global Economy

MADISON POWERS

OXFORD
UNIVERSITY PRESS

Oxford University Press is a department of the University of Oxford. It furthers the University's objective of excellence in research, scholarship, and education by publishing worldwide. Oxford is a registered trade mark of Oxford University Press in the UK and certain other countries.

Published in the United States of America by Oxford University Press
198 Madison Avenue, New York, NY 10016, United States of America.

© Oxford University Press 2024

All rights reserved. No part of this publication may be reproduced, stored in a retrieval system, or transmitted, in any form or by any means, without the prior permission in writing of Oxford University Press, or as expressly permitted by law, by license, or under terms agreed with the appropriate reproduction rights organization. Inquiries concerning reproduction outside the scope of the above should be sent to the Rights Department, Oxford University Press, at the address above.

You must not circulate this work in any other form and you must impose this same condition on any acquirer.

Library of Congress Cataloging-in-Publication Data
Names: Powers, Madison, author.
Title: A livable planet : human rights in the global economy / Madison Powers.
Description: New York, NY : Oxford University Press, [2024] | Includes bibliographical references and index.
Identifiers: LCCN 2023046752 | ISBN 9780197756003 (hardback) | ISBN 9780197756027 (epub) | ISBN 9780197756034 (ebook)
Subjects: LCSH: Environmental justice. | Human rights—Economic asepcts. | Environmental degradation. | International economic relations.
Classification: LCC GE220 .P72 2024 | DDC 333.72—dc23/eng/20231106
LC record available at https://lccn.loc.gov/2023046752

DOI: 10.1093/oso/9780197756003.001.0001

Printed by Integrated Books International, United States of America

Contents

1. Our Ecological Predicament	1
Convergent Crises	1
Summary of Chapters	7
2. Sustainability and Political Economy	16
Conceptions of Sustainability	17
The Logic of Capitalism	25
Psychological Explanations	30
Economic Growth	34
The By-Product of Inequality	42
Practical Implications	46
3. Market Fundamentalism	48
Market Fundamentalism and Neoliberal Policies	49
Three Rationales for Market Fundamentalism	52
The Non-Interference Conception of Freedom	66
4. Human Rights and Ecological Goals	74
The Normative Framework of Human Rights	75
Rights, Duties, and Structural Inequality	82
Three Problems of Application	90
Rights, Duties, and Violations	97
5. Market Power and Legal Advantage	114
The Consolidation of Market Power	115
The Realignment of State Power	128
Gaming the System of States	135
Control over Capital Investment	140
6. Land Use and Its Consequences	149
Farmland and Food Security	151
Impacts Beyond Land	158

vi CONTENTS

Forests and Biosphere Integrity	167
Land and Human Rights	179

7. Water and Social Organization — 182
The Management of Scarcity — 183
The Political Economy of Water Resources — 194
The Privatization of Essential Services — 204

8. Energy Transition Pathways — 216
False Hopes — 217
False Starts — 230
Path Dependencies — 238
Human Rights and Alternative Pathways — 246

9. Control over the Future — 249
Wealth and Power — 250
Sovereign States and Global Problems — 255

Notes — 263
Index — 307

1

Our Ecological Predicament

Convergent Crises

This book argues for a targeted human rights approach, assigning enhanced priority to a bundle of rights strategically important for counteracting ecologically unsustainable, economically predatory market practices that threaten our ability to maintain a livable planet. Specifically, it calls for enhanced protection for dual-purpose human rights. These rights not only secure the very basic elements of well-being that ground many of those rights, but they perform their normative function, in significant part, by imposing duties on states to protect the ecological conditions that sustain human life and make possible the satisfaction of basic needs and by giving individual right-holders more control over their ecological futures. High-priority, dual-purpose rights include rights of subsistence, food, and water, and rights that protect against serious environmental health risks and ecological degradation.

Climate disruption is perhaps the most obvious example of the rapidly unfolding ecological destruction unleashed by the scale, pace, and character of human impact on the rest of nature. However, humanity faces a more encompassing ecological predicament consisting of a cluster of concurrent, mutually reinforcing crises. The cluster also includes land-system change resulting in deforestation and soil degradation, loss of biodiversity and biosphere integrity, alteration of biogeochemical cycles, and decreased freshwater availability. Individually and in combination, these crises pose civilizational threats of such magnitude and complexity that

A Livable Planet. Madison Powers, Oxford University Press. © Oxford University Press 2024.
DOI: 10.1093/oso/9780197756003.003.0001

2 A LIVABLE PLANET

they challenge the ability of individuals to comprehend them and the capacities of institutions to respond.

There is no shortage of urgent ecological problems resulting from the ways humans and other organisms relate to each other and their shared physical environment, and plenty of other global crises pose civilizational challenges, but four reasons explain the focus on this specific cluster.[1]

First, the five crises are causally intertwined, resistant to resolution in isolation, often regionally variable in impact, but increasingly global in scale. Their unsustainable ecological effects are multiple, including resource depletion, ecosystem destruction, and planetary destabilization. Comprehensive and durable solutions to each crisis will require attention to the causes and consequences of other crises if we are to avoid cascading spillover effects.

Second, the urgency of each these five crises is reflected in the growing risks of irreversible transgression of planetary boundaries which mark the parameters of a "safe operating space for humanity."[2] The continued operation of key biophysical systems and processes within safe boundaries is critically important because they regulate the stability and resilience of the Earth system and maintain the conditions in which human societies have evolved over the past 11,000 years. For all five of these crises, it is now widely believed that the system boundaries have been crossed as the result of human activities.[3] Moreover, two of these five boundaries, climate change and biosphere integrity, are designated as "core boundaries" because a substantial and persistent transgression of each one, on its own, has the potential to drive the Earth system into a dangerously unstable state, and each one has pervasive influence on the functioning of the other biophysical processes.

A 2023 article in *Nature* authored by an international team of forty Earth scientists updates the planetary boundaries approach.[4] It expands upon and refines the work of seminal articles in the field from 2009 and 2015. Three of its central points are especially relevant to the framework developed in this book. First, it identifies more specific quantifiable indicators that can be used by policymakers to monitor eight of these systems and measure the impact of their activities. For example, separate indicators for groundwater and surface water are proposed, along with two complementary measures of biodiversity: (1) the area of largely intact natural ecosystems and (2) the functional integrity of all ecosystems, including urban and agricultural ecosystems. Second, the interdependence of systems is given added emphasis, for example, by observing the critical importance of preserving intact natural ecosystems for maintaining biodiversity and stabilizing the climate system. Third, indicators of planetary systems health are supplemented by more stringent indicators of "safe and just boundaries," thus recognizing the need for policy guidance sufficient to prevent substantial harm to ecologically vulnerable communities, future generations, and non-human species. All three points reinforce the importance of understanding our ecological predicament as a cluster of interrelated crises, and the significance of each point is reflected in subsequent chapters.

Third, a defining feature of our predicament is the socioeconomic origin of these crises. Their convergent effects result from or are exacerbated by the structure of the global political economy, especially the institutions that most influence market practices pertaining to the acquisition, use, and control of land, energy, and water resources. These institutions shape the production, consumption, and investment decisions that have transformed every region of the globe and altered the conditions that have supported life on Earth throughout the Holocene era.

Fourth, these highly consequential institutions and market practices are sustained and reinforced by dominant ideals of political and economic organization. Finding a pathway to a more just and sustainable global political economy therefore not only requires attention to day-to-day policy questions and expert evaluation of technological alternatives, but also deep engagement with questions of political philosophy. The centerpiece of that engagement in this book is the debate over the appropriate relationship

4 A LIVABLE PLANET

between states and markets. More specifically, the arguments center on the choice between a vision of markets as the fundamental principle of social organization and a human rights approach that counteracts the threats posed by ecologically unsustainable, economically predatory market practices.

The reason for concentrating on markets and their institutional underpinnings is that they jointly and systematically shape ecological conditions and, in the process, structure the life prospects of everyone subject to their profound and pervasive influence. If left unchecked by institutional mechanisms, the least sustainable market practices, especially the activities of powerful nation-states and transnational entities, will continue to erode the ecological conditions and deplete the resource base upon which the fulfillment of human rights depends. The impact of these practices is especially significant in a globalized world at a time when markets have become the central organizing principle of social life for so much of humanity and the countervailing power of political institutions has withered.

In other words, at the root of our ecological predicament is the fact that humanity, operating through existing mechanisms of the global political economy, is overwhelming the rest of nature, perhaps irreversibly. Achieving the goal of ecological sustainability thus requires substantial change in our relation to the rest of nature—and changing our relation to the rest of nature requires changes in the institutional basis of our economic relationships with one another. Progress on both fronts is inconceivable without transformation of the market practices and supporting institutions that contribute most to the creation or magnification of structural threats to the secure realization of human rights, especially for the world's poorest, least powerful people who often bear the greatest environmental burdens.

Consequently, our practical task focuses on a series of incremental steps for a transition to a more just and sustainable global political economy rather than a comprehensive ideal of a fully just

OUR ECOLOGICAL PREDICAMENT 5

global order. At minimum, these first steps should include efforts to advance an ecologically oriented human rights agenda. Its goal is implementation of an institutional framework that serves as an enforceable bulwark against predatory market practices that subvert the ecological conditions necessary for the secure realization of high-priority, dual-purpose human rights. These practices directly threaten the human rights of individuals and communities or undermine the ability of states to secure those rights for their residents. They enable powerful corporations and countries to hoard economic opportunities (including green technologies), crowd out sustainable alternatives, extract natural resources and other economic benefits from structurally vulnerable or subordinate communities, shift environmental and economic burdens, dodge political and market accountability, and hijack public institutions for private purposes.

A central feature of this targeted human rights approach is the accent it places on the state's expansive and open-ended duties to protect. Within the existing international framework, states are uniquely positioned to counteract structurally entrenched economic disadvantages and cumulative concentrations of power that systematically erode the ecological and economic conditions necessary for the secure realization of human rights. Nevertheless, the approach must acknowledge that states are unpopular. Marxists, libertarians, and anarchists, each for their own reasons, look forward to their demise or retrenchment, and many politicians and ordinary citizens appear to distrust them. However, the argument for state uniqueness and their irreplaceable, near-term strategic importance is not rooted in naïve assumptions about their benign nature, efficient operation, or robust capacities for independent action in a world of profound interstate power asymmetries. Nor does it assume that states should or will endure beyond the current era.

For now, if not the state, then there is no other agent that can approximate the wide-ranging capacity to protect human rights from clear threats, especially threats to economic and social rights arising

6 A LIVABLE PLANET

from structural features of economic organization. No matter what theory one adopts as the ultimate end of economic justice or ideal of governance, the pathway to change runs through states. Without initiating change there, however difficult the task may be, nothing else changes.

Concretely, change will require two transformations in the use of state power. First, it will necessitate expanded use of policy levers that regulate the background conditions pertaining to the distribution of economic benefits, ecological burdens, and decision-making authority over social investments and the production of the material basis of daily life. Such regulation means more state intervention in markets and profound changes in the political institutions in which they are embedded as well as changes in the constituencies that exercise control over state institutions. Second, it will require states to remove some key ecologically impactful decisions from the discretionary judgment of private entities which lack both political legitimacy and sufficient market incentives to pursue the common good.

This view of human rights, especially its account of the tasks undertaken by states in fulfilling their duty to protect, contrasts sharply with egalitarian critics of the global order who dismiss human rights as neoliberalism's "powerless companion."[5] State responsibility for human rights, properly interpreted, can be an instrument for great change.

In addition, such institutional changes are possible only with parallel changes in ideas, ideals, and ideology and, more specifically, dominant conceptions of justice and assumptions about the role of markets in ordering social life. Among other things, the necessary changes in ideas involve a reexamination of the rationales for markets as the presumptive policy prescription for social decision-making, reevaluation of justifications commonly offered for current approaches to development and economic growth, and a reconsideration of the moral legitimacy of largely unaccountable power exercised by some nation-states and other state-like transnational entities.

Summary of Chapters

Each chapter contributes to the task of explaining why timely exit from our ecological predicament will require coordinated, simultaneous solutions to multiple environmental problems, fundamental changes in the organization of global markets, and an updated vision of the human rights responsibilities of states and other institutions that shape market activities.

Sustainability and Political Economy

Chapter 2 addresses an overarching question. What makes the current organization of the global political economy unsustainable? The first section surveys several prominent conceptions of sustainability and defends a definition tailored for the specific task of assessing the multiple, mutually reinforcing ecological consequences arising from the configuration of global political and economic arrangements. Subsequent sections rely on that definition for examining four prominent "ecological critiques" of the organization of the global political economy, each pinpointing characteristics or features that make it unsustainable: (1) the "logic of capitalism," understood as the relentless pursuit of profits; (2) runaway acquisitive behaviors rooted in human psychology, whether artificially sustained by ideals of progress or inherent in human nature; (3) macroeconomic policies that make economic growth the synoptic goal of social organization; and (4) extreme socioeconomic inequalities that generate unsustainable patterns of consumption.

8   A LIVABLE PLANET

The conclusion is that each diagnosis of our predicament is useful but incomplete. However, the combined weight of these four critiques points to a future with less capitalism, less consumption, less emphasis on growth, and less socioeconomic inequality. Concretely, that means fewer social investment decisions driven by private profit; more policies that combat heedless consumption of resource intensive, environmentally destructive luxury goods; economic goals more aligned with the satisfaction of basic needs than aggregate growth; and a politics more attuned to constraining the concentration of political and economic power.

Market Fundamentalism

Chapter 3 illustrates how state intervention in market economies for the sake of social welfare goals or for the protection of economic and social rights provokes fierce opposition from an intellectually influential, politically entrenched ideal often referred to as *market fundamentalism*.

Although specific rationales differ somewhat, the core belief is that robust protection of market liberties should be the fundamental principle of social organization.

The first section explains the link between various market fundamentalist arguments and specific neoliberal policies designed to rebalance the power relations between states and markets. Their proposals for rebalancing are designed to curb the regulatory power of states, contract the scope of its institutional functions, transfer decision-making from the public to the private sphere, and, more generally, expand state deference to market outcomes.

The second section critiques three of the most prominent market fundamentalist rationales: (1) market liberties are foundational for all other liberties, (2) market liberties are necessary for self-defense against the moral and intellectual deficiencies of states, and (3) competitive markets are not only efficient, but also promote freedom, individual welfare improvements, economic fairness, and social stability.

The third section argues against the market fundamentalists' overarching conception of freedom defined strictly in terms of non-interference or, more precisely, the absence of coercive interference with an individual's choices and actions. The conclusion is that this conception fails to register some of the most important dimensions of any plausible ideal of a free person, and, if implemented in economic policy, powerful market actors are free to engage in unlimited pursuit of private benefit at the expense of the common good and the well-being of other parties.

Human Rights and Ecological Goals

Chapter 4 presents the central elements of a targeted human rights approach to our ecological predicament. There are three main components. First, some human rights deserve enhanced priority because they serve dual purposes. They protect the basic elements of human well-being that ground many of those rights, and they perform their normative function, in significant part, by securing the ecological conditions that sustain human life and make possible the satisfaction of basic needs. These high-priority, dual-purpose rights include rights of subsistence, food, and water and rights that protect against serious environmental health risks and ecological degradation.

Second, central to the approach is its conception of the state's duty to protect human rights. The primary state responsibility is to counteract structurally entrenched economic disadvantages and cumulative concentrations of power that systematically undermine their secure realization. More specifically, state duties to protect the economic and social human rights of its residents are fulfilled by policies that target ecologically unsustainable, economically predatory market practices that enable a relatively few

10 A LIVABLE PLANET

market actors to capture the bulk of economic rewards of global production and investment and shift their economic and environmental burdens and risks onto others, thereby undermining human rights fulfillment.

Third, the chapter responds to normative and conceptual objections to human rights theories generally and their specific application to complex ecological crises. The objections are too numerous to list in this introductory chapter and the responses are too lengthy to discuss in this limited space, but four examples of criticisms of human rights theories are illustrative. First, they cannot address morally troublesome inequalities, especially the structural inequalities that causally contribute to the creation and perpetuation of human rights deficits. Second, they cannot provide a solid foundation for comprehensive theories of ecological justice because they are concerned only with human well-being. Third, they cannot be applied to the diffuse ecological harms rooted in the structure of the global political economy unless they abandon or revise several traditional strictures on the conceptualization of human rights, correlative duties, and their violation. Fourth, any significant degree of reliance on state action is problematic because of the poor track record of governments in protecting human rights generally and their pivotal role in subverting economic and social rights.

Market Power and Legal Advantage

Chapter 5 surveys how the market fundamentalists' recommended changes in the global political economy undermined state capacities for protecting human rights. Institutional changes allowed market participants to rewrite legal rules to their advantage and use their market power to subvert competitive norms. These changes fostered new predatory economic behaviors and accelerated the growth of existing trends, enabling a relatively few market

OUR ECOLOGICAL PREDICAMENT 11

actors to use their enhanced economic position to (1) consolidate more market power, evade market discipline, hoard opportunities, and reduce accountability to consumers; (2) circumvent political accountability by disempowering democracies and hijacking state and international institutions for private purposes; (3) leverage enhanced capital mobility to game the global system of states; and (4) extract windfall profits from speculative, socially destabilizing, and ecologically destructive capital investments.

Because many of the most ecologically destructive, predatory market strategies are now globally pervasive and institutionally entrenched, they pose profound threats to people and the planet. They undermine the public good, destroy sustainable habitats, lock in disadvantage for subordinate groups, deprive vulnerable communities of the material basis for meeting their basic needs, and put at grave risk the stability of the global economy and vital planetary systems.

Land Use and Its Consequences

Chapter 6 examines the consequences of and some alternatives to humanity's most intensive land uses—activities having high ecological impact, typically extending well beyond the primary spatial area in which their activities are conducted. Because agriculture—primarily production of food, feed, and livestock—is responsible for the largest share of land conversion, the chapter begins by exploring the food security implications of modern, industrial-scale production techniques and analyzing the primary factors contributing to arable land scarcity, soil degradation, nutrient depletion, biodiversity loss, deforestation, and more.

The second section explores modern agriculture's adverse ecological consequences that extend far beyond the land itself, substantially affecting groundwater and surface water, oceans, ambient air quality, and the functioning of planetary systems, including the

12   A LIVABLE PLANET

climate system and biogeochemical cycles (e.g., phosphorus and nitrogen).

The third section examines the destruction and fragmentation of forests, one of the most immediate and far-reaching impacts of intensive land use. Many of the world's most fragile and ecologically critical terrestrial ecosystems are under pressure due to the expansion of the land area used for production of "high-risk commodities" (i.e., export commodities obtained from ecologically destructive agricultural techniques and other extractive activities). The section highlights both the regional and planetary consequences of deforestation and declining terrestrial biodiversity that accompany forest conversion. It illustrates the global market dynamics driving both crises, and it explains why forest and habitat preservation are crucial for human well-being.

The fourth section shows how multiple problems arising from modern land use practices are conceptualized as human rights issues and how they have been translated into concrete policy proposals, mainly by indigenous groups and cross-national peasant activist coalitions that have adopted a human rights perspective as the normative framework guiding their advocacy.

Water and Social Organization

Chapter 7 examines policies that affect human rights to clean drinking water and sanitation, along with water resource management and utilization practices that have significant implications for other human rights, including rights to health, food, and subsistence.

The first section of this chapter explores the causes, consequences, and severity of emerging water resource constraints. It then explains factors contributing to the complexity of managing water resources at the regional and basin levels, demonstrating that responsibilities for fulfilling the human rights to water within highly interdependent,

OUR ECOLOGICAL PREDICAMENT 13

densely concentrated human settlements are wide-ranging and necessitate highly centralized institutional coordination.

The second section examines key aspects of the global political economy of water resource acquisition and use. It first looks at policies designed to conserve a nation's resources by decoupling its economic growth from its domestic water consumption but often producing adverse effects beyond national borders. Moreover, the section surveys a variety of explanations for the prevalence of unsustainable policies that promote the production—and the export—of resource-depleting crops and water-intensive consumer goods contrary to recommendations for water-stressed regions to import rather than produce water-intensive crops and goods. Both policies implicate the ability of water-stressed states to fulfill their human rights responsibilities.

The third section discusses privatization of water delivery and sanitation services. It examines underlying political objectives and market dynamics along with the problems that have ensued. It assesses the ecological and human rights implications of placing highly consequential water resource decisions in the hands of private, for-profit institutions, and it critiques the normative foundations of policies that promote market allocation based on principles of full cost recovery.

Energy Transition Pathways

Chapter 8 shows how pathways for transition to a more sustainable mix of energy sources generate new ecological and economic risks, introduce market uncertainties, and disrupt established expectations: hence, the allure of sacrifice-free solutions and incrementally transformative pathways.

The first section considers pathways unlikely to produce timely changes because they depend on unrealistic assumptions regarding human behavior or the operation of markets. Examples include

14 A LIVABLE PLANET

overreliance on consumer-driven change, enlightened global leadership, and market-driven technological innovation.

The second section examines solutions that produce some positive results but only by creating problems within another sphere of activity, shifting problems onto other communities, or postponing or magnifying long-term harm. Examples include energy technologies that reduce fossil fuel consumption but result in unsustainable impacts on land, water, or biodiversity, and carbon offset schemes that fail to achieve the goals of nature-based climate solutions.

The third section explores a variety of *path dependencies*, or entrenched patterns of human behavior and social organization that lock in existing social and economic relations, thereby constraining feasible options for the future. Path dependencies include not only market practices that protect incumbent technologies, but also governmental policies that limit the ability to achieve the goals of rapid decarbonization necessary to protect the planet from irreversible harm. Examples of protective market practices are strategies that artificially prolong the commercial life of ecologically unsustainable products or crowd out more sustainable alternatives. Examples of highly constraining governmental policies include extensive state investments in fossil fuels, legal rules that protect businesses against liability for ecological harm or the risk from stranded assets, and national security goals and economic development objectives that work at cross purposes to sustainable energy aims.

The final section of the chapter demonstrates the high degree of alignment between the central arguments of this chapter and various policy proposals and strategies developed by indigenous and other advocacy groups that place a human rights agenda at the center of their work.

Control over the Future

Chapter 9 argues that the root of our ecological predicament is not simply that the affluent consume too much, but also that they control too much. Decisions about the basis of modern life and the fate of the planet carry too much risk or too much uncertainty to be left to a free market free-for-all, where the rule of the economically stronger routinely prevails. For example, concentrated wealth has an outsized effect on public investment and tax policy, channeling resources toward some economic beneficiaries and clustering ecological burdens elsewhere. An ecologically oriented human rights agenda, by contrast, can redistribute power, reorient state responsibility for securing human rights, and remove key social investment decisions from the discretion of private entities.

The bulk of the chapter explores the implications of and impediments to implementation of a human rights approach. It would not only require reversal of the power relations between states and markets, but it would also transform power relations across states and between the affluent and everyone else. Moreover, a human rights approach requires the reversal of two generations of global development goals dominated by market fundamentalist ideas and neoliberal legal norms.

Despite all the obstacles, less ambitious options have virtually no chance of success, and many of the more ambitious alternatives depend on the demise of capitalism or the system of states within the next few decades—or less—we have left before the planet becomes radically inhospitable to human life and more deeply antagonistic to the rest of nature.

2

Sustainability and Political Economy

This chapter addresses an overarching question. What makes the global political economy ecologically unsustainable? The question assumes that one or more aspects of its current organization is unsustainable, but disagreement arises among critics who focus attention on a singularly influential factor. This chapter sets the stage for its conclusions by evaluating several ecological critiques of political economy, each attempting to answer our overarching question.

The first section addresses a preliminary question. What conception of ecological sustainability is suitable for assessing the global constellation of political institutions and market practices that jointly and profoundly shape ecological conditions and channel their effects on human welfare?

There are many prominent definitions of sustainability. Some conceptions are useful for specific practical purposes but not appropriately tailored for our task. This section traces the evolution of prominent sustainability conceptions, examines their normative and conceptual underpinnings, evaluates their relevance for our task, and offers an alternative definition.

The second through fifth sections examine four ecological critiques of the global political economy. The first critique suggests that capitalism itself is the problem. The second critique points to psychological factors that drive a self-destructive consumerist ethos. The third critique emphasizes the impact of public policies that make economic growth the synoptic goal of social organization. The fourth critique identifies high levels of ecological harm as the by-product of high levels of economic inequality.

A Livable Planet. Madison Powers, Oxford University Press. © Oxford University Press 2024.
DOI: 10.1093/oso/9780197756003.003.0002

SUSTAINABILITY AND POLITICAL ECONOMY   17

The sixth section pulls together some conclusions from this survey. The cause of our ecological predicament is unlikely to be singular, but each critique yields valuable insights that can help identify and eliminate the specific market practices and institutions that impede the pathway to a more just and sustainable global political economy.

Conceptions of Sustainability

The concept of sustainability appears in a variety of academic and popular contexts, and its meaning varies depending on the practical purposes it is meant to serve. An examination of four aspects of the process of assessing the human impact on the environment point to the kind of definition we need. These include aims of assessment, scope of assessment, developmental bias, and assessment perspective.

Aims of Assessment

Sustainability conceptions are not designed for a strictly scientific assessment of the health and functioning of the biosphere, independent of its implications for humanity.[1] From their very first formulations, conceptions of sustainability have been used to assess how well alternative forms of economic organization support human life and well-being.

An early (if not the first) modern reference to sustainability is found in "World Conservation Strategy," a 1980 report produced by the International Union for Conservation of Nature (IUCN).[2] A central feature of the report is its contrast between the social and economic practices of some traditional subsistence societies and economically developed societies. It concluded that the developmental alternative would be better at meeting human needs

18 A LIVABLE PLANET

by conserving natural resources and preserving ecosystems upon which a flourishing society depends. Traditional subsistence economies, according to the IUCN report, struggle to secure even a basic level of human well-being for current generations, and they undermine long-term well-being prospects of future generations by relying on economic practices that involve high levels of resource depletion and environmental degradation.[3]

Disagreements among delegates attending the 1987 meeting of the World Commission on Environment and Development focused attention on the role of human well-being in the assessment of alternative forms of economic organization. Some delegates endorsed the priority of economic development for the sake of poverty relief and improved human well-being. They viewed the emphasis on human welfare as an alternative to what they viewed as the nature-preserving ecological goals championed by Western nations. Poverty, not pollution, some said, is the main global problem.[4]

The Commission's report, commonly known as the Brundtland Report, attempted to strike a balance between competing visions. It defined sustainable development as "development that meets the needs of the present without compromising the ability of future generations to meet their own needs."[5] Although the definition is widely noted for highlighting intergenerational justice as a central moral problem, the text of the Report offered little advice for adjudicating between the human well-being interests of current and future generations. However, the definition did underscore its anthropocentric premise. It left no doubt that the point of sustainable economic development is improvement of human well-being for the poorest people on the planet and the long-term well-being prospects for future generations of humanity.

Principle 1 of the Rio Declaration on Environment and Development, adopted by the United Nations in 1992, also made explicit the anthropocentric underpinnings of the Brundtland consensus: "Human beings are at the center of concerns for sustainable development. They are entitled to a healthy and productive life in harmony with nature."[6] The anthropocentric orientation continues in Agenda 2030, the 2015 United Nations roadmap for achieving the Sustainable Development Goals (SDGs). Its vision of sustainable economic development is defended on the grounds that it is indispensable for achieving poverty relief and improving the global standard of living, now and in the future.[7]

Even though rhetoric about the fate of the Earth is commonplace, sustainability concerns have never focused on whether the planet—or life in general—will survive. Nor are concerns about sustainability grounded in judgments about the intrinsic value of nature or the value of protecting natural areas from human intrusion. This is not to say that sustainability advocates are indifferent to such matters, but instead that the focal concern of a conception of ecological sustainability is the creation and maintenance of institutional arrangements that ensure that the Earth is—and will continue to be—hospitable to human life and well-being.

Developmental Bias

The history of the modern concept of sustainability also shows its pro-development bias from the start, promoted first by economically developed nations in drafting the IUCN report and then by Brundtland Commission delegates, especially representatives of nations eager to take the path of rapid development even at the cost of ecological goals emphasized by some delegates from more economically developed Western nations. This prompts a question: To what extent should the developmentalist bias be retained, modified, or abandoned, especially considering that it seems that there is a widespread consensus on its importance? My answer is straightforward. For a conception of sustainability to be useful for assessing the ecological implications of alternative forms of economic organization, it should not presuppose the necessity of

20 A LIVABLE PLANET

any model of economic development or build in a bias against it. Whatever the value of any model of economic development as a policy prescription or societal goal, the first step toward a useful analytic conception of sustainability is to draw a distinction between ecological sustainability goals and developmental goals. Critics rightly point out that the SDGs encompass competing objectives and obscure the potential for practical conflict between them.[8] Such issues should be left open for evaluation and debate, recognizing that the pursuit of ecological sustainability offers one potential pathway for securing human well-being in the long run and that economic development strategies provide another potential pathway in the near term. If the two pathways converge, then perhaps so much the better. But if, on balance, certain ecological concerns should give way to or, on the contrary, override economic development considerations, then a conception of ecological sustainability should afford a clear view of the competing values at stake and the necessity for tradeoffs.

Scope of Assessment

Sustainability conceptions can take a wide or narrow view of the ecological phenomena selected for assessment. Some sustainability conceptions are useful for understanding a specific kind of problem. For example, as applied to the management of fisheries or forests, "sustainable" is used as a rough synonym for "renewable." The idea is that fish and trees can be harvested in a manner consistent with a steady rate of replenishment.

A wider lens is suitable for a more comprehensive assessment of natural resource stocks. At the turn of the 19th century, Thomas Malthus, an English professor of history and political economy, raised the question of how a growing population could be fed given the limited land and other agricultural resources available. Conversations about natural resource limits as a constraint on

SUSTAINABILITY AND POLITICAL ECONOMY   21

economic growth were resuscitated in 1972 by the influential study, *The Limits to Growth.*[9]

More comprehensive sustainability goals, however, are necessary to assess problems beyond natural resource constraints. For example, a claim that activities or practices are sustainable often means that they avoid localized ecosystem harms, such as water pollution, or that they reduce greenhouse gas emissions that contribute to the planetary problem of global warming. In other words, a conception suitable for assessing the organization of the global political economy must be comprehensive, allowing for assessment of multiple unsustainable ecological effects, including resource depletion, ecosystem destruction, and planetary destabilization.

Assessment Perspectives

Ecological sustainability can be viewed from several perspectives. When viewed from an enterprise perspective, concerns about resource depletion, pollution, or carbon emissions, for example, are treated as business considerations to be assessed in terms of financial costs and reputational impact. A corporate sustainability officer seeks to balance society's environmental goals with a firm's own financial "bottom line."

By contrast, ecological concerns from a societal or state-centric perspective bring into focus a wider array of issues than a corporate sustainability officer must consider. Issues of energy independence, national security, and economic competitiveness are taken into consideration and recognized as potentially conflicting goals that must be balanced. For example, policy proposals for a "green new deal" attempt to align a country's international economic competitiveness aims with its carbon emissions targets.

Agenda 2030, the 2015 United Nations roadmap for achieving the SDGs, reflects the continuing prominence of the state-centric approach in global development circles. The goals contained in

22 A LIVABLE PLANET

Agenda 2030 are benchmarks for sustainable societies, emphasizing the responsibility of individual nation-states for their own ecological and economic conditions. It assumes that its list of 17 goals and 169 targets are achieved, if at all, by nations building them into their domestic policies and plans. Agenda 2030 acknowledges that problems like climate change require collective action and interstate cooperation, but nevertheless a sustainable planet is conceptualized as a world composed of individually sustainable national economies.

Three reasons demonstrate that it is no longer plausible to conceive of the perspective for assessment of ecological sustainability from the perspective of a single nation or society.

First, the global political economy is now the arena in which the fate of the planet will be determined. The global political economy, as commonly understood, refers to the totality of market practices that are embedded in multiple institutions and structured by a plurality of globally powerful actors. Although national governments, with their unique capacity to govern through comprehensive, legally binding rules, are perhaps the most important determinants of market practices, we need an expanded analytic framework to understand their dynamics.[10]

Robert Gilpin, for example, argues that a global perspective on political economy is necessary to take account of the growing significance of "the interaction of the market and powerful actors such as states, multinational firms, and international organizations."[11] Geopolitically powerful, economically advantaged states exercise their power to shape the trade, capital investment, labor, and taxation rules for their own advantage. In addition, some non-state entities exercise some of the powers historically possessed by states. These state-like entities include multinational corporations, hedge funds, and other institutional investors, along with supranational institutions such as the World Bank and the International Monetary Fund. To varying degrees, many of these entities exercise some of the capacities of states, but they answer to other constituencies

SUSTAINABILITY AND POLITICAL ECONOMY   23

such as shareholders, customers, and financial backers instead of citizens.

Second, a state-centric approach to issues of sustainability ignores the extent to which profound ecological threats are planetary in origin and driven by socioeconomic forces originating beyond the boundaries of any single nation-state. In advance of the adoption of Agenda 2030, prominent Earth scientists argued for establishing sustainability goals for problems other than resource depletion and local ecosystem degradation that, in principle, can be addressed by individual states. They urged top priority for tackling emerging threats of planetary destabilization.[12] The rationale for prioritizing the maintenance of safe planetary boundaries is straightforward. Planetary destabilization affects everyone, and its prevention cannot be achieved by better domestic management practices alone—for example, in the way scarce resources within a country might be conserved or pollution might be reduced within a state's territorial jurisdiction by adjusting its economic organization.

Third, nations that are successful in meeting their own ecological sustainability targets for resource conservation or localized ecosystem preservation often do so by reliance on market practices that undermine the very same sustainability targets for other nations. Countries can maintain their high standard of living by decoupling the productive basis of their economies from environmental damage not only by domestic adoption of less environmentally harmful production processes or using less water or fewer materials: they also can protect their own natural resources and ecological conditions by outsourcing the ecologically damaging activities of extraction, production, and waste disposal. Improvement in domestic ecological outcomes, if achieved by outsourcing, obscures the reality of worsened ecological outcomes for humanity.

The upshot of these three arguments is clear. The perspective necessary for understanding the origins of and requirements for responding to the planet's biggest ecological threats must take

24 A LIVABLE PLANET

account of the impact of the overall organization of the global political economy, not just the organizational features of domestic economies in isolation. It is a mistake to think that an ecologically sustainable society is strictly a product of its purely local socioeconomic conditions and institutions, and it is equally erroneous to think that a livable planet is a world composed of the sustainable political economies of separate states.

A Definitional Fresh Start

We are now in the position to offer a revised conception of ecological sustainability that satisfies these four assessment criteria. It is inextricably tied to the aim of securing human well-being. It embodies neither a pro- nor anti-developmentalist bias. The scope of ecological phenomena it assesses is comprehensive, and its assessment is conducted from a planetary perspective.

The central point of the most basic idea of unsustainability is this: if the social practices and institutions that make up the global political economy are unsustainable it is because of their tendency to be self-undermining. In general terms, social and economic practices, together with the background institutions in which they are embedded, tend to be self-undermining when they worsen rather than serve their fundamental purpose of securing or improving human well-being. Because social arrangements can be self-undermining in various ways, we need a more specific understanding of ecologically unsustainable practices and institutions.

Social practices and institutions are ecologically unsustainable when they exhaust the necessary resource base or otherwise degrade the environmental conditions upon which their continued existence and intended functioning depends.[13] In other words, an ecologically unsustainable global political economy is self-undermining insofar as the economic arrangements created for the promotion and protection of human well-being adversely alter the ecological conditions that sustain human life and well-being. An ecologically sustainable political economy, by contrast, is composed of institutions and practices that preserve and maintain the ecological conditions that make human life possible and play an essential role in securing the basic elements of well-being.

This definition, therefore, is suitable for understanding the insights generated by alternative answers to the question of what makes the global political economy unsustainable.

The Logic of Capitalism

One ecological critique places the blame for our ecological predicament on capitalist systems of economic organization. This critique adds a new dimension to the ongoing debate about the merits and shortcomings of capitalism. On the one hand, capitalism has been credited with many achievements, including the emancipation of the laboring classes from feudal subordination, producing a massive rise in the global standard of living, creating material conditions hospitable to the growth of democracy, and ushering in a long-term period of relative peace and reduced levels of interstate violence. On the other hand, critics argue that the benefits of capitalism are offset by its production of concentrated pockets of excessive wealth and human misery, the global expansion of labor exploitation and colonial subordination, and its tendency to undermine democratic control over key aspects of social life.

Capitalism's Two Structural Problems

An ecological critique of capitalism takes its cue from the argument that it is an inherently unsustainable form of economic organization in the sense that its continued existence depends upon conditions that tend to be undermined by the internal logic of

26   A LIVABLE PLANET

its operation. In its most familiar form, an internal logic critique elucidates capitalism as a system propelled by the relentless drive for increased profitability. For example, Marx and Engels famously argued that capitalism faces an inevitable structural crisis. Based on their observations of the stratification of economic classes in 19th-century industrial England, they predicted the inevitable immiseration of the proletariat while simultaneously ensuring that capital would continue to be concentrated in the hands of a relatively few owners of the means of production. In this scenario, the overwhelming proportion of the population would have no means for sustaining themselves other than by selling their labor. Given the stark inequality of bargaining power, the quest for profits would drive down wages to a level just barely sufficient to maintain the workers' capacities for engaging in productive labor. Over time, even subsistence would become harder to achieve, and the workers' opportunities for accumulating capital of their own would be largely out of reach.

Herein lies the first structural problem. Profitability is largely a function of two incompatible market realities. Profit depends on the capitalists' ability to tamp down the costs of labor, and yet, profit growth depends on producing and selling more material goods to more people who have sufficient means to consume them. Over time, the engine of profit, upon which the fate of capitalism depends, stalls. In other words, capitalism is depicted as economically unsustainable. It is a self-undermining system because its downward pressure on wages erodes the purchasing power of potential consumers needed to sustain its profit growth, which keeps the system going.

The debates about if or when the day of reckoning might occur are not central to our inquiry. The point is that an ecological critique, grounded in claims about the logic of capitalism, is modeled along the lines of the original structural crisis thesis developed in the Marxian tradition. The central claim of the ecological critique is that capitalism has an internal logic that is incompatible with the goal of ecological sustainability. In essence, the claim is that the main driver of environmental harm, or at least the main cause of its severity, is the endless quest for individual profit maximization. As we noted already, profit growth comes from producing and selling more material goods and services to more people who have sufficient means to consume more. So, the entire system depends on infinite growth in material production and new consumer markets, but we live on a finite planet, with limited resources and ecological boundaries that define a safe operating space for life on Earth. In other words, the newest twist on the idea that capitalism faces a structural crisis focuses on its tendency to exhaust resources and degrade the ecological conditions upon which its continued existence depends.

Arguments of this form are integral to contemporary theories of ecological Marxism, an intellectual project devoted to uncovering the deeper structure of its theory of crises or, alternatively, retrofitting that structure to encompass the ecological critique.[14] James O'Connor, for example, was an early exponent. He argues that there are two crisis-generating contradictions within the capitalist system.[15] In addition to the tendency of capital to keep wage-based labor costs low, thereby reducing the purchasing power required for buying the commodities upon which capitalism depends, it also tends to undermine the conditions of production by spoiling the natural environment upon which it depends for a steady supply of raw materials and resources.

The Impact of Capitalism, If Unchecked

Sometimes the critique claims that "the capitalist system itself is the cause of environmental destruction."[16] A few writers have suggested that a better name for our current era would be the Capitalocene, rather than the Anthropocene.[17] They note that systematic patterns of capitalist activities, not the activities of humanity in general,

28   A LIVABLE PLANET

have fundamentally transformed the planet. In the process, they have put at risk the future of a capitalist mode of social organization, thereby undermining whatever potential it has for improving the material basis of human well-being.

A nuanced formulation of the causal claim is proposed by Fred Magdoff and John Bellamy Foster. "It is our contention that most of the critical environmental problems we have are either caused or made much worse by the workings of our economic system."[18] They are not claiming that all ecological damage is due to capitalism. Nor are they committed to the claim that, in every instance, capitalism is the primary cause of environmental degradation and resource depletion. An important implication of their formulation of the nuanced causal claim is that it leaves room to explore other factors that contribute to our ecological predicament.

If we concede, as I think we should, that the most plausible formulation of the causal thesis is the more nuanced one, what remains viable in the logic of capitalism critique? I think the main point is most crisply put in the form of an incompatibility thesis. For example, Magdoff has observed that "capitalism is incompatible with a truly ecological civilization because it is a system that must continually expand, promoting consumption beyond human needs, while ignoring the limits of nonrenewable resources . . . and the earth's assimilation capacity."[19] This way of framing the issue makes a point about where the logic of capitalism, if unchecked, will take us. Capitalism is a system governed by a single self-defeating principle, namely the pursuit of private profit, and the acceleration of economic growth is necessary for the continued generation of profits. The principle is ecologically self-defeating because resource consumption is not infinitely expandable. Nor are the ecological conditions that support life infinitely resilient. And so, it is the logic of the system that leads to or exacerbates resource depletion, ecological degradation, and the transgression of stable planetary boundaries.

Importantly, the incompatibility of sustainable ecological conditions and unrestrained pursuit of profit does not entail that no other causal factors are in play, that the elimination of capitalism alone is sufficient for a transition to a more just and sustainable form of social organization, or that all ways of incorporating profit-driven activities in the organization of economic systems are equally destructive of the environment.

The logic of capitalism critique supports a narrower conclusion than the claim that no ecologically sustainable future is possible without the wholesale elimination of capitalism. The narrower conclusion is that the institutional structure of any sustainable future scenario must severely limit the scope of private profit-driven investment and production decisions. The profit-seeking logic of capitalism, at the minimum, must be institutionally constrained, specifically by limiting the extent to which key investment and resource decisions are left to markets, leaving owners of private capital free to call all the important shots on matters of collective consequence. On this point, the anti-capitalist critique is unassailable. A hallmark of contemporary capitalism is the outsized role of private owners of concentrated capital in shaping the organization of every aspect of social life through their market-driven investment and production decisions, stimulating overconsumption, and thereby driving the global economy toward perpetual growth and propelling the planet toward ecological imbalance.

Although the ecological critique of capitalism, on its own, seems to fall short of delivering the knock-out punch for the wholesale elimination of any remnants of capitalist social organization, the arguments prompt us to ask questions about the specific aspects of the economy that should be removed from the grip of market forces. For example, to the extent that market dominance of some sectors of the economy poses a threat not otherwise manageable to the secure realization of human rights, the case for removal is strong. Subsequent chapters incorporate this insight. They identify

30   A LIVABLE PLANET

types of market practices and institutions that should be targeted for restriction or elimination.

Psychological Explanations

The Infinite and Expanding Nature of Human Desires

An alternative thesis locates the origins of the sustainability problem and its potential solution, if there is one, primarily in facts about individual human psychology. The emphasis is on the dispositions and behavior of individual consumers rather than the way that the major production and investment decisions are structured in a capitalist economy. Excessive consumption is cast as a kind of ecological vice or personal failing, which suggests the paramount importance of changing the hearts and minds of the global affluent who consume the most. Proponents of this view often point to the fact that if the entire global population were to consume at the level of the United States, it would need the resources of four or five more Earths.[20]

Psychological explanations rest on an assumption about the infinite and expanding nature of human desire rather than on causal forces unique to capitalist economic systems.[21] As Vaclav Smil puts it, "objects of desire change, desire remains."[22] Alfred Marshall adopted a similar perspective. He sought to explain these changes by observing that the quantity and diversity of wants and desires expands with civilizational progress.[23] His analysis does not point the finger directly at capitalism. Instead, it is rising levels of affluence that generate wants, however affluence is created. In other words, there is a strong cultural component that explains the potentially unsustainable growth of consumption even though underpinning any specific culture are durable facts about human psychology. Human beings are "wired" to want more, consume more, and many cultures seem to view getting more as a marker of social progress.

SUSTAINABILITY AND POLITICAL ECONOMY   31

A particularly pessimistic version of the psychological explanation is known as the "Stone Age brain hypothesis," sometimes described by its critics as a form of *biofatalism*.[24] The hypothesis is that human brains evolved in ways that enabled them to flourish in conditions in which they lived in small groups, with little contact with or mutual effect upon other groups. Humans thus inherited problem-solving skills that equipped them for dealing with environmental and social conditions in face-to-face relationships requiring only a short-term planning horizon. On this view, humans are ill-equipped for the natural world that they have transformed. They are hard-wired for acquisition and hoarding behaviors that were once adaptive for survival in precarious circumstances but now predispose them to self-destruction. In the biofatalists' worst-case scenario, there may not be enough time to reverse evolutionary trends that threaten life on Earth.

A Problem Not Unique to Capitalism

Even if we reject the worst-case scenario, viewing our ecological predicament as rooted at least partially in human psychology poses a further question. Are our seemingly unlimited desires in some respect uniquely self-destructive within capitalist systems or perhaps more deeply rooted in the ideals of progress that co-evolved with its institutions? The answer would tell us whether changes in culture, institutions, or both would offer an effective strategy for humanity to escape its predicament.

Those who say that the problem is not unique to capitalism can point to pre-capitalist political writing, where the endless nature of human desire for material acquisition and its destructive consequences is a prominent theme. For example, in Plato's *Republic*, Socrates claims that the endless acquisition of money is self-defeating in two respects. First, it is the chief impediment to a truly rich and happy life.[25] Second, it is the main cause of civil

32 A LIVABLE PLANET

unrest, particularly when there are effectively two cities, "one of the poor and one of the rich living in the same place and always plotting against one another."[26] He argues that these self-destructive aspects of human psychology are so ingrained and dominant in most people that they are restrained, if at all, only by the firm rule of a Guardian class.[27] Authoritatively imposed institutional change, not a voluntary cultural shift in attitudes, would be the only realistic option for problems that troubled Socrates and for our ecological predicament.

Aristotle followed in Plato's footsteps, focusing on the vice known as *pleonexia*, a disposition to amass and consume more than others simply for the sake of one-upping, outdoing, or asserting superiority or dominance over others.[28] However, for Aristotle, human psychology is portrayed as more malleable, always requiring a mix of moral education and good laws and institutions that, over the longer term, combat and subdue the vices inherent in human nature.

Something like Aristotle's account of the social malleability human psychology is central to Marxist writings. Capitalism involves a socioeconomic belief system—an ideology—that makes market relations and exchange transactions the fundamental basis of all social goals and individual aspirations. Their point is that a market mentality bleeds into every aspect of the individual's life, crowds out other human values, and replaces the non-market value of human association and work with a desire to acquire more and consume more.[29] On this view, it is reasonable to think that hearts and minds, along with political and economic institutions, must be changed.

An enduring question for social scientists, then, is whether change in the material basis of production will bring about widespread psychological change or whether change in the social ethos is a prerequisite to system change. At issue also is whether such change is possible, and, if so, what it would take to dislodge the pervasive desire for "more and better" given that the prospect

SUSTAINABILITY AND POLITICAL ECONOMY   33

of improvement in material well-being seems so deeply rooted in ideals of progress, prominent not only in the cultures of the global affluent, but central to the aspirations of many residents of rapidly developing economies.[30]

Whatever the best answer to these causal questions may be, there is one clear implication. We must come to grips with the fact that psychological dispositions and habits take on a life of their own. Even if the logic of capitalism thesis turns out to be the best explanation of the origins of the most ecologically self-destructive consumer preferences, very substantial changes in human psychology will have to occur in tandem with changes in the material basis of production, driven to excess by the profit-seeking logic of capitalism.

The most hopeful picture is the educational pathway favored by Aristotle. Far less appealing is the draconian alternative—sometimes described as *ecofascism*—that takes its cue from the line of argument pursued by Socrates. If Socrates is right, creating institutions and developing social practices that lead to their eventual undoing is just what humans are prone to do, and not many are likely to change on their own.

Moreover, while psychologically oriented critics of the logic of capitalism thesis are right to note that environmentally destructive, profit-seeking, self-aggrandizing behavior is not unique to the capitalist era, their arguments do not rule out the possibility that these tendencies reach critical levels of urgency under certain ways of organizing capitalist institutions. Their arguments show that structural changes in systems of production and investment will not be enough to address the potential threats to humanity and their human rights caused by excessive consumerism. Unless we surrender to the pessimistic view, we will need to follow Aristotle's suggestion to change the culture primarily by designing better institutions and practices and dismantling the ones that are self-undermining, given the existence of deep-seated psychological dispositions that are difficult to dislodge. As suggested in

34 A LIVABLE PLANET

the first chapter (and elaborated upon in the next chapter), many ideals underpinning our current organization of the global political economy must be revised to make them suitable for the Anthropocene.

Economic Growth

Some critics see the main ecological problem associated with the global economy as a matter of macroeconomic policy rather than the logic of capitalism or individual consumer psychology. The suggestion is that whatever problems stem from private sector's relentless efforts to maximize profits or expansive appetites for consumption, they can be mitigated by abandoning the goal of maximizing gross domestic product (GDP). This version of the ecological critique views the obsession with GDP growth as a major cause of our predicament and an ideological impediment to a just and sustainable future.

GDP, a Flawed Metric

GDP is the monetary value of all the goods produced and services provided within a nation's borders in a given period (e.g., quarterly, annually). This single metric has been viewed as the most important marker of national and global well-being in political and policy contexts throughout the second half of the 20th century, down to the present. For example, the charter of the Organisation for Economic Cooperation and Development (OECD) explicitly makes GDP growth its highest priority.[31] Many economists and market observers typically view annual increases of 3–4% in national GDP as healthy growth rates. This measure remains the most common standard for judging economic progress and improvement of human well-being.

SUSTAINABILITY AND POLITICAL ECONOMY   35

A long line of critics argue that GDP is a flawed metric of global development and human well-being for several reasons. It doesn't matter what goods and services are produced as long as they have market value and that market value is increasing. For example, GDP goes up when money is spent in highly polluting industrial production, the construction and staffing of prisons, and dispatching garbage trucks to pick up food destined for landfills. All these economic activities add to GDP, but they are indicators of social dysfunction or ecological decline, not improvement in well-being. Equally important is what is left out of account, including the valuable goods and services performed outside of the market context. Unpaid work, for example, by members of the household who weed the vegetable garden or volunteer to plant trees in the neighborhood park is not counted. These activities add to human well-being and often improve environmental quality, but they do not register as positive achievements in GDP.

Also, there is another way in which GDP distorts our understanding of how well nations and their residents are doing. It measures increases in economic activity that occur within a nation, but it fails to reflect how much of that economic gain stays within that country. For example, oil and mineral extraction may increase the GDP of a country even though most of the money in circulation is deposited in offshore tax havens of the rich. The emphasis on the maximization of per capita GDP also fails to account for the within-country distribution of the economic benefits.[32] National economies that depend heavily on the extractive industries tend toward greater socioeconomic stratification, for example, with royalties pocketed by local elites while near-term economic conditions for the poor deteriorate and the long-term ecological conditions necessary for future prosperity degrade.

In other words, GDP registers as a positive achievement some economic activities that are detrimental to individual and societal well-being, including environmental harms, and it leaves out

36 A LIVABLE PLANET

non-market activities that add to quality of life, including environmental improvements.

More fundamentally, the goal of GDP maximization—or increased economic growth more generally, however it is measured—is subject to the same charge leveled against private profit maximization. The claim is that an undifferentiated, single-minded commitment to economic growth undermines the ecological conditions necessary for the continuous improvement of material well-being. Resources are exhausted, planetary boundaries are breached, and, perhaps worse still in the near term, these net environmental harms are not necessarily offset by other gains in well-being, given what GDP wrongly counts as a positive welfare benefit. Kenneth Boulding famously summarized concerns about the potentially self-undermining nature of economic growth policies by observing that "anyone who believes in indefinite growth in anything physical, in a physically finite planet, is either mad or an economist."[33]

Alternatives to Growth

One proposal is to reverse course, aiming instead for a no-growth economy or even degrowth.[34] For example, Tim Jackson, the author of an influential book, *Prosperity Without Growth*, makes the case for degrowth. He argues that we should give up on the aim of infinite growth of the global economy and, ultimately, retrench the world economy's material impact on the planet and simultaneously redistribute resources to meet human needs. One of its companion ideas, known as the *circular economy*, suggests that instead of expanding production, we should opt for repairing, repurposing, or recycling the materials already used. These are all fine suggestions. However, the implications of most degrowth proposals are stark. Without growth, the main source for increase in private profits disappears, and, without the expectation of greater

SUSTAINABILITY AND POLITICAL ECONOMY 37

profits, the engine of capitalist innovation and production stalls. A no-growth or degrowth policy would spell the end of capitalism as it has existed for the past several hundred years. The ecological sustainability gains might be desirable, all things considered, but, in the near term, the goal of lifting people out of poverty would depend entirely on a global transformation involving a massive redistribution of existing economic resources. Again, this, too, might be a good thing, but the practical question that besets both the logic of capitalism critique and the (less pessimistic version of the psychological critique) arises: Is it a realistic pathway to the kind of ecological transition needed within the timeframe it needs to occur?

Alternatively, in the near term, the macroeconomic goal of growth might be scaled back to encompass only genuinely beneficial, less environmentally harmful growth. The position is expressed under various banners, including "green new deal" proposals, green growth, and "doughnut economics." There are some important differences in emphasis and assumptions.

Green new deal proposals in the United States, United Kingdom, and Europe emphasize replacement of fossil fuels as a way of solving problems of structural job losses due to automation, deindustrialization, and the workforce impact of the energy transition necessary for combating climate change. A wholesale transformation of housing, transportation systems, and energy grids would result in a massive spurt of economic growth necessitated by the adoption of new technology and the creation of green jobs, but it is not an environmentally costless strategy in the near term. It will require more concrete and steel and more energy consumption, much of that coming, at least initially, from existing fossil fuel facilities.

Economist Kate Raworth argues for what she calls a *doughnut economy*.[35] We should be agnostic about growth. Instead, we should concentrate on public and private investment in things that keep the planet within the circle of the "doughnut," defined by reference to the notion of a safe operating space for Earth systems, together with priority for expenditures that maintain a standard of

38 A LIVABLE PLANET

living that fulfills human rights requirements. It is unclear whether her agenda ultimately requires capitalism to recede entirely or just a shrinking of its influence, perhaps by shifting the locus of many resource allocation decisions and social investment choices from the private arena of market participants to the realm of collective democratic control. However, her position is consistent with the narrow conclusion of the logic of capitalism argument, which calls for shrinking the domain in which capitalism is the primary determinant of social organization.

Growth Without Ecological Harm?

Ecomodernism, by contrast, is a strongly pro-growth position that challenges all the critiques discussed thus far. Its proponents believe that capitalism and economic growth can be sustained together with continuing improvements in material standards of living and a reduction in ecological damage.[36] It places its faith in market-driven technological innovation as the optimal, no-sacrifice solution for all environmental problems.[37] Clean energy, carbon capture and storage, water desalination, and genetically engineered drought-resistant crops are familiar proposals. An encouraging example of past responses to ecological challenges, one providing hope for the future, is the transformation of agriculture. Pro-growth advocates point out that although the global population increased dramatically in the 20th century, the total crop harvest increased at a far faster rate.

Moreover, beyond appeals to history, pro-growth advocates, including the ecomodernists, typically offer three arguments for their position. First, economic growth is indispensable for poverty alleviation. Second, an eventual reduction in environmental harms tends to accompany economic growth. Third, economic growth can be decoupled from environmental harm. All three arguments, however, are flawed or incomplete.

Consider first the claim that growth is essential for poverty alleviation. For example, if GDP grows by 3% per year, then GDP will double every 23 years. The OECD estimates that with a doubling of global GDP, the size of the global middle class (namely, those who spend between $10 and $100 per day) would expand from 2 billion people in 2015 to 5 billion people by 2030.[38]

However, this pro-growth argument only succeeds if the only path to poverty reduction involves growing the economic pie rather than redistributing it. Critics counter by saying that a high-quality life for everyone—even if the global population continues to grow—is possible within the planetary boundaries but not without fundamental restructuring of current institutions affecting economic distribution.[39] In addition, the OECD report acknowledges uncertainties that undermine their confidence in their own forecasts, including doubts about continued availability of cheap fossil fuels that propelled the growth experienced in the immediate past.[40] In short, growth alone may not bring about the goal of improved well-being for the global poor, and the goal of ecological sustainability may require either a no-growth or targeted-growth economic trajectory as the fossil fuel basis of modern growth recedes.

The pro-growth position might overcome objections to the first claim if its proponents are correct about their second claim, namely, that the adverse ecological impact due to growth will not last indefinitely. The argument is based on the environmental *Kuznet's curve*, which tracks evidence showing that, with growth in GDP, environmental pollution increases in the initial stages, but, as income per capita reaches a certain threshold, the trend reverses and begins to decline.[41] As the authors themselves noted, however, their projections are based solely upon measurements of air and water pollution in around 40 countries. It not only omits evidence from other countries, but, most importantly, it leaves out other ecological harms that we have shown to be relevant to a sustainability assessment. For example, it leaves out biodiversity loss, greenhouse

40   A LIVABLE PLANET

gas emissions, deforestation, and soil degradation. Recent evidence suggests that the environmental Kuznet's curve hypothesis does not hold up when it takes account of this wider range of environmental consequences.[42]

Also, for economic growth and ecological sustainability goals to be compatible, the arguments for the third claim must be successful. There would have to be significant progress in decoupling high material standards of living from ecologically destructive technologies. Strategies include dematerialization, decarbonization, and resource substitution policies. Beyond recommendations that we buy less, waste less, and repair more, many argue for faster uptake of more efficient technologies and adoption of resource substitution policies using materials that are renewable, less harmful, or not as scarce. However, efficiency gains tend to be offset by a limiting factor known as the *rebound effect*. Efficiency gains are often outpaced by the rebound in overall resource utilization. For example, the development of more efficient refrigerators tends to be accompanied by increase in the size and total energy consumption of refrigerators, and, with increased availability of alternative, less ecologically damaging building materials we build bigger houses. In short, we are back to the "hearts and minds" problem. Technology alone will not suffice, and treating GDP increase as the synoptic goal of social organization only worsens the ecological impact of unbridled profit-seeking activities and unlimited consumer appetites.

Moreover, as noted earlier in this chapter, some prosperous countries have been successful in decoupling their national material footprint (resource use) and environmental degradation from national economic growth by what effectively amounts to an accounting trick when viewed from a planetary perspective. Countries simply outsource production and extraction that depletes resources or degrades the environment.[43] The obvious problem from a planetary perspective is that the environmental gains of one country may not translate into global environmental gains because not all nations can outsource forever.[44] Also, pollution initially taken off the environmental ledger of an affluent, outsourcing country frequently reappears as toxic waste in its own landfills and streams, as well as harm to the global commons, including degradation of the oceans and the airborne drift of particulate matter from industrial production thousands of miles away. Eventually, the outsourcing of environmental harms becomes a self-limiting and self-undermining strategy. In other words, it is not a sustainable economic strategy.

The upshot is that the future of a global economy, one shaped by pro-growth macroeconomic policies, is clouded by the fact that the case for successful decoupling of growth from development has been predicated on doubtful assumptions about past conditions favoring economic growth continuing, an incomplete inventory of environmental costs, and a misplaced focus on measuring national rather than global impact. These three considerations reveal ways in which the efforts to combine pro-growth and pro-environment strategies are potentially self-undermining.

Moreover, environmentally destructive activities, supercharged by pro-growth macroeconomic policies, are not unique to countries that fit the model of traditional capitalist societies. Wherever such policies gain a foothold (e.g., China), their economies will have to change substantially, whether by abandonment of pro-growth policies leading to a likely decline in the material standard of living for the affluent or by more selective growth strategies that encourage only the kinds of growth that improve human well-being for the benefit of the least affluent.

Policies that raise the minimum standard of living, for example, by incorporating robust protection for basic social and economic human rights establish distributive priorities that put a moral brake on the aggregative, maximizing aims of a commitment to GDP growth. However, it remains an open question just how much, if any, the pursuit of poverty relief in conjunction with slowing the pace of ecologically destructive growth in GDP might affect the

42 A LIVABLE PLANET

timing of a transition to a more just and sustainable global political economy. One thing that is clear, however, is that our devotion to a model of endless and undifferentiated economic growth is a major impediment to a transition to a more just and sustainable global political economy, even if it is not the main cause of our predicament. In the near term, at least, the recommendations from proponents of doughnut economics seem most aligned with the human rights approach I defend.

The By-Product of Inequality

It is true virtually everywhere that the affluent cause more environmental harm than the poor or middle classes because they drive bigger cars, live in bigger houses, own more cars and houses, and spend more time and money on computers and airfares. A 2017 UN report estimates that fewer than 1 billion people consume 72% of the world's resources, while the bottom 1.2 billion consume only 1%.[45] More generally, the world's top 10% of income earners are responsible for between 25% and 43% of overall environmental impact, in stark contrast to the world's bottom 10% income earners, who produce only 3–5% of the environmental impact.[46]

It is true also that the ecological burdens of high consumption are unevenly distributed across countries. "Low-income countries have benefited least from growing global resource availability and have continued to deliver primary materials to high-income countries while experiencing few improvements in their domestic material living standards."[47] For example, the ecological footprint—which measures the number of biologically productive hectares needed to support individual consumption—for typical US and EU consumers is three to four times the global average.[48] Specific indicators of the water, materials, and energy footprints of consumption are much higher in high-income countries than

SUSTAINABILITY AND POLITICAL ECONOMY   43

in upper-middle countries and dramatically higher than in low-income income countries.[49]

In other words, studies of consumption patterns make clear that it is not humanity in general that has been the main driver of negative global environmental changes or unsustainable resource depletion. It is primarily the affluent—and especially the affluent residents of high-income countries. However, the story so far is about the consequences of affluence, not a story that explains whether or how environmental harm results from the mere fact that some countries and individuals have more—or even quite a bit more—than others. How, if at all, might economic inequality be bad for the environment?

There is no shortage of emerging empirical evidence showing that economic inequality—not merely affluence alone—is highly *predictive* of greater environmental damage and waste but we still need some explanation—or more plausibly, some explanations—for how inequality figures in these causal stories. There are several ways that a plausible backstory might be constructed.

For example, a familiar claim from the postcolonial and indigenous environmental studies literature is that the disposable income of today's affluent consumers is largely a consequence of inegalitarian economic regimes that were imposed on subject communities hundreds of years ago. At its core, it is a causal claim about the role of historical injustice in fueling inequality leading to contemporary environmental destruction. Such claims typically endorse proposals for reparations for resources wrongly extracted from their communities or demands for the repayment of an "ecological debt." However, arguments rooted in historical injustice are not advanced solely as claims for compensation for past harms. Often, they are claims about the special moral responsibility borne by the current generation of beneficiaries, not merely for rectifying unjust extraction in the past, but for taking responsibility for mitigating the continuing environmental harms of the present because they were made possible only by the enhanced and deeply

44 A LIVABLE PLANET

unequal purchasing power created by that extraction. In other words, on this account, the affluence that produces environmental harm is the product of the legacy of unjust inequalities.

Other approaches attempt to show that affluent inegalitarian societies—independently of how they became affluent—exhibit more ecologically destructive patterns of consumption than affluent societies in which the gradient of economic inequality is less steep. A growing body of empirical evidence confirms that residents of affluent countries where the gap between rich and poor is great cause more environmental damage than residents of other similarly affluent countries where economic inequality is less pronounced. In some highly unequal societies, both the rich and everyone else, including those in middle and lower distributional tiers, cause more environmental harm than their socioeconomic counterparts in less unequal societies. Citizens of affluent, inegalitarian societies emit more greenhouse gases per capita, buy more disposable goods, recycle less, use more water, generate more waste, eat more meat, consume more packaged products, drive more miles, take more flights, and in general engage in more ecologically harmful activities.[50]

And there's more. Where income differences are greater, there tends to be more industrial air pollution in urban areas.[51] Economically unequal societies tend to generate more carbon emissions.[52] Economic inequality is strongly predictive of greater magnification and acceleration of biodiversity loss.[53] And, in general, inequality is associated with more damage to the terrestrial biosphere from landfills, industrial sites, and mining.[54]

In short, there is considerable evidence that highly unequal societies—especially affluent countries—tend to cause more environmental stress for themselves, their least affluent citizens, and the world at large. However, it is an open question why this pattern seems so pervasive.

One explanation of inequality's role is the phenomenon of individuals "consuming more because others do."[55] There are

SUSTAINABILITY AND POLITICAL ECONOMY 45

a couple of variants on this theme. We could look to the kind of causal story often attributed to Thorstein Veblen's *The Theory of the Leisure Class*. High levels of "conspicuous consumption" might be due, in part, to a kind of competition for status recognition. On that view, we consume to "keep up with the Joneses" or, at least, to appear to do so. If there were no Joneses to keep up with, so the theory goes, the rest of us might consume less. No doubt there is some truth to that familiar story, but evidence shows that consumption patterns tend to top out at higher income levels, while acquisition of material goods remains steady or on the upswing among middle-income groups.[56]

Other factors could help fill in the gaps in the explanation of why individuals tend to consume more in highly unequal, affluent societies. For example, inequality might make people more oblivious to the ecological implications of their actions, especially when economic stratification goes hand in hand with residential segregation based on socioeconomic status. When production and waste facilities are located at a distance from the sites of consumption, there is a greater chance of a situation in which what is "out of sight is out of mind." In such cases, there is the pervasive risk that not knowing involves a measure of culpable ignorance on the part of people for whom it is not in their self-interest to inquire. Worse yet, having more might predispose people to greater indifference to the ecological consequences for others from their own actions. Some empirical research findings confirm the fact that faring better than others can breed indifference to the misfortunes of others, and even contempt.[57] Similar patterns of obliviousness and indifference accompany consumption of goods produced in sweat shops or derived from environmental sacrifice zones, where the dirty work of extracting, producing, and disposing of the material basis of modern life gets done.

One thing we can say with some certainty. Inequality does appear to have something to do with the trajectory of ecological damage that is now commonplace, even if the precise causal

46 A LIVABLE PLANET

mechanisms are poorly understood, or perhaps the hypothesized causal pathways are mutually reinforcing. Affluence is a part of the problem, but inequality appears to be another component of social systems that puts economic arrangements on an ecologically unsustainable trajectory.

Practical Implications

The survey of ecological critiques shows that are insufficient grounds for concluding that the primary cause of our predicament is singular or even for thinking that one causal factor is clearly more influential than others in all circumstances so that, once it is addressed, the remaining impediments are readily manageable. Instead of claiming that the fate of the environment stands or falls, for example, with the future of capitalist social organization, we need to take into consideration the wide range of obstacles on the pathway out of our predicament. If this conclusion is right, it might not be enough—or even necessary—to chart a course toward a just and sustainable future to settle some of the deepest debates over the best explanatory hypotheses of the origins of our predicament. Whatever initially set our current predicament in motion, numerous other institutions, social practices, and ideologies coevolved and often remain in place for reasons other than ones that best explain their genesis.

The critiques, taken together, however, do offer some practical guidance. They point to a future with less capitalism, less luxury consumption, less emphasis on aggregate economic growth, and less socioeconomic inequality and social distance between the beneficiaries of production and those who bear its disproportionate burdens. Concretely, that means fewer social investment decisions driven by private profit; more policies that combat consumption of resource-intensive, environmentally destructive luxury goods; an economy more aligned with the satisfaction of basic needs than aggregate growth; and a politics more attuned to constraining the concentration of economic and political power and the callousness it breeds. Moreover, the practical prerequisite for all of these changes is an enhanced role for states, contrary to conventional economic wisdom favoring markets as the fundamental principle of social organization. In subsequent chapters, I argue for the specific types of market practices that should be targeted for restriction or elimination because of their adverse impact on the secure realization of human rights. They are selected because they are among the most economically predatory, ecologically destructive features of the global political economy. However, we turn next to the dominant political and economic ideals underpinning the current organization of the global political economy. These ideals also impede a timely exit from our ecological predicament.

3
Market Fundamentalism

Implementation of a human rights approach for addressing the socioeconomic origin of our ecological predicament would require substantial reorganization of the political economy of individual states and the international order. It also would require repudiation of an intellectually influential, politically entrenched ideal often referred to as *market fundamentalism*. Although the rationales sometimes differ (but often overlap), the core belief is that robust protection of market liberties should be the fundamental principle of social organization. This principle guided the architects of the late 20th-century global political economy who sought to rebalance the power relations between states and markets, within and beyond the jurisdictions of individual nations.

More specifically, market fundamentalists sought to curb the growing regulatory power of states, contract the scope of governmental functions, transfer decision-making from the public to the private sphere, and institutionalize widespread state deference to the efficient outcomes expected from competitive market processes. The human rights approach, by contrast, recommends expansion of state power relative to market decision-makers by targeting ecologically unsustainable, economically predatory market practices. The task of this chapter, accordingly, is to examine market fundamentalist arguments that pose a challenge to the human rights approach outlined in the first chapter and developed in the next chapter.

A Livable Planet. Madison Powers, Oxford University Press. © Oxford University Press 2024.
DOI: 10.1093/oso/9780197756003.003.0003

Market Fundamentalism and Neoliberal Policies

Market fundamentalists endorse a portfolio of pro-market governance proposals that figure centrally in an economic policy agenda often referred to as *neoliberalism*. Within global development circles these policies are widely known as the "Washington Consensus," referring to the dominance of the pro-market worldview within the Bretton Woods institutions, especially the World Bank and International Monetary Fund (IMF), both based in Washington, DC, and heavily influenced by the US Treasury.[1] Such differences in terminology within and across disciplines can be confusing, and choice of labels inevitably invites criticism. It is not my goal to referee these disputes, but a few comments explain the reasons for my own taxonomy.

Some historians and social commentators adopt the market fundamentalist label because they wish to highlight the continuity of contemporary arguments for pro-market policies and the 19th-century laissez-faire appeals to the virtues of self-regulating markets.[2] Many economists also prefer the market fundamentalist label because of the centrality of an ideal of competitive markets in Neoclassical economic theory, its pervasive influence in the economics profession, and widespread invocation of the self-correcting nature of markets as the justification for neoliberal social policies.[3]

Other historians reserve "market fundamentalism" as a label applicable only to those theories that rest their case for competitive markets on the idea that they tend to be self-correcting under conditions of minimal state interference. Their stated aim is to highlight differences with various neoliberal theorists who rely on other rationales for their fiercely pro-market stance.[4] Moreover, various social scientists emphasize the evolution of meanings of neoliberalism, including uses of the term to connote not just a set of economic policies, but also an economically self-serving ideology

50   A LIVABLE PLANET

created by industrial Western nations or even a transformational way of life.[5]

I favor the approach of authors who appear to treat "market fundamentalism," "neoliberalism," and "Washington consensus" as rough synonyms, or at least focus more on the shared policy commitments, whatever the choice of label.[6] Simply for the sake of clarity, I reserve the term "neoliberalism" to refer to an economic policy agenda, and I use "market fundamentalism" as a theoretical umbrella to highlight—and, ultimately, to evaluate and critique separately—the diverse intellectual underpinnings of that agenda.[7]

The orthodox economic agenda relies on two complementary policy strategies. The first set of policies is designed to remove institutional shackles on the decision-making processes of market actors. The main examples are deregulation of market transactions within the private sector and liberalization (i.e., relaxation) of governmental restrictions on permissible forms of business organization, trade and investment activities, and capital flows within and across countries.

The second but equally important aim of market fundamentalists is to contract the scope of the state's institutional functions. This aim is best illustrated by examining the kinds of public policies they oppose. Their primary aim is to contract social welfare policies, which they oppose not only on grounds of presumed inefficiency, but also for broader philosophical reasons. They object to the legal implementation of economic and social rights and state intervention in the economy for the advancement of social welfare objectives, which they either view as morally illegitimate for government to embrace or believe best achievable through market mechanisms.

Examples of policies that market fundamentalists generally oppose include state limits on private capital accumulation; exclusion of certain goods and services from allocation as market commodities; the creation of wage and labor standards, economic safety nets, or universal income guarantees; reliance on taxation and other policy tools to limit inequalities in wealth, income, and differences in political power among economically stratified social groups; using non-market rules to determine access to natural resources or allocate the economic and social costs and benefits of activities affecting the environment; and so much more.[8]

One concrete mechanism for facilitating the elimination of such programs is privatization of existing state enterprises in sectors such as transportation, healthcare, water and sanitation systems, and other public utilities. Another mechanism, widely promoted by global and regional development banks, is the imposition of austerity measures (budget controls and sovereign debt limits) on debtor nations. The familiar refrain is the need to "starve the beast"—in other words, to disempower states likely pursue non-market social welfare policies by depriving them of financial resources. Unlike deregulation and trade liberalization, which are designed to limit government interference with business activities, privatization and austerity measures disempower the public sector by removing government from those activities that could be the province of private business. In other words, an overarching aim behind privatization and austerity measures is to transfer decision-making from the public to the private sphere.

Market fundamentalism, in the broad sense used here then, endorses a particular position on how markets should figure within an ideal form of capitalism.[9] It seeks to expand state deference to market outcomes in as many policy domains as possible. It therefore offers an austere vision of capitalist organization standing in opposition to a wide range state polices that either interfere with market processes by regulating the international flow of goods and services or supplanting the results of markets for the sake of social welfare objectives or egalitarian distributive goals.

Moreover, a reason for interest in these widely discussed matters is the fact that few areas of policy are more affected by the market fundamentalist position than those pertaining to the environment. Empirical research has shown that the state's role in regulation of market impacts on the environment diverges widely across varieties

52   A LIVABLE PLANET

of capitalist organization. Capitalist systems can be classified as ranging from more ecology-prone (protective) to more ecology-adverse (destructive) forms of capitalist organization.[10] Wholesale reliance on markets as the fundamental principle of social organization opens the door for market practices that are among the most ecologically unsustainable and economically predatory and thus a serious threat to the secure realization of human rights.

Three Rationales for Market Fundamentalism

Market fundamentalists appeal to a variety of rationales in defense of their ideal of political economy. In this section, I examine three.

The Foundational Role of Market Liberties

In *Capitalism and Freedom*, Milton Friedman argues that political freedom depends on the existence of economic freedom. In his words, "I know of no example in time or place of a society that has been marked by a large measure of political freedom, and that has not also used something comparable to a free market to organize the bulk of economic activity."[11] The core of his foundational argument is the claim that political and civil liberties are dangerously insecure unless some more foundational market liberties are protected.

Friedrich Hayek is the theorist who developed most fully the idea of the fundamental place of market liberties in a scheme of liberties. His version of the argument proceeds from what he calls the "conditions of freedom," which he defines as a "state in which individuals are allowed to use their own knowledge for their own purposes."[12] The conditions that he sees as definitive for life as a free person are realized only within a spontaneously generated social order. A spontaneously generated order emerges as a cumulative consequence of uncoordinated choices of separate individuals, each pursuing their own self-chosen ends. Markets are centrally important to the ideal of a spontaneously generated social order because they leave many details of daily life open to be chosen by individuals for themselves. In other words, individuals, on Hayek's view, are maximally able to use their talents and skills for their own ends and purposes when society guarantees a robust bundle of market liberties.

The liberties endorsed by Hayek and other market fundamentalists are quite comprehensive. They include the freedom to engage in market transactions such as saving, investing, and trading; freedom to enter labor contracts on mutually acceptable terms; and the liberty of individuals to acquire, retain, use, and transfer economic wealth and other resources as each judges best.

A society that engages in centralized economic planning, along with state provision of the goods and services chosen by its governmental officials or legislative bodies, stands in sharp contrast to the ideal of a spontaneously generated social order. These state interventions remove many decisions from the hands of individuals and vest concentrated power in bureaucratically organized states. Moreover, a society organized in pursuit of a common goal increases the instances of state coercion. The problem of increased state power, as Hayek saw it, is that no matter how valuable or noble the ends chosen by collective decision-making processes and coercively implemented by states, the activist role of the state thwarts the ability of individuals to use their own skills and knowledge to pursue the ends they judge most worthy. A spontaneous social order, by contrast, minimizes instances of state coercion. Markets facilitate the dispersal of power and create "conditions likely to improve the chances of all in the pursuit of their aims."[13]

Hayek, Friedman, and other like-minded economists and social scientists developed their ideas about the foundational role of markets against the backdrop of the totalitarian regimes of Nazi Germany and the Soviet Union. In 1947, the issue of state coercion

54 A LIVABLE PLANET

was front and center at the founding meeting of the Mont Pelerin Society, attended by founding members Hayek and Friedman. In its Statement of Aims, the founders proclaimed that the "central values of civilization are in danger" from political conditions that have "extended arbitrary power" and that these conditions "have been fostered by a decline of belief in private property and the competitive market."[14]

Hayek and other founding members of the Society made it clear that systems of totalitarian social control were not their sole targets. Their objections were lodged against any form of centralized economic planning, especially when done for the sake of social justice, whether undertaken by socialist, social democratic, or welfare capitalist states. Indeed, Hayek argues that pursuit of the goal of social justice is perhaps the "gravest threat to most other values of a free civilization."[15] All such regimes, however well-intended, are enemies of individual freedom, on his view, because there is no stopping point at which goal-oriented state intervention is safe for the cause of liberty. His claim is that there is a "self-accelerating tendency" of governments that intervene in markets for the sake of social justice to "progressively approach" totalitarianism.[16]

Friedman raised similar arguments against European social democracy. In his view, a persistent threat to liberty arises from any extensive use of state coercion, whether employed by dictators, monarchs, or "momentary majorities" in social democracies because it results in the substitution of the judgment of the state for the varied decisions of individuals.[17]

Even if we assume, for the sake of argument, that state coercion can pose an especially grave, perhaps morally unique, kind of threat to individual liberty, the foundational argument is subject to four objections.

The first objection is that the foundationalist argument fails to appreciate the intense competition among claimants of individual liberties. Substantive interventions—ones that are based on weighing up competing non-interference claims—are unavoidable in any reasonably complex society. The point is crystallized in Isaiah Berlin's elaboration on R. H. Tawney's famous remark that "freedom for the pike is death for the minnows; the liberty of some must depend on the restraint of others."[18] For example, many kinds of market transactions have non-consensual spillover effects on the environment and the health and property holdings of others. Liberty to pollute is a liberty to override the liberty of others to use their land productively and safely. A theory focused solely on minimizing state coercion fails to recognize the many day-to-day instances in which the primary consideration is not whether states should interfere with individual choices, but which choices should be foreclosed by state action so that the choices of others are left open.

This objection also goes to the heart of the fundamentalists' assumption that markets always diffuse power. Markets can concentrate power in ways that limit the choices available to other market participants. A blanket policy of state abstinence from all interferences with individual liberty is not a plausible institutional strategy, even from the perspective of someone who prizes the absence of coercive interference.

The second objection is that having more opportunities for the unimpeded exercise of market choice does not automatically enable more individuals to achieve more of their own self-chosen ends. While it is true that markets can aid individuals in getting more of what they prefer and less of what they do not want, the reverse also can be true. For example, individuals may strongly value protection against health risks from impure food or water and other harmful environmental exposures. But a policy that always leaves such matters to individual choice in the marketplace can lead to more consumers having fewer opportunities to realize what they value most. Two ways this can occur.

In one set of cases, the problem is that consumers are often unable to protect themselves against harmful products through the exercise of their own judgment, especially when issues of

56 A LIVABLE PLANET

science are complex and commercial marketing campaigns make it more difficult to make informed judgments about safety. In these instances, such risks are best dealt with through regulatory policies rather than reliance on the hit-or-miss effectiveness of consumer education.[19]

In another set of cases, consumer choice, even if well-informed, is insufficient for satisfaction of individual preferences for public goods, such as clean water or air. Only state intervention that restricts the market liberties of powerful commercial entities can ensure the satisfaction of such preferences. Although state action that removes some matters from market choice restricts the liberty of individuals to make some decisions for themselves, it nonetheless can result in more individuals getting more of what they value most highly, like health and environmental quality.

So, let's review what we have concluded thus far. Each of the first two objections to the fundamentalist argument raises a distinct point. The first objection demonstrates that liberty rights compete such that states must routinely make substantive normative judgments necessary to referee among competing claims of rights to non-interference. The second objection up-ends the assumption that the best way for individuals to satisfy more of their strongest preferences is always through the expansion of individual marketplace choice.

The third objection is that the obsession with minimizing instances of state actions that interfere with individual choice, or eliminating policies that remove decisional power from individuals, ignores important qualitative differences among choices. Much more is at stake morally, from the point of view of persons affected by state regulation, than simply the number of instances in which the power to interfere is constrained. Not all choices are on a moral par.[20] Some choices are relatively trivial in significance. The purely quantitative approach to limiting state interference is indiscriminate. It proceeds as if all forms of state interference with market liberties pose comparably profound threats to human freedom and are therefore equivalent in the burdens of justification that they must meet. For example, the consumer's freedom to choose plastic shopping bags that damage watersheds and aquatic life is not highly consequential for individual well-being or their ability to shape the important contours of their own lives. To the extent that individuals care about interference with their choices, it's not a simple matter of wanting protection of more or fewer choices, but the protection of choices that materially affect their overall quality of life or ability to control their own destinies.

The fourth objection is that the foundational argument gets foundational priorities the wrong way round. The protection of non-market liberties often depends on protection of certain background economic conditions. Political powerlessness, rooted in economic disempowerment, does not provide a secure platform for preserving guarantees of basic political and civil liberties. A degree of material security guaranteed by basic social and economic rights is widely viewed as a practical prerequisite for preserving a system of political and civil liberties from erosion at the hands of the economically more powerful members of society. John Rawls argued along these lines in his later writings. He explained that "the first principle covering the equal basic rights and liberties may easily be preceded by a lexically prior principle requiring that citizens' basic needs be met, at least insofar as their being met is necessary for citizens to understand and to be able fruitfully to exercise those rights and liberties."[21]

The upshot of the fourth argument is that guarantees of certain basic economic conditions are foundational, both for the security of a system of legally guaranteed political and civil rights and for the effective exercise of rights that are legally secure. However, neither point supports unlimited freedom to acquire vast property or to use property rights or natural resources free of regulation designed to protect others from harm. What is foundationally important in a scheme of economic rights is a secure material hedge against erosion of these basic civil and political liberties or deterioration

58   A LIVABLE PLANET

in the ability to effectively exercise those rights. Contrary to the market fundamentalist argument, there is not only a strong case for establishing a welfare floor as a hedge against loss of freedom. There also are reasons to think that establishing upper bounds on wealth acquisition by the powerful, along with restraints on its use in political processes, are foundationally more crucial for the protection of legal guarantees of civil and political liberties and the background conditions for their effective exercise.

Self-Defense Arguments

A second rationale for expansive market liberties is that social arrangements that leave more matters to individual choice in the marketplace provide a valuable means of self-defense against the predations of the state. The argument differs from the foundational argument. The self-defense argument views market liberty as instrumentally valuable for the protection against harm, not loss of freedom. The underlying assumption is that bureaucrats and legislators suffer from agential deficiencies that make them prone to decisions detrimental to the welfare of their citizens. The argument is rooted in skepticism regarding claims made by state actors about special expertise or superior knowledge as a rationale for preempting individual decisions in the marketplace. The argument also reflects suspicion of human motivations of the people who exercise political power. Specifically, market fundamentalists point to the potential for politicians in a democracy to adopt ill-conceived, socially destructive economic policies to curry favor with the populace or to cater to oligarchical factions seeking to capture the apparatus of the state for the advancement of their own narrow economic interests.

Such complaints, based on deficiencies in knowledge and moral virtue, if accurate, would tend to favor either a reversion to something akin to the 19th-century laissez-faire doctrine or else the need to find some workable criterion for distinguishing permissible from impermissible state action. Indeed, many market fundamentalists have taken a rhetorical turn toward libertarianism, a position which favors shrinking the state as much as possible, on every imaginable front. The logic of the argument is straightforward. If states are so often wrong about the reasons for their action and its implications, and so easily corruptible by both oligarchic interests and fleeting democratic majorities, then it is not clear that they can be trusted with any task. Anything short of a wholesale retreat seems like an unstable compromise.

For the market fundamentalists who concede, albeit grudgingly, that markets are not self-regulating and that sustainable competitive markets require the institutional support of the state, the self-defense argument is especially vulnerable to objection. It seems that there is no choice but to accept a somewhat more interventionist state. They must then answer an age-old question about where to draw the line circumscribing the legitimate use of state power. Both Hayek and Friedman proposed answers.

Hayek first distinguished between permissible and illegitimate forms of law creation. He rejects what he called "made law," the kinds of legal norms created by legislative bodies with the intention of achieving specific social or economic outcomes. By contrast, his favored form of law creation is exemplified in the Anglo-American common law tradition, where judges are presumed to establish narrowly tailored precedents that resolve specific problems of social coordination or conflict resolution. The assumption is that this institutional solution would tamp down the goal-oriented, self-consciously designed grand plans of legislators for reordering society. The upshot would be a gradual, organic, piecemeal evolution of legal norms, more in keeping with Hayek's ideal of a spontaneous form of social ordering achieved by uncoordinated marketplace decisions. The only safe path, on this view, lies in spontaneous social ordering by markets, supplemented by modest amounts of incremental, slow-paced legal rule-making.

60 A LIVABLE PLANET

However, Hayek was keenly aware of the practical limits of purely institutional solutions. An institutional division of labor would slow any legislative effort to implement a grand social design, but coercive state power, driven by grand visions of social transformation, is blocked most effectively by substantive legal rules. More specifically, legal rules should designate certain spheres of activity as ones in which government interference—including judicial interference—is prohibited. And one of the best ways of expanding that sphere is to bring more market activities within a constitutionally protected realm.[22] In other words, the self-defense argument favors contracting the scope of permissible state action so that individuals are better protected from harm caused by the pursuit of comprehensive goals for restructuring society.

Both parts of Hayek's solution face difficulties. The first problem is that he underestimates the extent to which activist judiciaries, animated by singular moral visions, can deliberately undertake conscious efforts to redesign the social order. The judiciary is not always, contrary to Alexander Hamilton's supposition, the least dangerous branch. Although, in Hamilton's oft repeated words, it has "neither sword nor purse strings," its decisions can be driven by grand visions of social transformation, often predicated on beliefs about its members' own superior knowledge and special expertise. We know that legal precedents that constitutionalize a zone of individual sovereign decision-making have a way of crumbling over time, whether by incremental erosion or sweeping reversal. The second problem also arises if we follow Hayek's general advice. If we tie the hands of government and defer to the spontaneous order generated by the market, we preempt any serious chance of tackling the convergent crises that constitute our ecological predicament. The ideal of a spontaneous social order now seems quaint and nostalgic in the age of the Anthropocene.

Years later, Milton Friedman, in *Capitalism and Freedom*, also took on the task of trying to draw jurisdictional boundaries of permissible state action. He developed his approach in the shadow of Karl Polanyi's influential argument against the "liberal creed" of self-regulating markets. Polanyi famously argued that markets are not self-sustaining and that, over time, competitive conditions would deteriorate, initiating new rounds of state intervention to correct the problems generated by laissez-faire capitalism.[23] While Friedman retained his belief in the long-run, self-correcting nature of market processes, he articulated a narrowly defined interventionist role for states in preventing market failures along the way. They should act as umpires. Government should confine itself to doing things "that the market cannot do for itself, namely, to determine, arbitrate, and enforce the rules of the game."[24] In practical terms, that means securing conditions for competitive markets and making sure that the price system works. For example, these aims could be achieved by policing monopolies, protecting private property acquired through market transactions, guaranteeing freedom of contract for individuals and businesses, and ruling out governmental interferences such as minimum-wage laws.

Friedman's version of the self-defense argument is compromised by two problems. First, the sweep of his doubts about the intellectual and moral virtues of states undermines even a limited role for states as umpires. If states are so thoroughly lacking in knowledge and good judgment, and so susceptible to corruption and forces of irrationality, it is unclear how they can be expected to fulfill their designated role as umpires. For one thing, states so prone to error and vice cannot be expected to stay within their prescribed institutional and jurisdictional boundaries. More generally, it would be unreasonable to trust the state to undertake even the function of an umpire unless, of course, it possesses a richly informed understanding of market conditions, probable consequences of various policies designed to ensure competitiveness, and the primary sources of market failure. However, because states are presumed to be prone to error, it is difficult to see how they could acquire sufficient knowledge to serve as umpires. And, of course, trustworthy

62 A LIVABLE PLANET

umpires also require moral virtues that the proponents of self-defense arguments think lacking in agents of the state.

Second, Friedman's self-defense argument errs in the opposite direction. It overstates the kind, quality, and extent of knowledge uniquely available to individuals pursuing their own purposes. It fails to acknowledge that market actors often do not foresee or care about larger-scale, longer-term consequences for others. Also, the argument implausibly neglects consideration of an epistemic advantage that states can have over individual market actors. States can overcome the narrowness of perspective, insufficiency of knowledge, and tendency toward corruption through deliberative processes on matters that pertain to the public good or affect large segments of the population. But, then again, he doesn't hold out much hope for the workings of democracy.

In short, self-defense arguments based on the presumed agential deficiencies of states rest on premises regarding deeply ingrained institutional frailties that undercut key aspects of the market fundamentalists' own position, especially among those who concede a limited state role as umpires. By the logic of their own argument, even the umpire cannot be trusted, and the only reliable defense against the predatory actions of states is their wholesale disempowerment. But that solution seems more suspect than ever. In the face of grave ecological crises, the market fundamentalist position would counsel states to defer to the verdict of markets, arrived at in characteristically slow, piecemeal fashion. That is more likely to be a recipe for collective self-destruction than individual self-defense.

Welfare Economics Arguments

A third rationale for market fundamentalism is rooted in Neoclassical welfare economics. The Neoclassical argument rests on the belief that economic reality regularly conforms to the model of competitive market equilibrium, where market failures are rare, thus ensuring the routine production of efficient outcomes. The close connection between efficiency and competitive markets is built into what is known as the *Fundamental Law of Welfare Economics*.[25] This defense of market fundamentalism exhibits considerable continuity with 19th-century laissez-faire thought, but, in addition, it often claims that efficient markets, when free of state interference, not only enhance freedom but produce outcomes that are fair, broadly beneficial, and socially stable.

Milton and Rose Friedman made famous the first steps in the argument, namely, that a great virtue of competitive markets is that they best promote economic efficiency *and* simultaneously maximize individual freedom.[26] The argument is complicated, but a simplified sketch of the basic steps will be sufficient to elucidate how the theoretical marriage between Neoclassical economic theory and political liberalism was crafted and its continuing allure in many quarters.

Neoclassical economics aims for efficiency, understood technically as a state of *Pareto optimality*. The Pareto criterion counts as efficient any state of affairs in which at least one person is made better off, and no one is made worse off. Individuals are made better off in the sense that they are able to satisfy their strongest preferences, as revealed in their market behavior.[27] The Fundamental Law of Welfare Economics presumes that the Pareto efficiency criterion will be satisfied under conditions of perfect market competition. Efficient market transactions not only result in a welfare improvement in the sense that individual preferences are satisfied, but every voluntary market transaction also involves an act of choice. It is therefore a small victory for the cause of freedom when individuals make market choices free from state interference. Many small market victories for the cause of freedom add up to a large victory when the aggregate of free, unobstructed market choices not only increases the sum of human welfare but simultaneously increases the sum of human freedom.

64 A LIVABLE PLANET

To put matters slightly differently, Neoclassical economic theory assumes that competitive markets result in long-term aggregate utility (welfare) gains—the total sum of individual preferences that are satisfied—but only so long as individuals are free to make their choices according to their own preferences. When more matters are left to market decision, leaving more individuals free to satisfy their own preferences, the result is the maximization of overall social utility *and* an increase in the overall social quantum of freedom. State interference with market choices, then, is seen to produce dual bad effects: it is a source of inefficiency, thus reducing individual and aggregate social utility, and it constrains the exercise of individual liberty.

Many versions of the Neoclassical rationale for markets go even further. They not only claim that efficient outcomes co-travel with enhanced freedom for individuals. The new, supercharged welfare economics argument also claims that efficiency secures the realization of other values. Some economists have described the Pareto criterion as a standard of fairness or equity that is so compelling that it is now widely accepted and that its general acceptance, in turn, contributes to social stability.[28] They ask: Who could object to outcomes in which at least one person is made better off and no one is made worse off?[29] Nothing but envy, they say, not a genuine complaint of unfairness, could explain its rejection. In other words, the supercharged argument promises a standard of social assessment that gives us everything we might want in one simple criterion for assessing social systems. The prospect that the Pareto efficiency criterion can serve as a synoptic social value contributes to the elevation of economics among the social sciences.

However, there are at least two major objections to the underlying notions of fairness (we will return to the issue of freedom in the next section). First, even if we set aside familiar objections to the idea that human welfare consists solely in mere preference satisfaction and we concede that individual market choices reliably make individuals better off than they would have been, they may still experience an extremely low level of welfare, even one that is below a human rights standard. Joseph Stiglitz observes that while markets might produce considerable social benefits for quite a few people "[m]arket processes may, by themselves, leave many people with too few resources to survive" and government, therefore, has an essential role "in ensuring social justice" for everyone affected by market organization.[30]

Second, William Easterly raises a different equity-based objection. Because the inequalities of reward from a transaction (or a series of transactions) can have serious effects on the distribution of advantages, we still can raise questions about fairness. Even if voluntary exchanges make both parties better off, market transactions do not necessarily make both parties better off to the same degree.[31] For example, successive iterations of wage bargaining may leave vulnerable employees better off than they would have been, but, over time, more economically advantaged employers are able to extract wage and other concessions, thereby inaugurating a downward spiral of decreasing welfare for the least advantaged.

Stiglitz and Easterly rather convincingly show two separate ways the standard of fairness often appealed to by Neoclassical economists should be rejected, at least if it is proffered as the sole metric of fairness. Even if we concede that markets may make people better off (by satisfying more of their strongest preferences), they can leave some people at a very low level of well-being, even below what is required under a human rights standard, and markets can leave people so much worse off than others that their bargaining power and long-term life prospects for welfare improvement are radically diminished, again eroding the conditions for secure realization of human rights.

Another objection goes to the heart of the social stability claim. John Rawls, for example, famously argues that income and wealth differentials arising from inegalitarian distributive schemes can have corrosive effects on democratic processes, enabling economic elites to fix the rules of social cooperation for their own advantage.

66   A LIVABLE PLANET

Second, this is a form of political unfairness that often translates into further unfairness in market power insofar as the rules work against the disempowered, leading also to a decline of public commitment to society's basic institutions.[32]

Rawls's points about fairness and stability differ from—but reinforce—Easterly's concern about accumulated market power differentials that are set in motion by bargaining disparities within individual market transactions. Rawls's point goes to the broader political consequences of power differentials at work within the institutions that structure those market transactions. There is nothing fair or socially stable about institutional rules, fixed for the benefit of the advantaged so that they can engage freely in market transactions, which set in motion a spiral of increasingly disadvantaging bargaining conditions for the less advantaged.

If the fairness and social stability arguments succumb to the combined weight of these multiple objections, the market fundamentalists' argument for rebalancing can prevail only if, as Hayek argues, freedom is a value of such moral weight that it trumps other values *and* the underlying conception of freedom itself is unassailable. The next section explains why we should reject the conception of freedom that underpins that argument.

The Non-Interference Conception of Freedom

The market fundamentalists' conception of freedom, as we have seen, is defined strictly in terms of non-interference, or, more precisely, the absence of coercive interference with an individual's choices and actions.[33] A gunman who demands "your money or your life" coercively interferes with individual choice, thereby leaving the victim with fewer options. This is a paradigmatic example of what it means to have power over a person, where power is understood as a particular kind of capacity—namely the capacity

MARKET FUNDAMENTALISM   67

to impose one's will on others.[34] The same is true for state coercion. If a state enacts a law backed by criminal or civil penalties, then that, too, is a coercive interference with individual liberty.[35] The social conditions under which their ideal of a free person is realized, therefore, consist in a system of institutionalized protections against both the gunman's threats and state interference with various liberties, including market liberties.

The non-interference conception is unobjectionable, as far as it goes. The real criticism is that exclusive reliance on this conception fails to recognize that there are multiple dimensions of human freedom and that the non-interference conception captures only a portion of the salient features of a plausible ideal of a free person.[36] A multidimensional approach, by contrast, recognizes that coercive interference with individual choice is one way—but not the only way—that individuals or entities can unjustly impose their will on others or hold power over them, inconsistent with their status as free persons.

For example, non-interference theories do not leave conceptual space to register the wrongness of relationships involving domination.[37] Cecile Laborde's definition is instructive: "domination refers to the relatively unrestrained and systematic (even if unexercised) ability of groups or individuals to exert power over others in pursuit of their own interest at the expense of those subordinate to them."[38] Her definition illustrates two key aspects of the injustice of domination left out of account by the non-interference conception.

First, power over others can involve control over the options available to others, even if there are relatively few instances of interferences with whatever choices remain available to them. The choices available to subordinate individuals or groups are ones that dominant persons, social groups, or institutional agents leave open for them to exercise. Subordinate persons are unfree to the extent that their fates are in the grip of others, leaving their options radically foreclosed. The non-interference conception, however, registers as losses of freedom only the losses of options resulting

68 A LIVABLE PLANET

from a direct interference with whatever choices are open to individuals.

Second, Laborde's definition emphasizes the importance of attending to power exercised by dominant parties over others "in pursuit of their own interest at the expense of those subordinate to them." A distinctively unjust aspect of a loss of freedom occurs when steep power differentials enable stronger parties to treat the subordinate party as a mere instrument or tool of their own wills. However, the injustice does not end there. The ability to dominate others confers enhanced power to engage in relatively unconstrained, exploitative advantage-taking or exclude others from beneficial forms of social cooperation and effective participation in public life.

There are many ways that domination can occur, as well as multiple ways that the power it confers can diminish an important dimension of what free persons value in their social relations with others. One familiar way is for social groups to gain effective control over the formal institutions of government, thereby allowing them to rig the rules of economic interaction for their own advantage.[39] For example, oligarchs, white supremacists, or patriarchal religious groups can establish self-serving rules pertaining to taxation, capital accumulation, access to education, and terms of employment. Subordinate groups are routinely and progressively disempowered as a result of the way these rules structure marketplace transactions. Those who are disempowered by the rules experience a loss in their standing as free persons, but not because of any direct coercive interference with their market choices. Their disempowerment is achieved by the exercise of control over the formation of background institutions and practices within which market transactions occur, which, in turn, reinforces relations of domination and the resulting patterns of disadvantage. The market fundamentalist conception cannot recognize the loss in this important dimension of freedom.

Not all forms of domination arise solely through control over the formal institutions of government. Domination also can arise through the ordinary workings of unregulated markets. Social groups or other entities, including multinational corporations, can be highly effective agents of domination even without rigging the formal legal rules of economic interaction. Instead of capturing the institutional apparatus of the state for their own benefit, their ability to subordinate others is enhanced when governments simply exit the arena within which the accumulation of asymmetric power in the marketplace could be prevented or undone by law or regulation. Power differentials thrive not only under political conditions in which non-state entities grab the reins of state power but also under conditions where states fail to restrain the exercise of asymmetric market power. While market fundamentalists are deeply opposed to the capture of state power for private purposes, the political conditions they endorse nonetheless facilitate market-based domination simply by leaving the economically less advantaged to fend for themselves. The non-interference conception fails to register these concerns as well.

There are further issues of freedom that the fundamentalists' conception fails to register. Not all social constraints on available options are a consequence of domination, whether achieved through capture of the institutional apparatus of the state or engineered through deliberate efforts to secure the state's exit from the arena within which the preventable accumulation of asymmetric power occurs.

Unjust differential freedom also can arise from social conditions generated from the cumulative, uncoordinated decisions of many individuals and entities whose intentions and understanding of the consequences of their actions vary considerably. Markets that are celebrated as an arena of morally neutral, spontaneously generated social order, when left unregulated, can produce durable clusters of disadvantage and deprivation that constrict effective social freedom for some groups relative to others. Two examples are especially

70   A LIVABLE PLANET

important: circumstances of forced choices and circumstances of foreclosed choices.

Exploitation involves forced choices, instances in which there is no coercive interference and where options are in fact expanded. Exploitation involves being unfairly taken advantage of for the benefit of another, more powerful individual or social group. Unfair advantage-taking need not completely vitiate voluntariness, result in the vulnerable parties being made worse off than they otherwise would have been, or pervade every aspect of life in the way robust forms of domination do—say, when it approximates the evils of slavery. An example is the multinational corporation that contracts with a local manufacturer for production of blue jeans. Assume that the corporation had no hand in crafting the local laws and played no role in the existing pattern of economic distribution and employment opportunities. The defenders of the "hard bargains" driven by sweatshop employers often note that not only are they not implicated in creating unjust background conditions, but their activities also do not result in a contraction of options but an expansion of opportunities. In such a case, the market fundamentalist would emphasize the voluntary nature of the employment agreement and the presumption of a welfare improvement for workers; therefore, they counsel against state interference with the market choices of the parties to the transaction.

By contrast, the relevant point here is that those who start out with few choiceworthy options due to differential bargaining power or material insecurity often end up with more constrained life prospects. Their range of available, choiceworthy social options contracts as disadvantage compounds and power differentials widen further in successive market transactions between parties who differ greatly in their relative social position. Over time, prevailing wages are driven down in places where economic opportunities are quite limited and employers are in position to force down already low wages. To reiterate, in this example, the employer did not create the circumstances of economic vulnerability in ways that the non-domination conception of freedom would condemn. And the employer did not coerce potential employees to work, a condition that the market fundamentalist would condemn. Loss of effective social freedom in this example results from impersonal market forces. It illustrates a loss in a dimension of human freedom that is neither reducible to concerns about domination nor recognizable to the market fundamentalist as raising an issue of freedom. The market fundamentalist can either view this outcome as morally unproblematic because there is no coercive interference, regrettable but not unjust, or see it as a temporary stop along the long-term pathway of a self-correcting market. Either way, on their theory, there is no loss of freedom warranting state interference in markets.

The problem of foreclosed choices, by contrast, arises where social structural factors exclude people from opportunities for full participation in the life of their communities, realms of power, sources of life satisfaction, and positions of authority and status, and, ultimately, deprive them of public recognition of their standing as moral equals. Instead of being forced to choose between bad or unfairly constrained options, as it is in cases of exploitation, individuals experience diminished social freedom because of outright social exclusion. They are shut out from the range of options available to others in their social environment. For example, residents of environmental sacrifice zones have no feasible housing alternatives other than living in communities where rents are low and risks are high. Such practices are not ones that market fundamentalists are equipped to condemn. Market liberty means a complete freedom to use market power for one's own personal ends, whatever the effects it might have on the range of options of other individuals and the members of social groups. On the market fundamentalist view, it is neither the responsibility of the state nor the responsibility of the polluting corporation to monitor the non-coercive, unintended constriction of the effective social freedom of marginalized social groups. The affected communities are left to

72   A LIVABLE PLANET

fend for themselves and use whatever market power they do have to alter their own circumstances, but they do not have recourse to state interventions, which are ruled out as unjust constraints on market liberties, judged more fundamentally important.

Of course, as noted already, problems of forced choices and foreclosed choices might well result from—and routinely do co-travel with—domination. In that case, individuals and groups who are so thoroughly lacking in control over their own destinies have no realistic choice but to submit to the grip of others and to live at the mercy of those have an outsized say in how things go. Because of the market fundamentalist's singular conception of freedom as non-interference, they cannot accommodate concerns about social exclusion and exploitation, whether these conditions result from patterns of domination, impersonal market forces, or, more typically, a combination.

The combined weight of the arguments in this chapter shows that there are serious problems inherent in the fundamentalist's understanding of state duties pertaining to the enforcement of non-interference norms. They fail to recognize the many instances in which governments must adjudicate between competing liberties, and they ignore the inescapable need for states to assess the relative gravity of their own and others' interferences with liberty.[40] They overestimate what individuals on their own can do to achieve their own ends and the extent to which they can rely on markets to satisfy their preferences. The more libertarian strand of market fundamentalism presupposes a high degree of individual capacity for self-defense and self-sufficiency even in complex social arrangements marked by globalized forces that are far beyond the individual's control. In this regard, they underestimate threats of harm from sources other than government. They fail to appreciate the importance of a proper balance of power, one that recognizes the importance of giving states just enough power to protect their citizens from harm caused by others, but not so much power as to be the main source of harm.[41] Democratic institutions at least aim for such a balance, not only by adjudicating competing claims of rights to non-interference, but also by policing conditions that incubate patterns of domination and social exclusion and the proliferation of forced choices and foreclosed choices. The rebalancing schemes proposed by market fundamentalists up-end the possibility of state action for establishing social conditions that support a multidimensional ideal of human freedom by advocating a blanket immunity from market interferences.

Moreover, the diminished, delegitimated state favored by market fundamentalists, especially the current libertarian strand, empowers and emboldens the already globally ascendant cadre of predatory economic actors, and it ignores the ecologically destructive consequences of their activities. Whatever the motives of its advocates, market fundamentalism serves the narrow interests of those who seek to consolidate and expand their gains by placing predatory market liberties on a par with other liberties. Their anemic conception of freedom shields them from proper recognition of problems of domination, forced choices, and foreclosed choices, and it fuels the global trend toward further de-democratization and greater economic disempowerment. All these freedom-constraining conditions are inimical to the secure realization of human rights, and the next chapter explains how human rights theory should take them into account in their conception of the state's duty to protect the human rights of the residents under their jurisdiction.

4

Human Rights and Ecological Goals

In this chapter, I argue for enhanced protection for a bundle of strategically important human rights specially targeted to counteract ecologically unsustainable, economically predatory market practices that threaten our ability to maintain a livable planet. These rights are referred to as *dual-purpose human rights* because they not only secure very basic elements of human well-being that ground many of those rights, but they also perform their normative function, in significant part, by charging states with the duty to preserve the ecological conditions that sustain human life and make possible the satisfaction of basic needs and by giving right holders more control over their ecological futures. High-priority, dual-purpose rights include rights of subsistence, food, and water, along with a family of rights protecting against environmental health risks and ecological degradation (e.g., the right "to a clean, healthy and sustainable environment," formally recognized by the United Nations General Assembly in 2022).[1]

A key to understanding the practical agenda of this targeted human rights approach is its conception of state responsibilities for their secure realization. I argue for the central importance of the state's expansive and open-ended duties to protect. Within the existing international framework, states are uniquely positioned to counteract structurally entrenched economic disadvantages and cumulative concentrations of power that systematically erode the ecological and economic conditions necessary for the secure realization of dual-purpose human rights.

This chapter's first section offers a brief sketch of generally recognized features of human rights that make them normatively

A Livable Planet. Madison Powers, Oxford University Press. © Oxford University Press 2024.
DOI: 10.1093/oso/9780197756003.003.0004

distinct. It surveys the diversity of grounds used to justify the inclusion of specific rights within a comprehensive list of basic human rights, and it demonstrates the extent of agreement on the inclusion of the subset of rights characterized as dual-purpose. It explains the rationale for and implications of assigning enhanced priority for these rights as a response to our ecological predicament.

The second section replies to objections to human rights theories based on their failure or inability to address a range of morally troublesome inequalities. I discuss three versions of the objection, but the primary target is the claim that they lack the theoretical resources necessary to identify and remedy structural inequalities that causally contribute to and perpetuate human rights deficits. I explain how an expansive specification of the state's duty to protect can counter this objection.

The third section examines three criticisms of the application of a human rights framework to problems posed by our ecological predicament. First, we should opt for voluntary, less socially restrictive approaches, such as humanitarian assistance. Second, the approach relies too heavily on a state-centric view of human rights responsibilities in a globalized world. Third, because the sole concern of human rights theory is human well-being, it cannot serve as the foundation for a comprehensive theory of ecological justice.

The fourth section steps back from a presentation of the central normative features of the approach to address conceptual issues that lie below the surface. I consider potential objections to the application of a human rights approach to ecological harms because, in complex cases, it would require revisions to a traditional conception of rights, their correlative duties, and their violation.

The Normative Framework of Human Rights

The positions adopted in this chapter proceed from key normative assumptions embedded in most human rights theories and

76 A LIVABLE PLANET

embodied in international legal conventions.[2] Human rights, as understood in this book, are moral norms. They frequently find institutional expression in international law, treaties, and conventions, and the co-evolution of moral norms and their legal counterparts has resulted in a remarkable cross-fertilization of ideas. However, the central idea of human rights, understood as moral norms, is that they are independent moral standards by which institutional arrangements, including human rights institutions and practices, can be appraised.

Moreover, human rights are moral norms of a special sort. Often they are portrayed as triggering claims against organized society for a stringent level of durable protection against grave threats to a relatively small number of vitally important human interests, most notably, the universally valuable basic requirements for a human life.

In addition, the interests protected by human rights warrant special societal protection because they are subject to unique and ongoing types of threats. The social guarantees provided by human rights are not meant to protect against every conceivable threat, including rare or random threats. Nor are they intended as a foolproof system of protection against every possible risk, even risks to an individual's most vital interests.[3] Human rights protect vital interests under social conditions in which they are vulnerable to persistent and serious threats that arise in the ordinary course of social interaction. Absent effective social mechanisms for protection, these interests are subject to a continuous, morally intolerable degree of jeopardy, which neither individuals acting on their own behalf nor humanitarian assistance can reliably offset.

As Henry Shue puts it, basic rights serve the vital interests of right-holders by providing "a shield . . . against at least some of the more devastating and more common of life's threats."[4]

Human rights function as a shield, in part, by insulating vital human interests from routine tradeoff for the sake of other goals. At the very least, they impose a very high burden of justification on public policies and private activities that tend to undermine the interests secured by human rights. Basic rights, therefore, constitute the minimum demands of justice, a "morality of the depths," as Shue puts it, marking a "line beneath which no one is to be allowed to sink."[5]

High moral importance alone, or even an elevated threat level, is still not enough to justify the very high degree of protection afforded by an institutionalized system of human rights. Such protection is justifiable only insofar as its social guarantees are practically indispensable for securing the vital interests under threat. The protected interests must be subject to grave and persistent threats that, in ordinary circumstances, only the institutional mechanisms of society can combat effectively. The reason for such a circumspect attitude toward human rights is that mechanisms for their implementation and enforcement impose serious demands on individuals and institutions. They tie the hands of democratic bodies and constrain the range of options available to private actors.

In short, the justification for human rights and their institutional protection rests on three foundational arguments: the special moral importance of the interests at risk, the seriousness and persistence of threats to those interests, and the practical indispensability of an institutional mechanism for protection. Human rights, therefore, are reserved for humanity's greatest moral and political challenges. Our ecological predicament is one such challenge.

Grounds for Specific Human Rights

Human rights theories differ in their list of rights, the foundational values and moral arguments that ground them, and the practical purposes for which they are intended. A brief survey of some leading theories shows that my approach does not hinge on acceptance of a specific theory of human rights or their foundational arguments. Consequently, my approach can be accommodated from within a diversity of theoretical perspectives.

78   A LIVABLE PLANET

One of the most common justifications for human rights is human welfare. Theories grounded in such considerations have obvious intuitive appeal. They provide straightforward justifications for rights that protect life and health or guarantee a minimum standard of living or subsistence. However, welfare-based theories differ in the welfare interests they rely upon and the inventory of rights they underpin. For example, highly restrictive welfare-based theories extend rights protection only to what is necessary for the satisfaction of basic biological needs, such as health and preservation of life. By contrast, David Miller's more expansive list of "basic needs" goes much further. It includes both biological needs (e.g., food, water, health, physical security) and social needs (e.g., education, work and leisure, and freedoms of movement, conscience, and expression).[6] In short, both restrictive and expansive welfare-based rights theories endorse rights that ensure survival and satisfaction of basic biological and subsistence needs given priority by my approach.

Some critics of strictly welfare-based theories, however expansively interpreted, doubt whether they can provide direct grounds for justifying human rights that protect individual liberties that are widely recognized as crucially important. One option is to justify civil and political liberties indirectly, for example, by reference to their (indispensable) instrumental role in securing the basic elements of well-being. Another approach expands the grounds of justification beyond conceptions of well-being. For example, James Nickel proposes a pluralist grounding. He argues that the diverse normative commitments of human rights are justified by a mix of considerations of fairness and the requirements of human dignity in addition to basic elements of human well-being.[7] These approaches differ in grounds for all of the rights they recognize as genuine human rights, but they agree on the inclusion of rights that ensure human survival and satisfaction of basic needs.

Some theories rely upon neither the direct nor indirect importance of welfare interests, but nevertheless they concur on the

HUMAN RIGHTS AND ECOLOGICAL GOALS   79

moral importance of welfare rights. For example, some theorists who express reservations about the universality of liberal democratic rights embrace universal human rights that secure the social and economic conditions necessary for subsistence or a basic level of material well-being.[8] Even some theories that ground all human rights in the value of exercising human capacities for autonomous deliberation and choice support welfare rights for instrumental reasons, for example, because effective agency requires a basic level of biological and material well-being.[9] In other words, two other prominent theoretical approaches, for divergent reasons, converge on the kinds of welfare rights that I include in my list of dual-purpose rights.

A demonstration of widespread agreement, of course, does not put an end to controversy, but it does delimit the battles that a defense of this approach must fight. Staunchly opposed positions remain. For example, market fundamentalist theories reject the existence of any economic and social rights because they generate duties that they view as requiring unjust interference in markets. Their arguments are critiqued in the previous chapter, and I do not re-litigate them here. Other theories dismiss such rights on conceptual grounds, and my response appears in the fourth section of this chapter.

Dual-Purpose Rights

The list of basic welfare interests singled out in this chapter is modest in comparison to the menu of grounds that underlie more comprehensive human rights theories, including one I defend elsewhere.[10] I agree with those who think that a theory of human rights that hews too closely to what is necessary for the satisfaction of basic biological needs is unsuitable as a generally applicable theoretical framework. The reason for adopting a different approach here is its singular practical purpose. Its aim is to identify a subset of

80 A LIVABLE PLANET

human rights that, if given robust institutional protection, directly and effectively address the roots of our ecological predicament.

The general rationale for enhanced priority for a subset of human rights is that they serve dual functions. They not only protect the basic elements of well-being that provide the primary grounds for those rights, but they do so, in significant part, by strategically advancing the goals of an ecologically sustainable global political economy. Sustainability, in this context, is understood according to the definition from Chapter 2. An ecologically unsustainable political economy is composed of market practices, supported by background institutional arrangements, that are self-undermining. These practices exhaust natural resources or degrade the ecological conditions that sustain human life and make possible the satisfaction of basic needs.

The market practices warranting heightened moral scrutiny have both immediate and substantial long-term impact on the prospects for preserving a livable planet. Dual-purpose human rights establish stringent moral constraints on the highly consequential market practices most likely to result in ecosystem degradation, deplete natural resources, destabilize the planetary processes that maintain the Earth system within safe operating boundaries, create serious environmental health risks, and damage elements of the biosphere essential for subsistence. Specifically, many of the most ecologically consequential market practices pertain to processes of acquisition, control, and use of land, energy, and water resources. Societal decisions about whether to monitor, regulate, or prohibit these practices should be guided by an assessment of their implications for the secure realization of rights of subsistence, food, water, and the various rights to a clean and healthy environment.

Moreover, dual-purpose human rights not only function as moral guidelines for assessing market practices and background institutions that sustain them. An enforceable system of human rights constrains the scope of discretionary judgment available to market participants whose activities have substantial environmental impact, thereby giving right-holders more control over their ecological futures.

A further feature of a conception of dual-purpose human rights is the extent to which it tracks and builds upon the foundational moral premises that underpin existing ideals of ecological sustainability. The twin objectives of dual-purpose rights—a minimum level of human well-being and ecological sustainability—align with the normative aspirations of contemporary sustainable development goals. Although (in Chapter 2) I argued against the pro-development bias built into the UN's formulation of these goals, they share a normative common core with the dual-purpose human rights approach. For example, the premise of Principle 1 of the Rio Declaration is that "human beings are at the center of concerns for sustainable development." In other words, the paramount concern of sustainability goals and human rights theory alike is the secure, durable realization of basic elements of human well-being, which both perspectives recognize as threatened by the degradation and exhaustion of the natural environment.

The list of strategically important dual-purpose rights also dovetails with similar lists of rights recommended for enhanced priority by coalitions of indigenous peoples and human rights activists from the Global South. The convergence in lists of high-priority rights and their arguments for that priority is important because it reveals how groups most directly and immediately affected by our ecological predicament understand its origins and the kinds of solutions required.

For example, the statement of principles by the Indigenous People's Network underscores their concern for protecting natural resources from overexploitation, but, in addition, they note the importance of preserving "healthy, diverse, and intact habitats" that indigenous peoples directly depend upon for subsistence.[11] Their arguments demonstrate their belief in the tight link between ecological conditions and the economic basis of their well-being, as well as the close connection between the condition of the planet

82 A LIVABLE PLANET

and the fate of its most vulnerable human inhabitants. In other words, their priorities reflect the special strategic importance of rights that constrain market practices that degrade or diminish the land, energy, and water resources upon which they depend.[12]

Similarly, the Bali Principles of Climate Justice, adopted by an international coalition of activists who gathered in 2002 at a conference known as Rio+10, emphasize the need for new policies that give priority to "fundamental rights to clean air, water, food, and healthy ecosystems."[13]

We can sum up this section as follows. The practical imperative of the targeted human rights approach to our ecological predicament is to elevate in public policy a short list of high-priority rights that directly align with urgent ecological sustainability goals by contributing to the preservation of the environmental conditions that are essential for the satisfaction of basic biological needs, human survival, and subsistence. To be clear, the intent of the proposal is not to downgrade or abandon other important human rights. Far from it. The point is that the dual-purpose rights proposed for greater policy emphasis and robust institutional protection are often shortchanged in public deliberation, and, when they are discussed in global development circles, the underlying structural socioeconomic conditions and market practices that place them in jeopardy are given little or no attention.

Rights, Duties, and Structural Inequality

A central feature of the human rights perspective I defend is its conception of duties to protect. I develop that conception in response to criticisms of human rights theories for their failure to address morally troublesome inequalities. Samuel Moyn, for example, argues that human rights are "not enough."[14] Unlike market fundamentalists who think human rights are too egalitarian, these critics are concerned that they are insufficiently egalitarian.

HUMAN RIGHTS AND ECOLOGICAL GOALS   83

Claims of this kind—the inequality objection—are open to several interpretations. I respond to three versions of the criticism, but I devote the bulk of attention to the most challenging objection by showing how my expansive and open-ended conception of the duty to protect addresses structural inequalities that place human rights in jeopardy.

Three Versions of the Inequality Objection

The first version of the objection claims that an emphasis on human rights in isolation from broader issues of justice, whether by design or inadvertence, can impede advancement of morally more ambitious and more urgent egalitarian aims. For example, global development goals that focus on the elimination of extreme poverty are often framed as human rights issues, but the concern is that this narrative tends to crowd out wider discussion of global economic inequality, its colonial origins, and its differential impact on disadvantaged or marginalized groups. Some theories are viewed by critics as especially problematic, for example, theories that fail to include rights of non-discrimination which are central to the struggle against political and economic exclusion.

However, recent surveys of empirical research suggest that the evidence for the detrimental impact from a focus on human rights or, perhaps even worse, a focus on an overly restrictive set of rights, is mixed and inclusive.[15] Nonetheless, it is important for theorists and advocates to emphasize the limited scope of human rights theories generally and to delineate the aims of their approaches to specific problems. My approach has limited and clear practical ambitions. It makes the case for heightened priority for specific rights that function as constraints on market practices that degrade or diminish land, energy, and water resources and thereby undermine the satisfaction of the most basic of all human needs.

84   A LIVABLE PLANET

A second and more troublesome version of the inequality objection is directed toward human rights theories that assume that the sole aim of justice is to secure minimum standards of well-being, not to compress differentials in well-being (or power, status, and so on) once the targeted threshold has been met. Such theories are criticized as powerless to address concerns about corrosive inequalities that undermine democratic institutions, social solidarity, or other values. The point of this version of the inequality objection is that the welfare floor guaranteed by a human rights theory, however generous and however expansively interpreted, is not enough for a just social order. In other words, egalitarians view some inequalities as unjust for reasons that transcend concern for the satisfaction of human rights. However, many theories—including my own approach—are not subject to this criticism because they do not equate human rights with a comprehensive theory of justice.

Moreover, it is important not to lose sight of the fact that a focus on a truncated list of welfare interests and a targeted set of human rights, if clearly intended for narrow practical purposes, can be an important theoretical virtue. Because human rights theories that place high value on basic welfare interests are compatible with a range of comprehensive theories of egalitarian justice, they can provide a roadmap for initial steps common to several pathways that may ultimately diverge in granular details. For example, my high-priority, dual-purpose list of rights does not take sides among egalitarians who differ on the kinds and degree of inequalities that are ruled out by their ideal of a fully just (domestic or global) social order.

My targeted human rights approach also has the advantage of bypassing other big questions about the structure of a fully just global order. It avoids debates about whether justice ultimately requires some form of global governance or the selective elimination of state sovereignty over issues of great planetary consequence. Also, it sidesteps disagreement among those who seek a better form

HUMAN RIGHTS AND ECOLOGICAL GOALS   85

of capitalism and those who argue for its ultimate elimination. The reason for abstaining from participation in these debates is that the first steps toward escape from our ecological predicament cannot wait until the demise of the fragmented system of sovereign states or until all the problems attributable to capitalism are addressed. As things stand, working within the framework of separate states is the default option, and chipping away at the ecologically worst features of global capitalism is defended as a strategic priority, not an end point. In short, the approach defended here is meant only for providing normative guidance for the transition to a more just and sustainable organization of the global political economy. It leaves considerable room for disagreement about the ultimate destination.

The third—and for our purposes, the most consequential—version of the inequality objection maintains that human rights theories are inadequate in another respect. Specifically, the objection is that human rights theories are deficient if they fail to identify and help rectify inequalities in the structure of social organizations that undermine the secure realization of human rights. The problem that this version of the objection isolates is not the lack of clarity in its statement of practical ambitions or its lack of theoretical resources to address inequalities that might remain after the minimum human rights demands are satisfied. The problem is that human rights theories can fail in their own terms. They seem unable to offer practical guidance for identifying and eliminating the structural inequalities that undermine the secure realization of rights.

While human rights theories might fail—and perhaps too often do fail—to make clear the linkage between structural inequality and human rights deficits, the omission is not an essential feature of such theories. I concur with Philip Alston's assessment: "It is patent nonsense to claim, as Samuel Moyn does, that 'even perfectly realized human rights, are compatible with . . . radical inequality,' or that human rights 'have nothing to say about inequality.' "[16] His

86   A LIVABLE PLANET

point, as I understand it, is that some inequalities are not compatible with perfectly realized rights, and theories that have nothing to say about what to do about those inequalities have more work to do.

Alston's remark therefore raises a question about the kind of human rights theory we need. My answer is that it should do more than generate a list of rights backed up by justificatory arguments supporting the selection of rights contained in the list. In addition, it should put its accent on developing an account of the duties or responsibilities that correspond with and effectively secure these rights. The crucial point is this. The view I favor is a structural human rights approach, where the linkage between rights and the structural conditions that secure or frustrate the realization of those rights is explicit and theoretically central.[17] I argue that the state's duty to protect the welfare interests secured by social and economic rights requires continuous economic intervention on multiple fronts to create and maintain background conditions that combat the structural inequalities that erode the secure realization of those rights.

The duty to protect, as I construe it, is expansive and open-ended in its requirements. State action must address multiple structural factors, including inequalities in the distribution of advantages, power, risks, and opportunities that render the realization of human rights insecure.[18] For example, without institutional arrangements that limit concentrations of private power and counteract the entrenchment of deep differential advantage, many individuals and groups are left structurally vulnerable to human rights deprivation, in large part because their economic and environmental conditions are disproportionately controlled by decisions left to the discretion of economic elites.

Concrete examples of the kinds of interventionist state action required include policies that protect human rights to food and water and protect against environmentally mediated health risks. These rights are easily thwarted by the lack of systems for preserving common pool resources such as water and air quality,

HUMAN RIGHTS AND ECOLOGICAL GOALS 87

as well as the absence of regulation of economic transactions that have harmful spillover effects on the environment and human health. Similarly, protection of a human right to subsistence is not readily achievable without curbing the excessive power of corporations over employees, their communities, and their environments. Equally important for securing these human rights is the protection of natural resources, fair and enforceable systems of land tenure and control, and regulations that prevent deforestation, pollution, and other forms of ecological degradation, especially when they are consequences of extractive activities or speculative investment that largely benefits non-nationals at the expense of local inhabitants. Moreover, as Dinah Shelton notes, "the absence of regulation, inappropriate regulation, or a lack of supervision in the application of extant norms may create serious problems with respect to the environment which translate into violations of human rights."[19]

In short, thinking about human rights in a vacuum, without articulating a concrete vision of the duties of a state, or focusing narrowly on the state's duty to ensure the provision of welfare-enhancing goods, distracts attention from the importance of specifying the practical requirements of duties to protect. Indeed, no plausible theory of human rights can stand on the sidelines, ignoring the implications of structural inequalities for achieving human rights objectives.

Ecologically Unsustainable, Economically Predatory Market Practices

We turn now to a more specific characterization of state responsibility for protecting high-priority, dual-purpose human rights by combating the ecologically unsustainable, economically predatory market practices that pose particularly grave threats to their realization.

88 A LIVABLE PLANET

The general idea of ecologically unsustainable market practices is straightforward. As spelled out in Chapter 2 and reiterated in this chapter's first section, they exhaust natural resources or degrade the ecological conditions that sustain human life and make possible the satisfaction of basic needs. Predatory market activities are defined, preliminarily, as economic interactions that substantially threaten human rights or undermine the ability of states to secure and enforce those rights for their residents. A more illuminating way to understand predatory market activities is to highlight the various forms those activities take. For example, they typically involve unilateral imposition of grave, non-consensual risks; grossly one-sided advantage-taking; the exercise of inordinate, unaccountable power over other human beings; and the exercise of power over matters that should be left to individuals to decide for themselves or reserved for the deliberative judgment of collective bodies. Such practices depend upon the support of background political and legal arrangements that Daron Acemoglu and James A. Robinson describe as *extractive institutions*.[20] They facilitate the ability of local and foreign elites to rule over and exploit others, extract wealth from those who are not in the elite, sequester economic benefits, and cement patterns of political subordination. We can add to their assessment the observation that they make it possible to offload environmental burdens, ensuring that neither the minimum demands of justice nor the goals of environmental sustainability are served.

More fundamentally perhaps, market activities can be seen as predatory if they do not serve their presumptive function of enabling market actors to derive profit from socially beneficial productive activities—as a rosier picture of markets would have it—but instead facilitate the extraction of profit without due consideration of social consequences, including their implications for human rights or the ecological conditions that sustain them. On this view, predatory markets are self-defeating. They produce effects contrary to the consequences that would justify their social acceptance.

Many of the ecologically unsustainable, economically predatory market practices and the extractive institutions upon which they depend can be classified under five general headings. They include practices that extract wealth from poor and powerless communities, in contrast to genuine investment in mutually beneficial economic development; hoard high-value economic opportunities, thus excluding rivals from access to the most desirable benefits derived from economic interaction and ecologically beneficial technologies; shift economic and ecological burdens and risk onto economically more vulnerable, politically less powerful communities and countries; dodge political, legal, and consumer accountability for the consequences of investment and production decisions; and hijack public institutions for private purposes instead of the common good.[21]

Moreover, deeply one-sided economic interactions are often dressed up as mutually beneficial, thereby obscuring two immediate but also far-reaching unjust consequences. First, they enable parties with stronger initial bargaining power to capitalize upon—and entrench—profoundly asymmetric, seriously disadvantaging distributions of benefits and burdens. Second, they routinely alter power relationships, thereby perpetuating disempowerment and diminished bargaining position for others. The joint result of entrenched disadvantage and power differentials is a social structure that renders human rights deeply insecure by undermining the economic and ecological conditions upon which their fulfilment depends.

By contrast, if we implement institutional strategies to protect high-priority, dual-purpose human rights for the least advantaged, least powerful people who are most frequently shortchanged by one-sided economic interactions, we go a long way toward protecting the ecological quality of the planet upon which human survival and well-being depends.

90   A LIVABLE PLANET

Three Problems of Application

This section responds to three potential criticisms of the application of a human rights framework to the problems posed by our ecological predicament. The first objection is that programs of humanitarian assistance are sufficient for the resolution of our ecological predicament. A second objection is that a human rights agenda relies too heavily on a state-centric conception of duty in a globalized world. A third criticism is that because the concern of human rights theory is human well-being, it cannot provide a framework for a comprehensive theory of ecological justice.

The Humanitarian Assistance Alternative

Critics might remind us that the legal implementation of a set of social and economic rights is defensible only if such arrangements are practically indispensable for securing the interests under threat. They might then argue that there are other less adversarial, less onerous ways to tackle the problems of poverty, promote a sustainable environment, and secure a global minimum level of economic well-being short of a major restructuring of the global political economy and the expansion of state power. The deficit in human well-being identified by the human rights approach could be remedied— perhaps even more effectively in the near term—such critics might argue, by coordinated altruistic efforts of wealthy individuals and foundations or through targeted global programs of assistance and technology transfer initiated by affluent states.

However, no amount of humanitarian assistance, however effectively targeted and coordinated, will substitute for a human rights approach. Even if every affluent person, country, and philanthropic organization on the planet regularly transferred enough wealth to meet the subsistence needs of the least well-off, it would not change the fact that the global poor remain powerless over

HUMAN RIGHTS AND ECOLOGICAL GOALS 91

the environmental conditions that determine their overall quality of life. Their economic life prospects and the environmental conditions under which they live remain subject to the discretionary good will of the affluent. Also, a culture of privilege that valorizes getting rich and "giving back" perpetuates the power of a global economic elite, allowing them to engage in ecologically unsustainable market practices and make partial amends on the back end.

By contrast, a human rights approach that furthers ecological sustainability goals offers durable solutions that this alternative cannot replicate. A rights-based approach backed by state efforts to combat underlying economic and social inequalities builds economic rights protections into the architecture of the social order.[22] Without institutional arrangements that limit concentrations of private power and counteract entrenched differential advantage, many individuals and groups would be left structurally vulnerable to a wide range of human rights deprivations, including depletion of natural resources and environmentally mediated harms to health.

A concrete example of social conditions in which dual-purpose rights have an important role to play is the global phenomenon of environmental sacrifice zones. These are geographic areas disproportionately populated by the environmentally most vulnerable, least powerful, and least well-positioned to adapt to degraded local environments and radically altered planetary conditions. Poor communities, and communities of color especially, are the primary sites of sacrifice zones. Their residents experience disproportionate harm caused by dangerous activities such as resource extraction, industrial pollution, toxic dumping, and land use decisions that geographically concentrate the adverse effects of natural disasters.[23] Moreover, environmental sacrifice zones disproportionately benefit the global affluent by offloading the ecological burdens onto less powerful communities, thereby insulating themselves from many of the worst environmental consequences of their activities.

92 A LIVABLE PLANET

Human rights, therefore, play an important and unique role in structuring power relations. Quite plausibly, as Shue remarks, "a fundamental purpose of acknowledging any basic rights at all is to prevent, or eliminate, in so far as possible the degree of vulnerability that leaves people at the mercy of others."[24] More specifically, Joseph Raz rightly observes that one of the most important functions of human rights—beyond the protection against specific threats to individual well-being—is to distribute power away from the powerful to everyone else, including in particular those people who are especially vulnerable to the abuse of states, corporations, and other internationally powerful organizations.[25]

My colleague Ruth Faden and I have made similar arguments. "When human rights protect against deprivation, they alter existing power dynamics by eliminating or reducing sources of vulnerability that powerful social groups and entities can exploit for their own advantage."[26] Circumstances of desperation effectively compel economically vulnerable and politically subordinate social groups to accept deeply disadvantaging, exploitative economic arrangements, thus reinforcing and magnifying the potential for further human rights deficits. Human rights remain permanently insecure under conditions characterized by deep asymmetries of power.

State-Centric Approaches

Critics of contemporary human rights theories, including the targeted approach, will point to interrelated concerns about reliance on states as the primary guarantor of rights. Many states have a poor track record in protecting human rights generally, and domestic elites often play a pivotal role in subverting socioeconomic rights. Absent effective institutional mechanisms that secure their protection, human rights claims are largely aspirational, and human rights rhetoric in such circumstances may engender false hopes in communities suffering grave hardships.[27] Even well-intentioned states find their policy options hemmed in by international power asymmetries.

A state-centric framework is not defended on the grounds that it is easy, especially in countries where institutional support is lacking and ruling elites are actively hostile toward human rights. However, these facts do not entail that nothing can be achieved by citizen groups that adopt a human rights approach in the absence of institutional enforcement mechanisms. Nor do they entail that advocacy must be confined within national boundaries or that human rights activism under deeply adverse international conditions must be a recipe for despair and disappointment.

Multiple normative and strategic advantages accrue to social movements that place a human rights agenda at the forefront of efforts to make transformational changes in state policy. Working from within states offers opportunities for democratic mobilization not readily available on a global scale, and, simultaneously, activists can increase external pressure for those changes in the international arena. Many indigenous movements and peasant groups now take this two-track approach. They address an audience that typically extends beyond national boundaries to motivate individuals, other states, and representatives of other institutions to join their cause.

Moreover, reframing an issue as a matter of human rights, rather than an ordinary disagreement over policy, has salutary effects on individuals and communities currently lacking institutional mechanisms for enforcement. It fundamentally alters the way individuals understand the origins of their circumstances and the moral gravity of their grievances. A profound psychological shift occurs when individuals no longer see themselves as supplicants, struggling to have their voices heard and their interests considered by those in power. The dynamics of social movements change when participants see themselves as entitled to have certain non-negotiable demands met and to exercise decisional authority over matters profoundly affecting them. As social uptake of this new

94 A LIVABLE PLANET

understanding increases, there are mutually reinforcing effects. A shared understanding adds confidence to individual judgment, builds resolve, promotes a sense of common cause, fosters social solidarity, and steels the nerves for collective resistance.

In addition, because the human rights approach is conceived as a mechanism for self-defense, it does not rely on the generosity of affluent states, the good will of conscientious consumers, or the green virtues of multinational corporations. Nor does it presuppose the existence of states already hospitable to human rights. Quite the opposite. The human rights framework is designed primarily for empowering the aggrieved in their struggle to defend the ecological conditions essential to the enjoyment of their rights, and that struggle characteristically begins close at hand.

Even as the default option for short-term change, critics may point to another obstacle. Many states lack the geopolitical power or economic independence to act effectively on their own, even if motivated to do so. The objection is powerful. Any argument for an expanded conception of state responsibility to protect human rights against threats arising from economically predatory and ecologically destructive market practices requires that states gain a high degree of effective control over the social and economic conditions within their borders. Impediments, for example (presented in detail in Chapter 5), include hypercompetitive forms of capitalism that have propelled aggressive market expansion, consolidated control over international supply chains, spurred foreign extraction and a global struggle for control over natural resources, and spread the influence of finance capital and speculative investment around the world. These developments make it clear that, without the ability of the state to defend against these external threats inherent in the organization of the global political economy, many individuals will remain inordinately vulnerable to other more powerful states and state-like entities that exercise some of the capacities of states.

However, recognition of the reality of limited state independence is not indicative of futility of the approach. It simply means that,

HUMAN RIGHTS AND ECOLOGICAL GOALS 95

frequently, states cannot meet their responsibilities on their own. Prospects for success often depend on the formation of multistate coalitions, unified resistance to market practices that confer excessive control over the conditions for extraction of domestic natural resources or deprive citizens of their own means of subsistence. Moreover, overcoming the problems of limited state power often demands opposition to local elites who often enrich themselves by exercising control over the machinery of the state, thereby enabling or encouraging ecologically unsustainable, economically predatory activities from the outside.

In sum, a state-centric human rights approach faces major challenges. However, the approach is not advocated because it is an easy pathway to change. No matter what ideal of the global order and the future of the system of nation-states we think best, the pathway to change runs through states. Without change there, however difficult it may be to achieve, nothing else changes.

Moral Relation to the Rest of Nature

Critics will object that the anthropocentric orientation of a human rights approach precludes direct recognition of the intrinsic value of the rest of nature. Human rights therefore offer protection for non-humans and ecosystems only indirectly and incompletely, given that such concerns acquire elevated instrumental importance only when the most basic interests that ground human rights are threatened. Even then, the concern is that there is only a partial alignment between the set of human interests that ground the portfolio of human rights and the inventory of non-anthropocentric interests implicated by ecological destruction. For example, the interests that ground human rights and the reasons for preserving other species, habitats, and wilderness areas may appear tenuous, and, in fact, they come into sharp conflict when clear and immediate human needs clash with the often uncertain overall ecological

96 A LIVABLE PLANET

value of preserving a particular species or protecting some type of land formation from human impact.

In other words, critics will say that the approach does not offer consistently aligned normative guidance for thinking about the morality of humanity's relation to the rest of nature. Theories that focus on a land ethic, wilderness ethic, or stewardship duties, by contrast, place concerns for species conservation and ecological preservation at the forefront of decision, and they do so for reasons independent of the instrumental value of sustaining resources for the sake of human well-being or preserving the ecological conditions essential for human existence.[28] Also, other approaches to environmental justice expand their repertoire of questions to consider what is required for "doing justice to nature."[29] There are two responses to these powerful criticisms.

First, the normative alignment is probably much closer than critics assume, especially when one takes a longer-term view. While explaining the value of ugly endangered species and dismal swamps to a skeptical legislator may be a difficult task, scientific opinion has moved far beyond such naïve views. The message from numerous United Nations agency reports is summarized by Tim Hayward, who observes that "it is reasonable to suppose that the more that humans come to understand about the interconnectedness of their health and well-being with that of nonhuman nature, the more inseparable appear their interests with the 'good' of nature."[30] For example, the value of biological diversity at both the genetic level and species levels is widely regarded as one of the most crucial requirements for maintaining the stability of planetary systems, generally understood as on a par with the functioning of the climate system.

In addition, there are many direct human benefits associated with preservation of forests, oceans, and soil microbes. Environmental assessment reports (e.g., the World Charter for Nature) dating from decades ago make it abundantly clear that there is no reason to presume that any aspect of the environment is dispensable, simply because its utility is currently uncertain, without risk of harm to the

HUMAN RIGHTS AND ECOLOGICAL GOALS 97

whole interrelated system upon which human survival depends. Chapter 6 supports such claims, demonstrating the significant extent of alignment of interests.

Second, I reiterate that the human rights approach defended here is proposed as a normative framework that has potential for changing our relation to the rest of nature by changing the structure of our economic relations with one another. It aims to provide practical guidance for dealing with problems in a sequenced, strategic way, beginning with efforts to mitigate threats that can be averted by intervention in highly consequential, large-scale human activities. For example, efforts to protect human rights will necessitate a shift away from concentrated sites of extraction, production, and waste disposal, and, as a result, such changes offer a surprisingly large moral down payment on what many who care about the environment for its own sake are most concerned to protect. Subsequent chapters demonstrate just how much a human rights approach will require humans to retreat from places and practices that figure centrally in the ecologically most destructive aspects of the global political economy.

Rights, Duties, and Violations

A traditional conception of the nature of human rights, their correlative duties, and the acts or omissions that constitute violations rests upon assumptions that challenge various aspects of the human rights approach and its application to complex ecological crises. This section provides a critical assessment of those assumptions and defends the approach against potential objections.

The Traditional Conception

Traditional conceptions of human rights are sometimes described as "naturalistic," reflecting their inheritance of key assumptions

98 A LIVABLE PLANET

from the natural law tradition.[31] Rights are timeless, invariantly applicable to all human beings in all circumstances, at all times. They are correlated with highly determinate (perfect) duties. The identities of duty bearers are ascertainable prior to the creation of states, and their duties are universal; that is, "owed" directly by all persons to all right-holders in virtue of their status as human beings (not as citizens or compatriots). Because duties are determinate and their assignment fixed, we have clear standards for identifying their violation, and violations give right-holders justifiably enforceable claims against anyone who has breached a duty owed to them.[32]

Timeless and Dynamic Conceptions

A view of human rights as generating timeless or invariant duties has obvious intuitive appeal, but it is deeply problematic. We can cite numerous arguments against the conception of fully specified rights that "all human beings at all times and places would be justified in claiming."[33] Responses that address perennial threats change. As populations cluster in urban areas and industrial and agricultural wastes become more concentrated, the requirements for securing access to clean water evolve. New threats emerge, for example, because smoke from coal stoves, once largely harmless, is no longer dispersed and air pollution reaches unhealthful levels. Old threats dissipate, for example, as vaccination programs render communicable diseases more manageable, making human mobility and population density less risky. Duties also change when human capacities change. The invocation of a right to a healthful environment has no point in circumstances in which there is no public health intervention for controlling a lethal pathogen. Duties and rights also change as knowledge evolves, for example, as the harmful effects of chemical compounds are understood.

A dynamic conception of human rights and their correlative duties, therefore, is needed to accommodate the fact that threats to human well-being are not constant across time and in all places and the fact that human knowledge and capacities to mitigate or manage risk of harm vary circumstantially.[34] A more general point raised by John Tasioulas is that "duties that a right generates are not comprehensively specifiable once and for all, instead, they can vary with changes in the nature of the agents, institutions, and social contexts in question."[35]

However, it is important to note that a shift from the traditional conception to dynamic conception of human rights responsibilities does not entail wholesale contingency. The stable feature of such duties is the point or ends they serve, namely, protection of the enduring interests that ground rights, not the concrete practical requirements for their protection or the precise specification of all duties.[36]

Pre-Institutional Assignment of Universal Duties

If the substantive content of duties can change over time and as a function of contextual factors, what about the identities of duty bearers? Onora O'Neill takes the position that they must be pre-institutionally ascertainable.[37] For example, the bearer of a negative duty, such as the duty not to inflict grievous bodily harm on innocent persons, is pre-institutionally fixed. Every living human being is under the duty not to inflict grievous bodily harm on another person. No background theory of social circumstances, institutional arrangements, or contingent relationships between parties is necessary to identify such duty bearers.

Positive rights, however, don't conform to her conceptual strictures. For example, there is no pre-institutional way of assigning primary duties that satisfy welfare rights, such as the right to food. She asks rhetorically whether there is a universal duty, binding on everyone, or a special secondary duty owed by farmers. Her answer is that no person or institution, absent assignment

100   A LIVABLE PLANET

according to a social convention, has such a duty owed directly to a potential recipient in need.

The implications of O'Neill's view radiate beyond her examples. If, as many theorists believe, states are under secondary duties, including duties of provision and duties to protect, then their assignment also must be a matter of social convention. If an element of convention is inherent in the process for identifying duty bearers, she thinks that such rights aren't genuinely moral rights after all, but mere artifacts of contingent human institutions. Moreover, these secondary duties, unlike pre-institutional duties, are not universal duties owed the world at large in virtue of their common humanity. They are owed to members of a common polity. Once again, we need a background theory that explains why some duties correlated with universal human rights are assignable only to specific individuals or institutions.

Here, we should take a step back to ask why O'Neill's austere naturalistic picture of human rights and duties should be persuasive. Specifically, we should ask why a conception of human rights that seems at home in the proverbial state of nature should have a grip on members of highly organized societies characterized by densely woven institutional arrangements and the accretion of social expectations. Charles Beitz offers a partial answer to that question, saying that we should replace such a view with an account of human rights that "is compatible with the basic fact that the state constitutes the basic unit of the world's political organization."[38]

Beitz's suggestion is not that radically revisionist, even from some natural law perspectives. The idea that the normative landscape of rights and duties can be transformed by institutional changes has been around at least since John Locke. He famously argued that individuals, upon entering political society (provisionally, most interpreters would say), surrender their right and duty to enforce what he calls the Fundamental Law of Nature.

Moreover, there are powerful reasons for preferring an alternative conception more compatible with evolving expectations for

HUMAN RIGHTS AND ECOLOGICAL GOALS   101

a division of moral labor. On such a view, some duties are assignable to every individual simply in virtue of common humanity, but others are assignable based on a variety of social contingencies.[39] In effect, this is the upshot of Henry Shue's proposal, now widely influential among human rights theorists. He argues that rights should be understood as generating a portfolio of duties, including duties commonly described as duties to respect, protect, or fulfill human rights. If we think a division of moral labor is more plausible than the pre-institutional model, as I believe, then it is reasonable to expect that duties within that portfolio will differ in their concrete requirements and their assignment. Differences may be based on numerous factors, including ways in which individuals and institutions stand in relation to the cause of the problem, or their capacities for preventing, mitigating, enforcing, or compensating for the harm, or their standing commitments to exercise those capacities, and so on.[40]

The alternative to a conception of pre-institutionally identifiable duty bearers is a pragmatic and contextual approach. It is pragmatic in the sense that it takes its cue from assumptions about the problems for which human rights theory is useful to address, assuming also that the problems are not necessarily identical to ones faced in some vision of the state of nature. It is contextual in the sense that it proceeds from an assessment of how agents stand in relation to the origins of and capacity to address those problems. The upshot is that not only can the specification of duties "vary with the nature of the agents, institutions, and social contexts in question," so, too, can their assignment vary.

Secondary Responsibility

The existence of secondary state duties to protect is a premise in human rights documents and conventions. However, the point of a pragmatic approach is that a contextualized argument can be used

102   A LIVABLE PLANET

to justify a division of moral labor and the assignment of secondary duties. A three-part argument supplies a rationale for these widely shared state-centric assumptions.

The first step of a three-part argument follows Mill and Beitz in their understanding of rights in a modern context in which nation-states have become dominant forces in the affairs of humankind. A right, as Mill says, is founded on interests of such importance that the individual is justified in making a claim against the state for protection. Although his aim is to illustrate the high moral stakes required for a moral norm to earn the status of a right, equally important is the implicit acknowledgment of the unique power that states exercise, conferring upon them a default role as potential rights enforcers.

The second step expands upon the first argument by taking note of a state's unique capacities, in contrast with the bare fact that it occupies a unique niche in global power relations. No other agent in the existing international order has the institutional capacity to create and maintain the minimum economic conditions and distributive safeguards necessary for the secure realization of human rights. As argued earlier, states are unique in their capacities for making continuous and simultaneous adjustments to multiple social factors, coordinating the decisions and actions of others, employing institutional mechanisms for monitoring and enforcement, and altering the distribution of advantages and the concentration of political and economic power which, if unchecked, poses grave threats to human rights.[41]

A third step in the argument draws upon widely recognized ideals of state sovereignty and political legitimacy. One highly plausible account of political legitimacy asserts that a government is justified in the exercise of sovereign state authority over a territory and its inhabitants if it satisfies two criteria. States exercise legitimate authority only if they respect, promote, and protect the human rights of everyone within their borders and respect the

HUMAN RIGHTS AND ECOLOGICAL GOALS   103

human rights of non-nationals over whom they have no direct political jurisdiction.[42]

Many, if not most, states fail the tests for legitimacy in some respects, but the probability of their success is not the point. No other agent—including supranational entities or socially responsible transnational corporations—has a comparable presumptive claim of moral legitimacy for assuming a plenary and wide-ranging role in protecting human rights and undertaking the full range of activities outlined in the second step of the argument. For example, we may want more in the way of human rights stewardship from the International Monetary Fund and transnational corporations, but it is unlikely that we want them to assume more state-like powers.

The three-part argument makes a purely pragmatic, contextual case for assigning special responsibilities to states for the protection of the human rights of persons over whom they exercise pervasive and profound influence. States operating under the current global order have unique human rights responsibilities because they are uniquely positioned with the power to protect and enforce human rights and because they can accomplish what no other agent has sufficiently wide-ranging capacity or presumptive moral authority to undertake on behalf of persons subject to their jurisdiction.

Indeterminacy of Secondary Duties

The conception of the duty to protect, as developed thus far, involves a high degree of indeterminacy. Indeterminacy is inherent in the task of simultaneously adjusting a variety of overlapping and mutually reinforcing structural factors causally implicated in the production of human rights deficits. By contrast, duties of justice, including duties correlated with human rights, are traditionally described as *perfect duties*. They are satisfied by discrete and highly determinate (i.e., perfect) duties. Imperfect duties—paradigmatically duties of beneficence—are

104 A LIVABLE PLANET

understood as less determinate, defined by reference to the ends they serve and thus more open-ended. If we concede the open-ended nature of the duty to protect, then either we must revise the traditional distinction between perfect and imperfect duty, or, if no revision seems credible, we must revisit my expansive construal of the duty to protect.

Amartya Sen has offered one avenue for navigating the issue. He suggests that human rights are correlated with a mix of perfect and imperfect duties.[43] However, if state duties correlated with human rights resemble imperfect duties, it is important to note that the similarities are limited. Imperfect duties of beneficence are highly discretionary. Benefactors are free to pick their beneficiaries, choose the means and amount of assistance they provide to others, and so on. Given the latitude in choice of beneficiary and manner of bestowing benefit, there is no one who can claim a right to any form of assistance, let alone a determinate benefit. If there is latitude inherent in state duties to protect human rights, then it cannot be viewed as comparable to the scope of discretion available to those who bear imperfect duties of beneficence. The scope of state discretion must be more circumscribed if it is to be plausible. States should not get to pick and choose whose rights are protected, which rights to deemphasize, or interpret their duties in ways not strictly answerable to the underlying values or purposes served by those rights.

The upshot is that a reinterpretation of state duties as imperfect is not a plausible option. Instead, such duties are better construed as hybrid, neither fully imperfect nor quite like perfect duties. While the requirements of duty may be unclear in specific cases (e.g., whether some state action satisfies the duty to protect), there are plenty of clear cases in which duty is breached because the interests served by rights, which give them their point, constrain the actions and policies that can count as fulfillment or a violation. Moreover, this constraint limits the scope of reasonable disagreement about fulfillment or violation even if we concede that, in many if not most circumstances, more than one set of state interventions can be effective in achieving the ends that ground those rights.

Rights Violations

Complex ecological crises such as climate disruption pose another problem from the traditionalist's perspective. These crises present a different challenge to our ability to identify primary human rights violations, further complicating the way should we think about violations of a duty to protect. Such crises are examples of uncoordinated "group harms," Derek Parfit's label for types of harms that result only from "what we all do together."[44] We know about the adverse outcomes of climate disruption including floods, droughts, heat waves, or other extreme weather events, which in turn reduce agricultural yields, increase heat-related deaths, and much more. We also know that it threatens the secure realization of human rights to food, water, health, and subsistence. However, it is virtually impossible to definitively link any specific loss or increased risk to any specific causally responsible individual, activity, law, or policy.

Moreover, the unintended harms or risks typically flow from actions that are not widely regarded as inherently wrong, or they are only recently recognized as potentially harmful. They typically arise in circumstances in which no one individual's action causes harm or increases the risk to an identifiable individual (including members of future generations), and prevention of the expected aggregate harm is unlikely unless everyone, or nearly everyone, reduces or ceases to engage in activities that collectively and cumulatively result in harm. In such cases, it is not clear what, if anything, makes an activity wrong or a breach of human rights duties.

Climate change is not unique. Deforestation, species loss, habitat destruction, and fundamental alteration in the hydrological cycle are ecological harms that often occur as the cumulative

106 A LIVABLE PLANET

consequence of otherwise harmless or minimally harmful activities undertaken by multiple individuals and entities over time and sometimes for the sake of socially beneficial objectives.

Therefore, we need some way of resolving these problems if a human rights perspective can have practical value for addressing environmental harms and risks that are both exceedingly complex in their origins and increasingly routine in their destructive impacts. Two strategies are adopted. The first strategy offers reasons to revise the traditionalist's understanding of what constitutes a primary rights violation. The second strategy argues that, even if we are uncertain or cannot agree whether a primary rights violation has occurred, we still can provide a coherent picture of acts or omissions that constitute a violation of a state's secondary duty to protect.

Let's begin with the revisionist strategy. Three points show reasons for relaxing some traditional assumptions about rights violations.

First, it is worth emphasizing that one fairly common understanding of the function of rights, including human rights, is that they do more than protect individuals from actual harm from discrete acts. Rights function as prohibitions on types of action that, as a rule, pose unacceptable risks to vital human interests. Often, we make judgments about the types of activities that violate rights by concentrating on the typical circumstances of occupants of certain roles, such as automobile operators, train conductors, gun shop owners, handlers of explosives, and state officials. We assign responsibility to those in the best position to take preventive or precautionary action, taking into consideration the relative financial or cognitive burdens of attending to the potential for harm from their activities.[45] As a conceptual matter, this means that rights violations do not always require actual harm to specific persons, only the violation of certain norms designed to protect right-holders against types of risky behavior.

I might not raise the risk of any climate-related harm by driving my gas guzzler on the weekends, but I engage in a risky type of

HUMAN RIGHTS AND ECOLOGICAL GOALS 107

conduct. Traditionalists, however, will bristle (quite rightly) at the thought that, absent a substantial increase of risk, my recreational driving should be viewed as a human rights violation. Accordingly, we need much more refinement of the argument to determine which, if any, causal contributors are rights violators.

Second, neither increased risk nor causal contribution to an outcome alone—however large or small—settles anything morally. Judgments about the assignment of moral responsibility turn on the identification of salient causes. A commonplace observation in both legal and moral theory is that very often there are multiple causal factors at work in the most ordinary circumstances. Consequently, we always need some way to discriminate among the diverse (actual or potential) causal contributions to decide which contributions are the salient ones, warranting an assignment of moral (or legal) responsibility.[46] For example, we often take special note of the presence of a culpable indifference to the welfare of others. Hazards from driving can result from a combination of multiple factors, including snow-covered, unplowed motorways, traffic congestion, and poorly engineered roads, but we are more likely to pin greater responsibility on the speeding drunken driver. The example is quite ordinary, but it illustrates the inescapably conventional nature of judgments about the activities that constitute rights violations.

In other words, we are not always obliged to untangle complex causal chains to assign moral culpability. Still, a traditionist might continue to balk at the suggestion that driving a gas guzzler could be a salient risk or cause on a moral par with drunken drivers.

Third, judgments of special moral salience are not static, such that activities historically seen as business as usual with merely unfortunate side effects remain forever beyond the reach of human rights protection.[47] Some activities in the context of our ecological predicament are so utterly reckless, considering what we now know, that we can no longer dismiss them on the grounds that no discrete activity will be necessary or sufficient for harm to materialize or for

108   A LIVABLE PLANET

pushing the level of risk beyond some threshold of unacceptability. However, as the harmful effects of certain kinds of activities become common knowledge, we are justified in updating our assessment of the most routine, previously accepted activities.[48]

For example, it is now exceedingly difficult to dismiss as mere business as usual the widespread practice of deforestation in the Amazon and other tropical forests. While no single cleared tract, however large, is likely to be the trigger for a dieback that has disastrous consequences, these activities are an integral part of a widespread and highly consequential global pattern of behavior that, if unabated, will lead to climate change acceleration, a critical loss of terrestrial biodiversity, fundamental changes in the planetary hydrological cycle, and more immediate harms to members of indigenous communities who depend on forests for moderating tropical temperatures, their subsistence, and much more.

I might get off the moral hook for my gas guzzling driving habits, but ecologically destructive, economically predatory market practices central to the organization of the global political economy strike me as fundamentally different.

The upshot of these three points is that the supposedly insuperable problem of holding specific individuals or entities responsible for human rights violations resulting from their participation in the production of group harms is overstated. Human rights protect everyone against certain kinds of risk or harm, but the kinds of risks or harms that warrant protection against evolve, and the identification of participants who bear special moral responsibility is never a simple factual task of finding the causally responsible agents who directly harmed or compounded the risk to a specific rights-bearer. Our uncertainty about what to say about individual gas guzzlers does not undermine our ability to update our understanding of human rights and their violation.

Let's consider the second strategy. Suppose we conclude, as some theorists have argued, that there is no defensible way of identifying a primary rights violation in the kinds of environmental harm cases

HUMAN RIGHTS AND ECOLOGICAL GOALS 109

now commonplace. Should we then conclude that judgments about violation of duties to protect unravel? After all, it might seem that the duty to protect, if it means anything, is a duty to prevent and punish human rights violations.

The task of the second strategy is to explain why there is no compelling argument against holding to account the institutional agents charged with protecting against known threats—however produced—for the secure realization of basic human rights. Two reasons lend support for this conclusion.

First, arguably, the moral case for treating state agents as guarantors of the human rights of their residents is even greater when the threats to their secure realization result from group harm and the primary agents of injustice are numerous, differ in their causal contribution and culpability, or no longer reside within feasible jurisdictional reach. Consider the implications of rejecting this view of secondary responsibility. Individuals who lack the ability to press claims against identifiable individuals and entities whose discrete actions are causally traceable to the resulting harms (or elevated risk) would be left with no remedy. This is not a problem of marginal consequence. The absence of uncontroversial breaches of primary human rights duties by specific economic actors is now the ordinary situation. In the typical circumstances of massive environmental harms, the threats to the secure realization of human rights are produced by multiple causal contributors, often without coordination or common goals.

The point can be made concretely. Examples include large-scale extractive enterprises, plantation agriculture, concentrated sites of industrial pollution, and the combination of various economic activities that propel widespread deforestation or rapid resource depletion. These are the kinds of activities that, in the aggregate, predictably undermine the secure realization of human rights to health, food, water, and subsistence, and states should counteract these threats. If there is a secondary duty to protect the public against grave harm or elevated risk of harm to the vital interests

110 A LIVABLE PLANET

that human rights are intended to secure, there is no obvious conceptual or practical rationale for restricting that duty to instances in which discrete actions of individuals constitute clear and uncontroversial primary violations. Where the harm (or risk) is predictable, the aggregate causes are now well-understood, and the state has institutional mechanisms for altering the social conditions that generate threats to the secure realization of human rights, a failure to take reasonable steps to prevent grievous harm is a clear violation of its duty to protect.

Moreover, given the plenary powers of states to monitor activities and adjust institutional factors within complex causal chains that result in human rights deficits, it is not necessary to know the identity of specific rights violators or the specific conduct that constitutes a discrete violation for holding states responsible for taking protective action that no other agent is positioned to take under the current configuration of the global order. Persons whose rights are threatened by the confluence of ecologically unsustainable, economically predatory practices thus have solid grounds for holding states accountable for their failures to exercise their unique powers, institutional capacities, and presumptive moral authority to protect them against predicable harms.

Although I think that the initial revisionist strategy has considerable merit, if the arguments for its conception of primary rights violations fail to convince the traditionalist, we are not left without a basis for recognizing human rights violations in group harm cases.

Duties to Future Generations

Future generations will experience the adverse effects from many complex cases of ecological harm, potentially greater than the harm to many members of current generations. However, another problem arises if we accept a traditional conception of rights as justifiably enforceable claims. The notion of a violation of a duty owed to the individual right-holder goes beyond the idea of a breach of a very stringent universal moral standard. It implies the existence of someone who is aggrieved in a special way and is personally entitled to insist on protection, demand remedy or compensation if there is a breach of duty to them, and, if all else fails, a right to actively resist injustice. Much of what makes human rights normatively distinct and politically powerful is the idea that duty bearers are accountable directly to right-holders for their actions.

Nevertheless, retaining the idea of rights as justifiably enforceable claims runs into difficulties in its application to problems of intergenerational justice. The challenge is to explain how the identities of right-holders are determined. More specifically, many moral philosophers question whether it is coherent to say that distant generations—whose members are not yet in existence—can assert claims against current generations for protection against harm, such as a lower expected standard of living or a seriously degraded environment. The identity—and indeed, the very existence of the members of future generations—turns on decisions of current generations.

There are many layers in this problem, but, at the most basic level, the challenge stems from the fact that there are no existing human beings who can claim that they have been made worse off or claim that they have been exposed to an unacceptable risk by the actions of current generations, however reckless those actions may seem in the abstract. How can persons who do not and may never exist be considered as rights-holders who have justifiably enforceable claims?

A comprehensive theory of human rights owed to distant generations whose members are not yet born has much work to do if these concerns are to be addressed to the satisfaction of its critics. However, I see two readily available options for short-circuiting these objections.

One option is to dispense with the traditional criterion of rights as justifiably enforceable claims.[49] Instead, we might think

112   A LIVABLE PLANET

of human rights as universal moral standards of appraisal, largely aspirational in character, understandably subject to flux and imprecision, where failure to act confers no special standing on identifiable right-holders who are entitled to make claims based on what is due to them. On this view, current generations and distant generations alike would not have justifiably enforceable claims. The overall merits of this proposal are beyond the scope of evaluation in this chapter, but I will note there is a steep price to pay for this maneuver. It does not preserve an important place for individualized accountability in human rights discourse.

I suggest a second option. The human rights approach I propose bypasses concerns about the coherence of conceiving rights as claims by members of distant generations not yet born. Persons whose lives intersect, including relations between the oldest and youngest living generations, many of whom can be expected to be alive 80 years from now, unquestionably have rights they can claim against individuals and entities exposing them to unacceptably risky types of conduct or fail to carry out their responsibilities to protect them against the risky behaviors of others.

My proposal is not a solution to the future generations problem. It only offers near-term practical guidance for the just structuring of socioeconomic relationships among contemporaries The time horizon of roughly 80 years, or the span of a few overlapping generational cohorts, is a purely conventional choice, but it is not a fatally arbitrary timeline for two reasons.

First, the time horizon marks the outer limits of feasible planning estimates, given current scientific knowledge of natural processes and understanding of social organization. Second, a period marked by roughly the end of the current century is the upper limit of the time humanity has left to address the full range of convergent crises and avoid tipping points that usher in cascading human catastrophes. The rights of existing people—including the very young—are being adversely affected now, and the window of opportunity for addressing crises that magnify these threats to

HUMAN RIGHTS AND ECOLOGICAL GOALS   113

their human rights is closing rapidly. For issues of climate change, water availability, land use, biodiversity, and more, we have but a few generations left, at most, to avoid severe, perhaps even irreversible consequences. Whether potential members of distant generations can assert human rights claims is a question of philosophical importance, but it does not require an immediate answer given the compressed time frame for action.

Responses to the various conceptual challenges to a human rights approach and its application to complex ecological crises complete the defense of an approach that recognizes the need for enhanced priority for a limited set of dual-purpose basic human rights and the centrality of state duties to protect, which require wide-ranging state interventions in the economy. The purpose of intervention is to combat structural inequalities that undermine the secure realization of human rights. The primary targets of state intervention are the ecologically unsustainable, economically predatory market practices, especially practices pertaining to the acquisition, control, and use of land, energy, and water resources. These practices should be constrained by implementing policies that protect human rights to subsistence, food, and water and protect against serious environmental health risks and degradation of the ecological conditions that sustain human life. The next chapter continues the argument. It provides concrete examples of these market practices, reveals their pervasiveness in the current organization of the global political economy, and illustrates the urgency of adopting a targeted human rights approach.

5

Market Power and Legal Advantage

Human rights in the global economy are structurally insecure. Widespread uptake of the market fundamentalists' recommendations for the rebalancing of power between states and markets created new threats to human rights and undermined state capacities for their protection. The reordered global political economy enabled the strongest market participants to rewrite legal rules to their advantage and use their market power to subvert competitive norms. The spread of ecologically unsustainable, economically predatory market practices allowed a relatively few companies and countries to capture the bulk of economic rewards of global production and investment and shift their economic and environmental burdens and risks onto others, thereby undermining human rights fulfillment.

Of course, structural threats to human rights are nothing new. Human rights have always been vulnerable to the asymmetric power exercised by autocrats, oligarchs, imperialists, ethnic nationalists, and patriarchal religious leaders. Furthermore, the restructured global economy not only threatens the dual-purpose rights strategically important for responding to our ecological predicament. It also generates or exacerbates threats to other human rights. For example, forced labor is a familiar feature of global supply chains, and militarized police forces often suppress political protests directed against exploitative economic conditions. The parallel threats are unsurprising. The structural economic conditions that foster heedless resource extraction, overconsumption, and ecological damage also facilitate labor exploitation and political repression. However, this chapter retains

A Livable Planet. Madison Powers, Oxford University Press. © Oxford University Press 2024.
DOI: 10.1093/oso/9780197756003.003.0005

its focus on specific ways in which the changes in the global political economy undermine state capacities for protecting the economic and social rights that are strategically most important for maintaining a livable planet.

The first section shows how powerful companies (and countries) use their enhanced economic position to consolidate market power, evade market discipline, hoard opportunities, and reduce accountability to consumers. The second section explains how some market actors can avoid political accountability by disempowering democracies and hijacking state and international institutions for private purposes. The third section describes widely employed strategies for leveraging capital mobility to game the global system of states. The fourth section demonstrates how the restructuring of the global political economy facilitates extraction of windfall profits from speculative, socially destabilizing, and ecologically destructive capital investments.

The Consolidation of Market Power

The expansion of global markets is driven by the search for new sources of commodities, labor, and natural resources. That's not the whole story. Economic globalization also is propelled in specific directions by the desire to exploit favorable market conditions and craft or utilize existing legal rules for managing risk and uncertainty. In some instances, the aim is to eliminate competition insofar as feasible, while in other situations, the aim is to capture the most lucrative position in global value chains, secure privileged access to resources, offload market risks, or escape accountability to both markets and states. Market fundamentalists describe these conditions as market failures, and they view them as relatively rare or readily reversible. Critics, by contrast, cite decisive evidence showing that the anti-competitive use of concentrated market power is a pervasive and centrally defining feature of many key

116 A LIVABLE PLANET

sectors of the modern economy, including pharmaceuticals, agriculture, health insurance, media, energy, finance, and more.[1]

Here and in subsequent chapters, examples from the agricultural sector are highlighted for three reasons. First, the sector exemplifies many of the key trends in virtually every sector of the global economy.[2] Most of the main anti-competitive devices are in play: subsidies, subventions, bailouts, market manipulation, non-competitive contracts, rent-seeking, and regulatory arbitrage. Second, the sector figures centrally in all five ecological crises. Agriculture is one of the main causes and casualties of climate disruption and a key factor in the choice among energy alternatives. It places the largest demands on the world's water, and it is a primary driver of soil depletion, deforestation, biodiversity loss, and dysregulation of global nitrogen and phosphorus cycles. Third, agriculture is a major issue in trade policy conflicts, debates about pathways to global development, and analyses of the impact of speculative capital investments.

Market Concentration and Supply Chain Management

The first step in any business strategy, if designed to circumvent market discipline, is to consolidate market power. In practical terms, that often means selecting mechanisms for exercising control over global supply chains. Indeed, one of the defining features of the global reorganization of production and patterns of transnational investment is the concentration of market power in the hands of a few sellers, buyers, or both. In the agricultural sector, for example, market power has concentrated in the hands of a decreasing number of producers, commodity buyers, and retailers. Four companies produce 50% of seeds, six manufacturers produce 75% of fertilizers and pesticides, and four conglomerates control 75% of the global grain trade.[3] Four meat packing companies in

MARKET POWER AND LEGAL ADVANTAGE 117

the United States process 83% of beef and 66% of pork.[4] Similar patterns of oligopolistic market concentration among commodity traders, manufacturers of production inputs, and meat processors are now worldwide.

Perhaps more importantly, markets characterized by a small, concentrated pool of global buyers—*oligopsony*—have transformed global supply chains in the agriculture sector. A small pool of large-scale purchasers of food for retail grocery chains, fast food outlets, and other multinational food processors have become "lead firms" linking a network of producers in almost every country to consumers all over the world.[5] Oligopsony is now the most prevalent model of market organization, dominating most of the world's regional markets.[6]

The most immediate, tangible impact of oligopsony has been its alteration of the way production is organized and the benefits of production within supply chains are distributed. To begin with, market concentration among buyers is responsible for the rapid disappearance of traditional "spot markets." This form of market organization gets its name from the physical marketplaces where independent producers and potential buyers meet and reach a sales agreement on the spot. Many of the major agricultural commodities in the United States and elsewhere are produced under exclusive sales contracts with purchasers acting on behalf of an increasingly small number of global buyers.

A growing share of fruits and vegetables in the United States is produced on contract with "first handlers"—the packers or food processing companies—who agree in advance to purchase of a farmer's entire crop at predetermined prices, and 40% of cattle are sold through "captive supply chain" contracts, providing for the sale of a feedlot's entire production to a designated meatpacker.[7] By 2003, almost 40% of all US agriculture was produced under contract.[8]

In addition, large-scale purchasers often prefer agreements that allow them to exercise control over every aspect of the supply

118   A LIVABLE PLANET

chain without having to invest directly in production. For example, an astounding 95% of chicken consumed in the United States is produced under contract with "integrators" who control every aspect of production from supply of chicks and feed to management and delivery of broilers.[9] These "hierarchical supply chain contracts" are favored because they give purchasers a way to ensure a reliable supply of standardized agricultural products sufficient to meet the requirements of a global enterprise, restrain and stabilize commodity prices, and minimize the need for future rounds of market negotiation.[10]

Supply chain reliability, price stability, and quality control were thus among the reasons that contract agriculture grew in importance and replaced older vertically integrated models in which every facet of production and distribution—e.g., from seed to shelf—was owned by one entity.

Vertical integration as a mechanism for supply chain management fell out of favor across a range of industries, perhaps most notably within the international garment manufacturing sector. An important impetus for the shift in the textile sector was the recognition that investments at the retail and commodity production stages are the least profitable and most risky components of any business. Global clothing brands discovered that they could manage the risk of excess inventory of raw materials by parceling out production tasks to facilities owned by contingent contractors who produce garments to specification on a "just in time" basis. The garment industry also manages risk of excess inventory of finished goods by selling franchises to independent owners and operators of retail outlets. Changes on both ends of the supply chain allowed manufacturers to offload risks of economic loss due to changes in consumer preferences or reduction in their purchasing power.

Agribusiness learned a valuable business lesson. Agricultural commodity production is an especially risky venture because of weather variability and product perishability. Vertical integration

MARKET POWER AND LEGAL ADVANTAGE   119

thus became less attractive because of the combination of low profit margins and the high risk at the production stage of the enterprise. Moreover, contractual management of supply chains is attractive because it serves many other critical business goals and solves problems specific to global enterprises. Although the geographic elongation of supply chains, both within and across nations, opens new opportunities for lowering production costs, it presents new challenges arising from operation in multiple jurisdictions. Contract production offers a solution. It allows businesses to avoid risks associated with changes in legal and regulatory climate, stranded assets in politically unstable countries, and long-term financial commitment to fixed workforce pools and pension obligations.[11] With apologies to Marx, it is often financially better to control the means of production than to own it and better to control the labor of others than to employ them.

While agribusinesses obtain clear benefits from the contract model, it results in greater economic precariousness for farmers, reduced bargaining power for workers, and diminished accountability to communities. Contract agriculture under the oligopolistic market conditions described earlier leads to the effective exclusion of small farmers from lucrative markets. Because buyers can lower their transaction costs by contracting with a smaller number of growers, producers must expand their operations to make it worthwhile for purchasers to offer them a contract. A familiar refrain among farmers is that "Big only buys from Big." Ultimately, even when farmers expand their operations, they are forced to sell to one of a very small number of buyers whose dominant position in an oligopolistic market enables them to dictate prices and drive down farm income, sometimes below the costs of production. For some products (e.g., the broiler industry), the evidence of marginal and declining rewards for those at the commodity production stage of the supply chain is quite dramatic. In the United States, the net income of many producers is only slightly above the household

120 A LIVABLE PLANET

poverty level, but the costs of maintaining contractually required facilities leaves them in debt, often over a million dollars.[12]

Contract agriculture under oligopolistic market conditions does not only result in an upward redistribution of economic reward and a downward redistribution of risk. There are the broader social consequences, especially when production is geographically concentrated. Broiler production in the United States provides the most thoroughly studied case study illustrating the reasons for geographic concentration and its consequences. In 1950, 95% of broiler producers were independent, but less than 30 years later, a handful of chicken processors heavily concentrated within a few localities within the Southern United States accounted for 90% of the broilers produced in the United States.[13]

The underlying incentive structure of the *Southern Model*, as it is now widely known, is rooted in the typical characteristics of the processing sites. The geographic areas chosen by the industry are predominately poor and disempowered communities which offer a substantial pool of flexible farm labor, low prevailing wages, lack of unions, and weak environmental, worker safety, and wage laws.[14]

The geographic concentration of contract agriculture in such communities also has significant effects on the livelihoods and life prospects of residents outside of the agricultural sector. In jurisdictions without strong unions or labor protection laws, labor patterns generally have shifted away from formal arrangements for full-time employment. Unemployment insurance, workers' compensation benefits, regular shifts and full-week work hours, and other forms of workforce security all become less common, thereby increasing worker insecurity and exacerbating vulnerability to lost wages and uncompensated health losses.[15] Local communities also suffer environmental harms from geographically concentrated agriculture. Because of a lack of regulatory oversight, the concentration of chicken, hog, and large-scale crop production operations routinely overwhelms the capacity of rivers, streams, air, and soil to absorb and dilute the pollution.[16]

MARKET POWER AND LEGAL ADVANTAGE 121

The global expansion of the contract model is unsurprising, given its enormous corporate advantages. In addition, international economic development agencies promote it as a vehicle for poverty relief among the rural poor and a mechanism for small landholders to tap into potentially lucrative global agricultural commodities markets.[17] However, the empirical literature shows mixed results for farmers in low- and middle-income countries.[18] Critics of the global expansion of the contract model cite these results, as well as evidence of the environmental and economic consequences gleaned from the US experience, as reasons for caution.

The socioeconomic and environmental effects of geographic concentration of production are replicated in other economic sectors, for example, where "company towns" spring up around a single dominant industry, such as garment manufacturing, mining, oil and gas fields, or chemical processing plants. The contract pro-duction model is used in some of these industries, such as garment manufacturing, but the larger point is that whatever supply chain management technique is used, the concentration of market power in the global political economy is highly beneficial for business, but it imposes heavy burdens on politically powerless, economically dependent communities. The concentration of market power everywhere and in every sector, especially when that power is used to shape the background institutional rules, not only confers control over the livelihoods of employees or contract workers, but also control over the environmental and economic conditions of entire communities.

Export-Driven Production

A staple of policy advice from the International Monetary Fund (IMF) and the World Bank is the recommendation that developing countries adopt a specific kind of export-led growth strategy, often focusing on large-scale production of one or two commodities.

122   A LIVABLE PLANET

Export-driven agricultural production in particular is touted as a way of promoting rapid economic development in the world's poorest countries, reducing the sovereign debt of nations struggling with payment obligations to foreign lenders, and improving the economic prospects of farmers.

The most fundamental rationale for such a policy recommendation is the argument from comparative advantage. The idea is an old one, traceable to 19th-century classical economists, including James Mill, John Stuart Mill, and David Ricardo.[19] A country tends to fare better economically by concentrating on the goods that it can produce at comparatively less costs than required to produce other export goods. For example, if a country can produce palm oil cheaper than it can produce steel, other things being equal, it is better to export palm oil and import steel.

Assessments of the comparative advantages enjoyed by economically less-developed countries often point to the merits of focusing on the agricultural sector. Advisors take note of their surplus of unskilled agricultural labor and economically unproductive land and the lack of a skilled industrial workforce, industrial infrastructure capacity, or sufficient capital to develop that infrastructure. Moreover, the case for export-driven agricultural production is promoted on the grounds that production for global export markets is generally more lucrative than domestic cash crop markets.[20] Also, public investment in rural agriculture, under the right conditions, produces more economic growth than many other sectorial investment strategies, concentrates more of the benefits of growth among the rural poor, and diffuses that economic benefit throughout rural communities because of the multiplier effect of increased farm incomes on non-farm incomes.[21]

However, the age-old economic development advice is subject to morally significant exceptions, widely referred to as the "commodity trap."[22] Commodity-producing nations tend to lag in the economic gains realized by developed nations over the long run. As explained earlier, producers of agricultural crops or other raw commodities for export operate at the least profitable and most risky link in the economic value chain. The overwhelmingly profitable position is at the "bottom," or final phase of the value chain, where finished products are sold, typically to affluent customers in overseas retail markets.[23] The accumulation of durable economic disadvantage is a major reason why the commodity exporting strategy is described as a potential trap—the risk to a developing country and its enterprises of getting locked into the least profitable position within global value chains.

Moreover, countries whose economies are based primarily in raw, unprocessed commodities—agricultural or natural resources— also tend to deindustrialize.[24] Once economies deindustrialize and become less diversified, they lose out on opportunities for economically more rewarding manufacturing and processing activities. Also, their economic fates become overly dependent on the performance of a single commodity, leaving a country at the mercy of fluctuations in global export prices.

Dani Rodrik points to some further consequences specific to the overreliance on export-led growth strategies based on agricultural commodities. When more farmland is used for large-scale exports, much of the wealth generated by global trade gets captured by the owners of large plantations.[25] This sets off an economic chain reaction. The cost of land then rises, often dramatically, leaving the rural poor less able to afford enough land and, consequently, putting them at increased risk of losing their livelihood from subsistence farming.[26] Consumers are disadvantaged as well. As the cultivation of export crops displaces agriculture for domestic use, consumers must rely more on food imports. The poor are hit especially hard when global spikes in grain prices put imports out of reach.

More generally, overreliance on international trade as an economic development strategy brings problems of its own. For every dollar of increase in the gross domestic product (GDP) of a developing country achieved through increased international trade, roughly $50 of income is transferred from the lowest economic

124 A LIVABLE PLANET

strata to the middle- and upper-income strata.[27] (This is not a typo!) Even worse, much of the new wealth generated by global trade is captured by existing economic elites.[28]

In short, the export-led agricultural approach provides strategically good business opportunities for corporations based in economically developed countries, and it is highly beneficial for consumers in affluent countries, making food cheaper and more abundant year around. However, large-scale production, propelled by market concentration and the globalization of supply chains, enhances the ability of transnational corporations to capture the lion's share of profits in economically vulnerable countries.[29] In a way, these results should not be entirely surprising. A recommendation to place all investments in a single sector is rarely sound financial advice for nations or individuals. Moreover, as we saw earlier, because global commodity buyers are interested primarily in large-scale contract purchases, small producers must either expand operations or form grower alliances, or they are forced to sell to the few intermediaries that have the market power to drive down prices. It's no wonder that plantation owners flourish while small landholders continue to struggle.

Global Land Acquisition

Market fundamentalists support foreign direct investments in large-scale agricultural production facilities for many of the same reasons they recommend rapid and wholesale transformation of agriculture for export commodity production. It is commended as a way of enhancing rapid economic growth, providing less-developed nations with needed capital and technology, and creating employment opportunities.[30] Sponsoring nations and multinational corporations have their own motivations. In many host countries, land and water resources are relatively cheap,

MARKET POWER AND LEGAL ADVANTAGE 125

governments are welcoming, land acquisition laws are lax, and regulatory oversight is weak.[31]

The market dynamics of what many critics call the "global land grab" often mirror the "natural resource curse," the name given to the portfolio of adverse consequences of foreign investment in extractive industries such as oil and minerals. Countries blessed with rich stores of natural resources (whether it is oil or soil) but lacking in other immediate economic opportunities have many well-known adverse effects. They invite exploitation from the outside, enable autocratic leaders and local elites to prosper, and divert money from public purposes to pay bribes, fund patronage, and purchase military armaments used to remain in power through repression.[32]

Some specific effects produced by foreign investment in traditional natural resources are produced by global farmland acquisition. Foreign investors, with no long-term stake in the host countries, have powerful incentives to extract high profits, deplete resources, produce goods for export to the global affluent, invest little for the improvement of the local economy or relief of poverty, leave behind problems of environmental degradation, convert small holders to low-wage informal sector workers, and dispossess traditional landholders.[33]

The dispossession of the rural poor from traditional ancestral lands or public lands is an especially serious problem arising from both natural resource extraction and the global farmland acquisition for growing export crops. Land is easily expropriated for use by the state, local elites, or foreign business interests because of deficiencies in the legal rules of ownership in many countries. The United Nations estimates that 4 billion people worldwide lack legal title to the land they occupy or have limited recourse to basic rules of law that establish property rights and provide remedies for dispute resolution.[34]

To make matters worse, agricultural purchase and leasing agreements often contain vague promises of environmental

126　A LIVABLE PLANET

protection and provide little or no direct economic remuneration to the host nation beyond the unenforceable promise of overall increase in GDP or the illusory creation of jobs.[35] Because foreign investors have no long-term stake in either preserving the land for posterity or supporting the local economy, they are unreliable stewards of the ecological conditions that sustain the community. For example, even the World Bank notes that the industrial cultivation of export crops in many less-developed regions of the world has damaged soil and water quality so much that a third of the productivity gains have been lost.[36]

Moreover, foreign investors lack incentive to set aside a portion of their crops for domestic sales for the same reasons global development experts advise small holders to sell commodity crops in more lucrative global markets, where consumers with sufficient financial resources to pay the most for their products are found. Markets cater to purchasing power, not needs.

In other words, the lack of a publicly known, regularly enforced, and system of transferable property rights, together with the predictable high levels of environmental degradation and the lack of demonstrable economic benefit for the local community, virtually guarantees that the rural poor will remain poor and powerless, constantly at the mercy of local elites and foreign businesses, and worse off in terms of food security, land tenure, and environmental health risks.

The push to expand export-driven commodity production and the quest for new offshore sites for large-scale agricultural production are driven by the same economic dynamics. Affluent countries and multinational corporations have increased incentive for expanding their international access to land and water resources for the benefit of their own citizens and customers as global land and water resources dwindle. Conversion of prime agricultural land for export production, whether undertaken as part of a domestic economic development agenda or driven by the business plans of foreign investors, puts the global poor at greater risk for

MARKET POWER AND LEGAL ADVANTAGE   127

deprivation. They experience a decrease in domestically produced affordable food stocks, accelerated depletion of land and water resources, and environmental degradation from the industrial-scale application of chemical inputs, the cultivation of ecologically unsustainable crops, and deforestation.

Because the globalized food production system depends on the efficiencies obtained from a concentrated market led by small number of purchasers who, in turn, do business with a small number of large-scale producers, there is a built-in incentive for growing a very limited number of commodities. The resultant decrease in crop diversity, together with the concentration of production risks from weather and pests, poses a systemic threat to overall food security and the resilience of the entire global food system. These risks, however, are disproportionately greater in lower and middle-income countries. A small price change for affluent consumers is an inconvenience, but it is an especially serious threat to life for the roughly 2 billion people who make less than $2 per day, and whose food costs account for 50–80% of their household budgets.[37] Knowledgeable observers anticipate these challenges to intensify episodically as ecological conditions worsen.[38]

The overall argument of this first section can be summarized as follows. The specific patterns of globalization of agricultural production and investment are fueled by capital concentration that makes possible a high degree of market concentration, which, in turn, paves the way for new approaches to supply chain management and resource acquisition. None of the market strategies could be successful without considerable reliance upon state policies of regulatory forbearance and the active encouragement of international development agencies. The result has been the availability of relatively cheap food for the global affluent. However, these benefits come with considerable moral costs. The global system of agriculture has concentrated profits in corporations based in the developed countries, offloaded economic and environmental risks to poorer countries and poorer regions of affluent countries,

128   A LIVABLE PLANET

disrupted local economies, exacerbated overall economic inequality within and across nations, depleted and degraded water and soil resources at the sites of industrial-scale production, and undermined food security. These systemic consequences originate in the grossly unequal distribution of market power and legal advantage, and, ultimately, these factors threaten the human rights of some of the world's most economically vulnerable people.

The Realignment of State Power

The realignment of power between states and markets can take various forms. The first part of this section discusses policy mechanisms that disempower states. Well-known examples include neoliberal policy prescriptions such as deregulation, privatization, and budgetary austerity. However, market actors also adopt strategies to increase their power relative to states by enlisting and controlling state power for their own purposes. The second part of this section surveys four such strategies: preferential regulation, rent-seeking, quasi-mercantilist diplomacy, and schemes for risk transfer and enterprise protection. The policy mechanisms and market strategies are connected. The policy mechanisms for disempowerment of states endorsed by market fundamentalists remove key obstacles to the capture of state power for private purposes.

Structural Adjustment

Deregulation, privatization, and budgetary austerity are well-known components of the neoliberal policy portfolio imposed on debtor nations as a condition for loans and assistance by the IMF and World Bank. Collectively, the key elements of loan conditionality agreements introduced in the 1980s were known as "structural adjustment" policies. Although the name has been officially retired,

MARKET POWER AND LEGAL ADVANTAGE 129

the institutional policy priorities remain in place. The distinctive point highlighted here is the way in which the three policies work in conjunction to disempower states, increase market power of private entities, and render human rights less secure.

Deregulation removes legal restraints on business enterprises, freeing them from environmental protection rules, wage and employment standards, various capitalization requirements, and public disclosure procedures. Without widespread deregulation, the patterns of market consolidation discussed in the first section would not be possible. Privatization removes large swaths of the economy from the public sector, and its overall social impact is a function of the way it works in tandem with deregulation. It's not only that the activities of privatized entities are not accountable directly to the electorate in the way public utilities are. Deregulation also lets them operate free of extensive state oversight. The private provision of water and sanitation services is an important example discussed in Chapter 7.

Budgetary austerity measures also operate in conjunction with deregulation and privatization policies. Debtor nations are urged to adopt austere, stripped-down budgets to facilitate repayment of accumulated debt to the IMF, investors in sovereign bonds, and private bankers. Deregulation is part of an overall plan designed to regain fiscal stability by stimulating private-sector growth and increasing public-sector tax revenue. In addition, privatization of transportation, water and sanitation services, and healthcare is promoted, not simply on grounds of greater efficiency, but because it removes public payroll and other expenditures from government balance sheets.

Criticisms of structural adjustment and the imposition of austerity measures are familiar to many readers by now. For example, the wholesale interference with domestic policies of states in Latin America, Africa, and elsewhere are condemned as neocolonialist efforts to reassert political control over newly decolonized nations and retain privileged access to their resources.[39] Critics also object

130 A LIVABLE PLANET

that wealthy nations that fund and direct the operations of the IMF and World Bank use their power to advance the narrow economic interests of businesses based within the major donor nations, often to the detriment of debtor nations.

In addition, international financial institutions use their power as lenders of last resort to alter domestic social programs to suit their ideological preferences, and, in effect, they conduct a non-voluntary social experiment on a grand scale.[40] The budget cuts demanded by austerity regimes have immediate negative impact on the ability of states to meet the basic needs of their citizens, fulfill their human rights responsibilities, and protect the environmental conditions essential to the well-being of current and future generations. The cuts include reductions in enforcement of public health and environmental standards, reduction of public employee wages and pensions, and elimination of minimum wage laws and economic safety net programs. These budgetary changes fundamentally alter the societies where they are imposed. They make labor pools more flexible and desperate, and they undermine state ability to preserve the quality of environmental conditions. Apart from these objectional social consequences, external control over domestic social policies constitutes an unjust imposition of ideals of social justice that citizens may not share or, at any rate, that they have a right to determine for themselves through democratic processes.[41]

Treaties and Trade Agreements

Structural adjustment policies and austerity regimes are perhaps the most familiar ways, but not the only means by which the disempowerment of states has been achieved. For example, trade rules found in various multinational agreements such as the North American Free Trade Agreement (NAFTA; now the US-Mexico-Canada Agreement USMCA), the cluster of agreements that

MARKET POWER AND LEGAL ADVANTAGE 131

underpin the World Trade Organization (WTO), and provisions within the constitution of the European Union tie the hands of future democratic majorities. Key provisions of these treaties restrict social welfare policies that might interfere with free trade across member states. Such agreements have the same effect on national economic sovereignty of signatory states, for the same ideological ends as the structural adjustment policies.[42] In addition, among the most controversial elements of various free trade treaties are binding rules that not only prioritize free trade over social welfare and environmental goals, but also confer legal standing on private entities to challenge the environmental and employment policies of member states.

Moreover, the European Union has institutionalized a budget austerity plan modeled along the lines proposed by market fundamentalist James Buchanan.[43] He argued for implementation of a "debt break," ideally, in his view, a constitutional provision that limits public spending, either through a balanced budget requirement or public expenditure debt limit tied to economic metrics such as GDP. The intent is to limit legislative enactment of deficit spending measures, especially long-term borrowing used to finance multiyear social welfare programs. In other words, the aim is to "starve the beast," and (as we saw in Chapter 3) an intended result is de-democratization.

A lesser-known instrument for disempowering states is the bilateral trade agreement mechanism. It substitutes the foreign law—most often the business-friendly corporate law of New York state or the United Kingdom—for domestic laws of nations where transnational corporations are doing business abroad. Estimates suggest there are as many as 2,000–3,000 such treaties in existence, conferring upon the world's most powerful market actors the ability to create their own rules tailored for their own benefit and adjudicated in venues favorable to their interests.[44]

Whatever the specific institutional mechanism—structural adjustment, external imposition of budget austerity measures,

132   A LIVABLE PLANET

multilateral or bilateral trade agreements—the intended effect is the same. They transfer power from states to markets or specific market participants, curtail market regulations, substitute market mechanisms for collectively run public programs, and tie the budgetary hands of democratic majorities.

Hijacking State Power for Private Purposes

Market fundamentalists, as discussed in Chapter 3, often defend state disempowerment on the grounds that robust, wide-ranging state regulatory capacity is dangerous because it attracts private interests that seek to capture it for private purposes. However, as the power of states was scaled back, the increase of relative private-sector power has made capture both easier and more attractive. This section will be brief, providing only basic points about four strategies described more extensively in specific examples in subsequent chapters.

The first strategy involves *preferential regulation.* Both international treaties and the bilateral trade agreements demonstrate that business interests sometimes favor preferential regulation over outright deregulation. Often it is better for them to write the rules in their own interest than to eliminate rules.[45] For example, provisions central to most bilateral trade agreements establish the rules, procedures, adjudication venues, and remedies for enterprises doing business in foreign jurisdictions.[46] Wherever multinational corporations go, they bring their own rules with them, or they prevail upon states to adopt local laws that entice risk-averse foreign investors.

The second strategy is known as *rent-seeking.* In practical terms, it means that private entities routinely seek to enlist the support of states in their efforts to extract profits, using their ties to governments to manipulate public policy to bypass market competition. For example, some enterprises seek to steer government

MARKET POWER AND LEGAL ADVANTAGE   133

contracts in their direction, preferably without the requirement of competitive bidding and, ideally, through open-ended, costs-plus contracts that create a perpetual motion machine of profit generation. Military hardware production contracts, water and sanitation management contracts, and global shipping contracts for the delivery of international aid are prime examples.

Exclusive government contracts allow private firms to expand their profits by eliminating the transaction costs and market uncertainty of competition. They also freeze out potential market entrants. Businesses like these arrangements because they know that competing in markets is often a far less rewarding and less reliable business plan than enlisting the power of government to make sure that the playing field is not level. Once again, we see how the consequences of state deference to market actors diverge substantially from the grand designs and expectations of market fundamentalists. Weakened states are easy prey for firms seeking to hijack governments to evade or reduce market competition.

The third strategy involves the *commandeering of international diplomacy*. While the wholesale integration of states and enterprises that defined classical mercantilism may seem like a relic of the past, private enterprises still tap into rich veins of economic nationalist sentiments to help them secure global conditions hospitable to their own business interests. A recent example of this quasi-mercantilist strategy is the enlistment of the US Department of State to dissuade other countries from banning the sale of US fracking technology abroad.[47] The more familiar long-term example is the symbiotic relationship between states and aviation industries that jointly work to sell airplanes and military hardware as a way of advancing both national security and domestic economic goals. The ideal of free, unobstructed markets never enters the equation.

A fourth strategy involves mechanisms that *shift private investment risks to states*. For example, US banks in 2008 procured bailouts for investments and loans that they not only knew in advance were risky, but also knew that government would step in if

134   A LIVABLE PLANET

things went badly. They were confident that they could make the case later that they were "too big to fail" and that criminal prosecution would be extremely unlikely. Corporations also undertake certain activities such as loan underwriting, sale of flood insurance, and vaccine development only when they obtain government assurance that their losses will be indemnified and that their legal liability will be limited should harm result. These are functions that markets typically will not fulfill unless conditions of market competition are suspended and mechanisms of legal accountability for product defects and consequential harms are set aside.

Risk shifting also is achieved by the private-sector enlistment of the regulatory power or financial resources of government either by putting a ceiling on market loss or building a floor of assured income. Private enterprises seek government protection from capital losses caused by economic and political adversaries. Examples of government policies that shield businesses against economic loss are "ag-gag" laws which prohibit filming of factory farms and laws which restrict or criminalize environmental protests and labor organizing activities. Classic examples of the strategy of building an income floor include direct subvention for private enterprises, for example, agricultural price supports, key industry subsidies, and public funding of research and technology transfer to the private sector.

In short, even though economists make the case for disempowering the state by appealing to the social value of market competition, it is often a better business strategy to enlist state power to circumvent the discipline imposed by markets and eliminate the legal rules that hold market actors liable for the consequences of their profit-seeking activities. This sort of business strategy might sound odd or of marginal significance given the extent that the value of competition is emphasized by economists and pro-market propogandists. However, the strategic importance of loosening the grip of market competition is an important staple of contemporary business thought. An enormously influential 1979 article by Michael Porter in the *Harvard Business Review* made the case for monopolies and other anti-competitive practices as central to any plan for increasing corporate growth.[48] The fabulously successful and closely watched investor Warren Buffett has been a prominent proponent of investing only in businesses that can build a "moat" around their enterprises, insulating them from the threat of competition.

Contrary to the rhetoric of market fundamentalism, enterprises with considerable market power and political influence often view competition as an undesirable—and eliminable—source of risk and uncertainty. Sometimes deregulation best serves their business purposes, but, at other times, preferential regulation, rent-seeking, quasi-mercantilist policies, or mechanisms for direct subvention and loss protection work best. However, the availability of these anti-competitive business strategies depends heavily on the success of state disempowerment advocated by market fundamentalists.

Gaming the System of States

Multinational corporations do business wherever there are attractive opportunities for obtaining natural resources, labor, or geographic access to lucrative markets. However, these opportunities are not the only draw for global enterprises. Transnational corporations, financial institutions, and an army of lawyers and international wealth managers routinely engage in a practice known as *regulatory arbitrage*. They pit nations against one another in a competition for investment based on which countries provide lenient taxation policies and business-friendly regulatory climates beyond what international and bilateral treaties already provide.

Although shopping the world for permissive legal regimes has become widespread over the past 40 or so years, the idea has been around for quite some time. Fredrich Hayek suggested that the global economy itself should be converted into an arena of market

136   A LIVABLE PLANET

competition, where states are forced to compete for capital investment based on favorable political and legal arrangements. As Hayek saw it, the rationale for such competition is that it would counteract state monopoly on coercive power and tame the efforts of individual states to adopt social welfare and labor policies that distort the price mechanism. In other words, states would compete for investment based on which country taxes and governs least. Deregulation, privatization, and austerity policies provide the basis for such competition.

Regulatory Arbitrage

Illustrative examples of regulatory arbitrage include efforts to extract business concessions and relaxed environmental and employment laws. Potential investors also seek to lower minimum capital requirements for financial services, eliminate or reduce fees for land reclamation security bonds imposed on extractive industries, and, more generally, temper any laws that might effectively raise production costs. They also seek to lower the costs of doing business by demanding state subsidies, infrastructure improvements, and the issuance of taxpayer-backed bonds to fund construction of factories or shipping facilities.[49]

Moreover, the model of regulatory arbitrage that pits nation against nation is not confined to the global arena. It has long been employed in federalist systems such as the United States, where states are pitted against states, and cities are pitted against other local jurisdictions.[50] Manufacturing firms and regional distribution organizations often make their locational decisions based on criteria like those employed by agricultural processing businesses discussed earlier in this chapter. A cadre of experienced consultants generally take the lead in the negotiation process, known in the United States as "buffalo hunting." Even when the winning state or city is not the one that offers the greatest regulatory or tax relief, the competitive process confers a bargaining chip. It allows businesses to press for concessions not otherwise available to them and certainly not available to smaller competitors.

The competitive process for extracting governmental concessions is now entrenched as a routine part of global business. In effect, from 2003 until 2021, Hayek's dream of a global market for deregulation and preferential regulation was institutionalized by the creation of the World Bank's registry known as the "Doing Business Report." It ranked 189 countries based on the ease of doing business. The Bank's own online information repository takes credit for incentivizing more than a quarter of the 2,100 reforms registered since its creation. Such regulatory changes are defended on the grounds that they improve the economy by relaxing onerous burdens that businesses typically face, such as mounds of paperwork and unwarranted bureaucratic delays. However, critics observe that many of the changes did much more. They lowered labor and environmental standards, diminished business contributions to social security funds, and made it easier and cheaper to transfer public lands to foreign buyers searching for oil fields, mineral deposits, freshwater resources, forest land convertible for industrial-scale agricultural use, and other governmental concessions that harm the poor.[51] The Doing Business Report was discontinued, but not because of these adverse effects. The Bank acted in response to complaints about ethical lapses in compiling the rankings, and its own statement on the matter made it clear that its promotion of the deregulatory policies would remain in force.[52]

Many observers argue that regulatory arbitrage thus far has not resulted in a global race to the bottom.[53] They correctly point out that transnational corporations make locational investment decisions based on a host of considerations, including access to markets, workforce characteristics (e.g., low prevailing wage or high prevalence of specific skills), access to vital transportation hubs, or quality of life factors. In fact, the largest constellation of foreign direct investment involves recipient nations and companies

138   A LIVABLE PLANET

and contributing nations both of which rank relatively high in both taxation rates and regulatory oversight.[54] The important point, however, is that many jurisdictions are not as well-positioned to resist the overreaching demands of potential investors, and, consequently, many transnational companies have strong incentive to search for locations for operations that require few skills, have adverse environmental impact, or offer little benefit for—or even create a drain on—the local economy. Economically weaker nations—or less economically developed states within a federalist system—are no match for hypermobile corporations that can credibly threaten to end or not undertake business investment in a legal jurisdiction they cannot effectively dominate.[55]

Tax Competition

A global system in which countries specialize in the creation of "tax havens" works in tandem with international competition for regulatory relief. Tax havens do more than simply offer lower rates of taxation on the operations conducted within their borders. They are jurisdictions that cater to transnational corporations and wealthy individuals seeking to avoid high taxation and public scrutiny of their profits from elsewhere in the world.

The mechanisms are often enormously complex, but the point, with respect to multinational corporations, is that they get to pick the country where they declare their profits and channel their wealth into tax-free or low-tax jurisdictions by creating shell corporations. These shell corporations derive their name from the fact that they are often little more than "letterbox" operations, a convenient postal address with no substantial business presence. They are created solely for the purpose of reducing or avoiding taxes and escaping strict financial regulations in the countries where they conduct most of their business or derive most of their income.[56] In short, tax havens tailor their laws to offer lower tax rates (or no tax), shield tax data from other jurisdictional taxing authorities, and allow businesses to conduct their financial transactions with few restrictions on and little oversight over the source and disposition of the deposited funds.

The international practice of reliance on tax havens is not limited to a few small, unsophisticated legal jurisdictions or clustered primarily in poverty stricken or (stereotypically) corrupt island nations. Luxembourg, the Netherlands, Hong Kong, Switzerland, and Ireland are among the world's largest tax havens. Although the Cayman Islands are among the most well-known "offshore" tax havens, its governors are appointed by the British crown, its laws are subject to British approval, and legal disputes are resolved under British law.[57]

Moreover, the use of offshore financial centers is not an economic anomaly or a vehicle used mostly by drug cartels and other criminal syndicates aiming to hide their ill-gotten gains. It is now an essential component of wealth management plans for multinational corporations and the world's richest individuals. Much of the wealth generated from strictly legal global trade is deposited in offshore accounts, insulated from scrutiny and sheltered from high taxation rates. Roughly 40% of all multinational profits is routed through tax havens, and, for the multinationals based in the United States, the percentage is 60%.[58] Moreover, IMF researchers estimate that 40% of all foreign direct investment that flows into these tax havens creates no genuine economic benefit for the recipient nation.[59]

Nor is the system of offshore tax havens a phenomenon of marginal economic or distributive significance. Estimates of the magnitude of corporate and individual tax revenues lost because of tax competition vary, unsurprisingly, given the shroud of secrecy created by a complex web of domestic and international legal rules. One widely cited estimate is that $483 billion in tax revenue is lost each year to tax abuse by multinationals and wealthy individuals, but equally important is the pattern of upward transfer

140　A LIVABLE PLANET

of wealth to the world's most affluent countries. Member countries of the Organisation for Economic Cooperation and Development (OECD) are responsible for 78% of the annual tax loses, and the United Kingdom alone is responsible for 39%.[60] Furthermore, as Brooke Harrington documents, wealth managers exacerbate global inequality by keeping wealth in families for generations.[61]

The precise amounts of revenue losses are subjects of ongoing debate and refinement, but there is widespread agreement about their impact. They deprive many countries of revenue, exacerbate global and intergenerational inequality, and shield assets from efforts to hold corporations and shareholders accountable for environmental and other damages they may have caused. Even countries that are net beneficiaries of tax competition, at least for a time, experience a loss in capacity to regulate their own economies due to the hypermobility of global capital.[62] In short, tax competition is a perfect example of economically predatory, ecologically destructive market practices that have moved from the periphery to the core of the global political economy.

Control over Capital Investment

The current global order is defined by market mechanisms and institutions that not only skew the process of capital accumulation, but, equally important, they skew its investment. The trend toward *financialization*—the growing share of the financial services sector in the global economy and its staggering influence on other sectors—has led many observers to label the current era of economic history as "financial capitalism."

The financial services sector is often celebrated because it serves two major functions thought essential to the global economy. In theory, it directs funds from savers and potential investors to borrowers and companies who need capital for socially beneficial productive activities such as manufacturing, healthcare, energy generation, mining,

MARKET POWER AND LEGAL ADVANTAGE   141

and transport. The global phalanx of banks, pension funds, insurance companies, private equity funds, sovereign wealth funds, private money managers, and other institutional investors are thus seen as essential to efficient—and socially beneficial—capital allocation. In addition, financial institutions are credited with playing an essential role in risk management. For example, if they properly exercise their duties of due diligence, they can vet creditworthy enterprises and weed out inefficient practices, and they can establish secondary markets through which debt is sold to other investors, thereby spreading the risks of lending. If all goes well, the global economy is well-served by institutions that perform these two essential market functions of capital allocation and risk-spreading.

However, the financial services sector in its current form falls far short of the ideal for two main reasons. First, much of the capital extended to borrowers is not used to increase socially beneficial production or trade but to help other financial-sector borrowers profit on interest rates, dividends, or, most significantly, capital appreciation of assets. For example, only 10% of bank lending in the United Kingdom is for businesses outside of the financial sector.[63] In other words, the lending practices crowd out, rather than facilitate, the flow of capital to borrowers who might use it for socially beneficial productive activities.

Second, the size and influence of the finance sector confers upon private owners of concentrated capital an immense power to determine what gets produced, where, by whom, and the conditions of state oversight over production.[64] They do much to determine whether incumbent fossil fuel technologies remain in place; how water resources are used and distributed; the method, location, and types of crops that are grown; and the fate of forests, oceans, and more. In other words, the financial sector has a lot of unaccountable power over the future of the planet, and it uses much of its power to fuel speculative investment in non-productive activities rather than, say, climate-proofing coastal cities or rebuilding crumbling water and sanitation infrastructure.

142   A LIVABLE PLANET

Moreover, the 2008 financial crash revealed two additional, highly problematic, deeply intertwined aspects of the international system of finance: the increase in sector profits derived from speculation (instead of production) and the rise of the shadow banking system.

Speculative Investment

A major problem for the financial sector is not only its misallocation of capital, but also the dangerously large sum of capital tied up in bank loans made for highly speculative investments in real estate or other assets such as high-yield corporate bonds or foreign land and water resources. These purchases are described as speculative because the loan repayments for the underlying asset outstrip the expected regular income stream from commercial rents, bond premiums, or dividends. These are highly leveraged investments, meaning that the debt-to-equity ratio is very high, leaving very little cushion for recouping potential losses or shortfalls in expected asset appreciation. In other words, these highly leveraged investments are nothing more than bets that the long-term appreciation in asset value will be sufficient to repay the loans, knowing that regular income from productive uses of capital will not be enough.

Because loans on highly leveraged investments are such risky bets, it is generally seen as necessary to remove them from the books of ordinary banks. Novel market practices have been devised to spread the risks in secondary markets where buyers purchase the rights to future proceeds of loans. Hundreds of billions of dollars in these bank loans, along with corporate bonds from bank portfolios, are repackaged into tradable securities, for example, financial instruments known as collateralized loan obligations (CLOs). In theory, CLOs and other securitized investment vehicles sold in secondary markets are designed to mitigate the risks that banks take

MARKET POWER AND LEGAL ADVANTAGE 143

on when they borrow heavily to lend money to businesses and commercial real estate purchasers. However, there are (at least) five serious problems in the way these practices affect the distribution of risks and rewards.

First, if commercial real estate values or corporate bond prices fall, leading the highly leveraged borrower to default, downstream purchasers of the CLOs suffer in a chain reaction of losses. In fact, a cascade of default is a serious risk. About 60% of the US companies rated by Moody's have a credit rating of "speculative," otherwise known as "high yield" or "junk bonds."[65] Even in the market for the safest corporate bonds, money has been chasing higher returns by lending extensively to institutional borrowers that have some of the lowest credit ratings. They fall into the category known as BBB, just a notch above "junk" bonds. By some estimates, bonds rated BBB represent more than half of the investment-grade US corporate bond market.[66]

Second, the purchasers of securitized loans or bonds are often among the institutions that create the securities in the first place as a mechanism for spreading their risks more widely. But instead, some institutions, including ordinary banks, most at risk and most in need of mechanisms that limit excess financial exposure are buying portfolios of highly leveraged debt from other lending institutions. If all this sounds like the 2008 asset bubble, famously precipitated by the decline in value of repackaged home mortgage debt—well, it is. By some estimates, it is even worse. The amount of money at risk from the highly leveraged loans taken on by businesses exceeds levels of debt that led to the cascade of defaults, foreclosures, bailouts, and global economic shocks more than a decade ago.[67] The point is not that another crash is imminent or inevitable. I have no financial crystal ball. The point is that systemic financial risk is built into current market practices that benefit a few by imposing—without disclosing—risks on the many.

Third, highly leveraged asset markets have massive and immediate redistributive effects. For example, corporations use the

144 A LIVABLE PLANET

proceeds of these loans to fund stock buybacks for large insider shareholder executives. It's arcane stuff, but the relevant point is simple. Instead of using the loans to hire new employees, develop new products, or expand production, the buybacks—or stock repurchases—raise a company's earnings per share and, ultimately, the value of the shares. For corporate officers who get much of their compensation from the sale of their shares of stock rather than salary, the increase generates a large windfall profit. In other words, overleveraged corporate debt is not used to finance potentially socially beneficial activities, such as the development of green technologies, but for enrichment of the corporate elite and large investors.

Fourth, many of the highly risky securitized financial instruments are contracts known as *derivatives*. They are named for the fact that their market value is based on the expected yield derived from the underlying bundle of assets, not tangible assets that can be valued more accurately in the open market. The underlying assets often include corporate bonds, real estate loans, or any other assets, including agricultural and water resources, and even sovereign debt of debt-ridden nations, all folded into tradable, high interest–yielding derivative contracts and sold to other banking institutions, hedge funds, diversified mutual equity funds, university endowments, and pensions. The risk is not just the previously noted concern that the capacity for loan payoff is dependent on asset appreciation rather than based on expectations of a stable income stream. An indicator of how speculative—and risky—these investments in the aggregate are is the fact that the total value of financial exposures from derivative contracts alone is estimated at somewhere between two and three times the total market value of all tangible assets in the world.[68]

Fifth, funds known as *special purpose vehicles* (SPVs) are another important component of the financial sector. They allow multiple investors to create new finance streams used to fund the privatization of traditional government activities such as hospitals, schools, and water and sewer services. A typical example is the use of SPVs to construct facilities that governments then rent under long-term leasing agreements, often coupled with lucrative management contracts that outsource a range of government services to private-sector investors. Politicians and credit rating agencies like these arrangements because they remove the costs of operation and construction debt from the government books, thereby improving their credit worthiness for taking on more debt. However, critics point to numerous instances in which these private financing initiatives dramatically raise the costs of debt service and operation of privatized services to the taxpayers. In fact, few privatization schemes would be undertaken absent the guaranteed revenue stream made available to SPV groups who often use their political influence and personal connections to get sweetheart deals available to no one else. Moreover, the revenues they generate routinely flow into tax havens, escaping taxation and transparency in the use of the proceeds.

The Shadow Banking System

The main lenders fueling the global frenzy of speculative investments are not ordinary banks, which are subject to at least some measure of regulatory oversight. The primary market actors are members of a heterogeneous collection of hedge funds, pension funds, private equity funds, asset managers, and investment brokers collectively known as the "shadow banking system." The system is so named because its participants operate without the same regulatory oversight as traditional banks. Like the system of tax havens and the practice of regulatory arbitrage, the shadow banking system, with its lead role in spurring speculative investment, is no anomaly or matter of marginal significance. At the close of 2022, the shadow banking system (i.e., non-bank financial intermediaries) held more assets than commercial banks and

146 A LIVABLE PLANET

central banks combined and more than double the amount held just three years after the 2008 financial crisis.[69]

Obviously, the lack of regulation and monitoring, along with the sheer size of its hidden market influence, makes it difficult to detect systemic risks before they turn into full-blown crises. But the shadow banking system not only opens the door to risky loans and financial system collapse. It also facilitates funding for projects of dubious social value that, at least in principle, banks subject to greater public scrutiny might avoid with the exercise due diligence, if for no other reason than reputational concerns.

A final point on the economic front is that the shadow banking system is not a freestanding problem. It is now the primary conduit through which 40–50% of all income from global trade ends up hidden in offshore tax havens.[70] These two institutions—the shadow banking system and the offshore tax havens—jointly define what counts as business-as-usual in the contemporary global political economy. Many productive sectors of the economy, including agribusiness, have become more integrated within global networks of financial institutions. They are locked into patterns of business practice that work in tandem to deprive nations of tax revenue, increase the concentration of capital in the hidden portfolios of the global rich, stifle innovation and crowd out more productive uses of assets, increase the systemic risk of financial collapse of the global economy, accelerate the extraction of dwindling resources from low-income countries, and drive up asset prices—especially, land—beyond the reach of local residents.[71]

Moreover, as Wolfgang Streeck observes, "financialization turns the financial sector into an international private government, disciplining national political communities and their public governments, without being in anyway democratically accountable."[72] The sector's effects on global power relations can be put into perspective by looking at three aspects of the structure of financial institutions illustrated in recent studies.

First, of the 200 richest entities on the planet, 159 are transnational corporations, not countries.[73] Second, 737 corporations control more than 80% of the value of more than 43,000 transnational corporations, with 147 "core" entities exercising control 10 times bigger than what could be expected based on their wealth alone.[74] Third, a stunning 75% of these core entities are financial intermediaries, including both traditional banks and shadow banking institutions. The point is not that these entities work in lockstep or in coordinated fashion. But, on a global scale, there is a remarkably small cluster of entities—mostly financial institutions or entities closely tied to those institutions—that have outsized and largely unaccountable control over economically and ecologically consequential decisions affecting everyone.

This section completes the task of the chapter, leading to one overarching conclusion. No progress toward a transition to a more just and sustainable global political economy is possible until there are fundamental changes in the processes of capital accumulation, market concentration, supply chain management, the dynamics of international investment, and the system of finance that underwrites predatory market activities. These market strategies are predatory insofar as market actors are able to extract profit without due consideration of social consequences and "live off the work of others," as James K. Galbraith points out, "not by their functional contribution to the productivity of the system."[75] Predatory market strategies also erode state capacity for governing, undermine the public good, destroy sustainable habitats, lock in disadvantage for subordinate groups, artificially inflate the costs of food and other essential commodities, deprive economically vulnerable communities of the material basis for meeting the basic needs guaranteed by human rights, and, ultimately, risk the stability of the global economy and vital planetary systems.

So long as the various institutional agents serving the global affluent have the power to support their high standard of living through economic activities that pose grave risk to the conditions

148 A LIVABLE PLANET

on which the lives, livelihoods, and satisfaction of the human rights of the least advantaged communities depend, there can be no movement toward a more humanly just world or the preservation of the ecological conditions that support all life on Earth. A transition to a more just and sustainable future for the planet is inconceivable without fundamental changes in the balance of power between states and markets, and between market-dominant states and market-subordinate states.

6

Land Use and Its Consequences

Humans are a terrestrial species unlike any other. They occupy almost all of Earth's habitable land. No other species engages in comparably intensive land uses—ones having high ecological impact, typically extending well beyond the primary spatial area in which their activities are conducted. Land transformation is accelerating at a rapid pace, increasing in its intensity of impact and expanding across a wider geographic space.

A recent assessment estimates that more than 70% of the Earth's ice-free land (including habitable and uninhabitable land) has been transformed in varying degrees by human activities.[1] Three centuries ago, humans were intensively using only 5% of the Earth's land area, but the current figure is conservatively estimated at around 50%.[2] Nearly 60% of terrestrial Earth is under moderate or intense human pressure (e.g., carbon dioxide [CO_2] emissions, material extraction, nutrient depletion, habitat destruction, freshwater appropriation).[3] By some estimates, more than 75% of Earth's habitable land areas are degraded (e.g., by desertification, pollution, erosion, or deforestation) to such a degree that the well-being of 3.2 billion people is now at risk, and the proportion of affected land is projected to rise to 95% by 2050 under a "business-as-usual" scenario for land use.[4]

Major contributions to the land footprint include the conversion of forests and savannahs into pasture or cropland, construction of human settlements, mining and well drilling, creation of transportation corridors, and the diversion of water. Humans are running out of the space they need to do what is necessary to support life in the way to which many have become accustomed and to which

A Livable Planet. Madison Powers, Oxford University Press. © Oxford University Press 2024.
DOI: 10.1093/oso/9780197756003.003.0006

150 A LIVABLE PLANET

many others aspire, and many of these land use practices are unsustainable. In other words, they are what we described in Chapter 2 as ecologically self-undermining. They exhaust the necessary resource base or otherwise degrade the environmental conditions which support human well-being. Human flourishing, and indeed human existence, depends on the capacity of the species to extract benefits from their terrestrial habitats, and yet the current level of extraction is incompatible with maintaining that capacity.

The first section explores the food security implications of agricultural land use. The largest share of anthropogenic land-use change is undertaken for agricultural purposes, but the farming practices that have made it possible to feed an expanding global population now threaten the capacity of the land to meet basic human nutritional needs. The section explains features of widespread food production practices that make them unsustainable and unpacks the debate over the choice between intensification and extensification of the land use footprint of agriculture.

The second section examines intensive land use practices having impacts that extend far beyond the land itself, substantially affecting groundwater and surface water, oceans, ambient air quality, and the functioning of planetary systems essential for sustaining life on Earth, including the climate system and biogeochemical cycles (e.g., phosphorus and nitrogen). Decisions about the future of farming become more complex and a sustainable pathway forward becomes more narrowly constrained once these consequences are considered.

The third section examines the destruction or fragmentation of forests, one of the most immediate and far-reaching impacts of intensive land change. These fragile terrestrial ecosystems are increasingly under pressure from the global expansion of land used for production of "high-risk commodities" (i.e., export commodities obtained from ecologically destructive agricultural and extractive activities). This section explains why forests are crucial for human well-being, surveys the human and ecological consequences of

LAND USE AND ITS CONSEQUENCES   151

deforestation and declining terrestrial biodiversity, and illustrates the global market dynamics driving both crises. The section ends with an assessment of some proposed nature-based solutions, explains their socioeconomic and ecological shortcomings, and shows how they perpetuate an unsustainable business-as-usual approach to land use.

The chapter concludes with a brief section explaining how the land use issues raised in this chapter are conceptualized as human rights concerns which, in turn, have been used by indigenous and other advocacy groups as a normative guide to their concrete policy proposals.

Farmland and Food Security

This section and the chapter more generally focus heavily on agricultural land use for four reasons. First, land use is the centerpiece of current discussions of the global food security challenge. The Food and Agriculture Organization (FAO), for example, warns that "degradation and deepening scarcity of land and water resources" poses a profound challenge to the task of feeding a global population expected to grow well beyond 9 billion by 2050.[5] Second, roughly half of the land occupied by humans already is devoted to food production.[6] Central to a sustainable form of food production is the ability to restrict the agricultural land footprint, given the competing uses of habitable land suitable for production of food, feed, fuel, and fiber, along with competing non-farm uses. Third, few land uses have more ecological impacts, not only on soil, but on freshwater availability, the increase in atmospheric greenhouse gases, deforestation, habitat destruction, and biodiversity loss. Fourth, land is the locus of an intense global competition for scarce resources. Land is the single most important economic asset for the vast proportion of the world's population that depends on agriculture for their livelihood, but land security is under pressure from

152   A LIVABLE PLANET

the owners of highly concentrated, hypermobile capital in search of increasingly scarce land for production of export crops, fuel, and forest products and the extraction of minerals.

Food Security Challenges

Food security is often understood along the lines of various FAO definitions proposed in a series World Food Summits. According to its one of its most comprehensive definitional proposals, "[f]ood security exists when all people, at all times, have physical, social and economic access to sufficient, safe and nutritious food that meets their dietary needs and food preferences for an active and healthy life."[7] Some variant of this definition is mirrored in the major human rights conventions and national constitutions that recognize a right to food.[8]

Moreover, the definition aligns with UN Sustainable Development Goal (SDG) 2, aiming to "end hunger, achieve food security and improved nutrition, and promote sustainable agriculture."[9] One of the targets by which its attainment can be measured closely tracks the broad FAO definition. Its stated aim is to "ensure access by all people, in particular the poor and people in vulnerable situations, including infants, to safe, nutritious and sufficient food all year round."[10]

However, knowledgeable observers of the global system of food production ask whether humanity is entering into a new, historically unprecedented era of ecological limits. It is widely estimated that, by 2050, the world will need to increase food production by at least 50–60%, and some projections consider scenarios in which the necessary increase will range as high as 70–100%.[11] One influential study that estimates that the global average of agricultural production will have to increase by 60% by 2050, compared with the levels of 2005–2006, forecasts a much greater increase in developing countries, on the order of 77%.[12] Estimates vary due to differences in underlying assumptions, with slightly lower estimates reported in more recent meta-analysis of projections.[13] However, whether the best projection turns out to be nearer the higher or lower end, there is no disagreement about the essential nature of the challenge ahead and its primary causes.

The food security challenge is often described as caused by a confluence of demand-side and supply-side (or production) pressures.[14] One aspect of the demand-side challenge is that, by mid-century, there will be many more people to feed, when world population is expected to increase from 7 billion to 9.7 billion, and perhaps even to 10.9 billion by the end of the century.[15] Another demand-side factor is a global shift in dietary habits. As the more affluent residents of the low- and middle-income countries become richer, they increase variety in their diets, with a larger share of their protein requirements obtained through the resource-intensive production of livestock animals.[16] Increased production of animal products will require more land and water; increase the pollution of air, soil, and water; and generate more greenhouse gas emissions than most plant-based foods.[17] These environmental consequences are highly significant, given the fact that 75% of land clearing for agriculture is undertaken for farm animal production.[18]

Soil Degradation

Land availability is a limiting factor in any future scenario. The FAO's 2015 report, *The Status of the World's Soil Resources*, estimates that 33% of existing agricultural land is moderately to highly degraded due to erosion, salinization, compaction, acidification, and chemical pollution of soil and concludes that conditions are getting worse in far more cases than they are improving.[19] Some more recent estimates are closer to 24%.[20] Although estimates vary somewhat, there is widespread agreement that a higher degree of agricultural land degradation is concentrated in many economically less-developed nations. Because almost 40% of the agricultural land is seriously degraded in countries where roughly 76% of the global population derive most of their protein from plants, many of the world's poor will face even greater nutritional challenges.[21]

The primary activities leading to soil loss differ by region, but among the most important factors are overgrazing, increased soil or water toxicity due to chemical inputs, and water erosion caused by deforestation or other land use decisions.[22] Although the FAO's report card on the state of the world's soil resources identifies a diversity of causally important activities and types of land degradation, studies reveal that the consequences for the future of farming are much the same everywhere. The rate of topsoil depletion vastly exceeds the rate of replenishment in all regions of the world.[23] The depletion-to-replenishment ratios routinely range from 10-to-1 in parts of the American agricultural heartland to as much as 40-to-1 in parts of China.[24] Some of the most intensively farmed areas (e.g., in Iowa and surrounding states that produce corn and soy for export) are losing soil at a rate 16 times the pace of natural replenishment.[25] The 2019 Climate Change and Land report by the Intergovernmental Panel on Climate Change (IPCC) paints a starker picture for some parts of the world, indicating locations where soil is being lost more than 100 times faster than it is being formed in heavily ploughed areas (and 10–20 times faster even on fields that are not tilled).[26]

Although the FAO's 2020 update is less pessimistic than earlier forecasts—which warned that some regions would experience complete soil exhaustion in 40–60 years—the diagnostic focus has sharpened, now identifying agricultural practices as the key driver of degradation in every part of the world.[27] More specifically, they conclude that the main causes of damage to soils are intensive agriculture, with excessive use of fertilizers, pesticides, and antibiotics that kill soil organisms, reduce fertility, and leave the soil more prone to erosion. Such problems are expected to

LAND USE AND ITS CONSEQUENCES 155

worsen because of the combination of rising global temperatures due to climate change and the global expansion of chemically intensive farming methods. For example, the IPCC Working Group II estimates that, by 2100, between 8% and 30% of the land currently used for agriculture and raising livestock is expected to become "climatically unsuitable," depending on how much more warming occurs.[28]

The problem of soil degradation is especially challenging in some parts of the world, in particular Africa and dryland regions of Asia that are most prone to further increases in desertification from climate change.[29] Desertification, which the IPCC defines as "land degradation in arid, semi-arid, and dry sub-humid areas, collectively known as drylands, resulting from many factors, including human activities and climatic variations." Drylands are home to approximately 38% of the global population, around 3 billion people. The largest number of people living in drylands are found in South Asia, followed by sub-Saharan Africa and Latin America. Overall, "about 90% of the population in drylands live in developing countries," the IPCC report notes. Dryland populations are highly vulnerable to the effects of desertification and climate change because their livelihoods are heavily dependent on agriculture, one of the economic sectors most susceptible to disruption from climate change.

Because recent estimates project that somewhere between 30% and 40% of the world's land under cultivation is likely to become too degraded to support agriculture over the long term, two main options have dominated the discussions of the future of food production. Sites of agricultural production can be extended—extensification, as it is known—but only at the expense of other uses for land, including sites now devoted to human settlements, thus risking further displacement of subsistence agriculture communities and more encroachment on the world's forests. An expanded land footprint is not a viable option. The alternative is agricultural intensification—typically employing more chemical

156 A LIVABLE PLANET

inputs to maximize the yield on current sites of production, thereby freezing the land footprint of food.

Africa is an especially illuminating example of how little room remains for expanding the land footprint of agriculture. The United Nations Convention to Combat Desertification (UNCCD) estimates that about two-thirds of African lands are now either desert or drylands.[30] The Montpellier Panel, an eminent group of agriculture, ecology, and trade experts from Africa and Europe, reach similar conclusions, estimating that 65% of Africa's arable land is already too damaged to sustain viable food production.[31] To put these startling facts in a socioeconomic context, agriculture accounts for 65% of full-time employment in Africa, 25–30% of its nations' overall gross domestic product (GDP), and over half of the continent's export earnings.[32]

Synthetic Solutions

An important proposal for coping with the emerging scarcity of farmland is to make more intensive use of land rather than extend the cultivation footprint of agriculture. The main premise of the intensification argument is straightforward. High-yield production of most staple crops requires soil that is rich in essential nutrients. In particular, agricultural production is dependent upon the abundance, availability, and balance of nitrogen with phosphorus. Nitrogen is essential for the leafy green vegetative growth and longevity of plants, and it is largely responsible for the protein content of cereal grains. However, one problem is that soils of many regions lack sufficient naturally occurring nitrogen levels to support robust plant growth. They require synthetic nutrient supplementation, especially for producing crops not otherwise suited to local conditions.

Moreover, even in regions where nitrogen is naturally abundant it is often found in a form that few living organisms can use. Most plants—other than legumes, such as peas, beans, and other

LAND USE AND ITS CONSEQUENCES · 157

pulses—are unable to use the nitrogen gas that makes up 78% of the earth's atmosphere. For the most part, agriculturally useful nitrogen must be "fixed," that is, pulled from the air and converted into usable inorganic compounds, such as ammonium (NH_4) and nitrate (NO_3). The most optimistic case for successful intensification is premised on the prospect of increased production and dissemination of synthesized nutrients, together with ambitious programs for technology transfer and refinement of chemical inputs and application techniques that reduce their adverse ecological consequences. While the expanded use of synthetic agricultural inputs as a means of land sparing is supported by agribusiness, some members of the conservationist community also favor freezing the land footprint of agriculture so that wildlands are preserved.[33]

The grounds for optimism are rooted in the history of the Green Revolution. Until the invention of the artificial nitrogen fixation process, known as the *Haber-Bosch process*, the production of agricultural crops depended on the limited quantity of available (reactive) nitrogen naturally occurring in soils and ecosystems. The process became the basis for all synthetic nitrogen fertilizers, and their production has grown exponentially since the end of World War II, accounting for the bulk of human contribution of new nitrogen to the global cycle.[34] Commonly accepted estimates of the proportion of current global crop harvests made possible by the application of synthesized nitrogen fertilizer range from 40% to 48%.[35] To put matters slightly differently, at the higher end of the range, the estimate is that agriculture would have supported 3.5 billion fewer people without nitrogen fertilizers.[36] Optimists also point to the fact that the land footprint of agriculture has grown more slowly than productivity. For example, for the period between 1967 and 2007, global crop yields grew by 115% while the area of land in agriculture increased by only 8%.[37] Based on 2014 data, only 30% of the arable land area was needed to produce the same quantity of crops relative to 1961.[38]

Recent research suggests that, with existing technology, a 48% global reduction in nitrogen fertilizer use is possible through

158   A LIVABLE PLANET

proper irrigation, crops that more efficiently utilize nitrogen, and changing the forms of nitrogen used in fertilizers. However, achievable benefits require large-scale global application, optimal soil and other local ecological conditions, substituting more expensive hybrids for existing crops, and economic resources simply not available in many parts of the world.[39]

To be clear about what the data cited by optimists mean, many of the crops produced with the aid of synthesized nitrogen increased yields that feed livestock. Animal protein thus became a rapidly expanding share of the human diet only because of the productivity gains achieved by the combination of fertilizers, irrigation, crop breeding, and the mechanization of planting and harvesting. A smaller proportion of food consisting of animal protein would have made these productivity gains less urgent. Consequently, it is important to consider the broader implications of a livestock-intensive, chemically intensive pathway for feeding the world.

Impacts Beyond Land

The intensification option, as it turns out, has its own problems, including multiple negative environmental effects that now figure centrally in the arguments by advocates for a rapid and wholesale retreat from reliance on synthesized chemical inputs. There are at least three reasons for questioning whether the current chemical pathway for feeding the world is possible within ecologically sustainable parameters: its role in producing water pollution and related ecosystem damage, its contribution to climate change, and its disruptive effect on biogeochemical flows.

Water Pollution and Ecosystem Damage

First, there is the problem of water pollution. For example, the US Environmental Protection Agency regards agriculture as the

LAND USE AND ITS CONSEQUENCES   159

leading source of impairment of the nation's rivers and lakes.[40] More than 60% of coastal rivers and bays in the United States have been moderately or severely degraded by nutrient pollution, especially nitrogen.[41] Agricultural chemicals are a major source of water pollution in other developed countries as well.

The pollution is a consequence of the amount of nitrogen residue that concentrates in ground and surface water, runs off into inland waterways and pollutes distant watersheds, and often ends up in coastal waterways and oceans. The problem is that only 25–50% of the nitrogen contained in the fertilizers applied to the soil is absorbed by plants.[42] The rest is either absorbed in the ground or it runs off into surface waters, producing various secondary ecosystem harms, including acidification of soils and invasion of nitrogen-loving weeds and highly concentrated toxic substances in rivers, streams, and lakes.[43]

One of the most well-known problems is eutrophication of coastal marine ecosystems—commonly known as "dead zones"—resulting from excesses of both nitrogen and phosphorus. These nutrients fuel the explosive growth of algae, ultimately depriving aquatic organisms of the oxygen required to support them. These "anoxic" (oxygen depleting) events are particularly common in marine coastal environments fed by large, nutrient-rich rivers (e.g., Mississippi River feeding the Gulf of Mexico; Susquehanna River feeding the Chesapeake Bay).

Under conditions created by large-scale agricultural practices, where extensive plowing is the norm, soil degradation and its knock-on effects on water are accelerated in two ways. First, plowing reduces soil fertility by destroying naturally occurring organic matter. Modern tillage agriculture thus deprives soil of the basis for producing the essential nutrients it needs, thereby increasing dependence on synthetic nitrogen fertilizers. Second, destruction of the organic matter breaks down the soil structure that otherwise would allow it to absorb and retain water. When the soil is broken down, more soil washes away, carrying more nitrogen and phosphorous into rivers and streams, thereby requiring

160   A LIVABLE PLANET

application of a greater quantity of fertilizer to make up for what is lost by the runoff. To put the problem into perspective, "each 1 percent increase in soil organic matter helps soil hold 20,000 gallons more water per acre."[44]

The depletion of soil fertility, together with the breakdown of soil structure and decreased capacity for water retention increases the need for heavier applications of fertilizer to produce high yields.[45] The result has been described as a "treadmill effect": the more that is used, the more that is needed. With heavier applications, more runoff and more water pollution. One of the most destructive and widely studied examples is the massive problem of recurring algae blooms in the Lake Erie basin caused by large-scale production of corn and soy in the midwestern United States.[46] As one soil conservationist summarizes it: "If you have an agricultural system where the farmer can only survive by polluting Lake Erie, then there's something fundamentally wrong with that system."[47] To put the US experience into perspective, the recent research that projects a 48% increase in efficiency in the application of nitrogen fertilizers, using existing technology, assumes a global average of 42% absorption and a US average of 67%.[48] That means that in locations where relative efficiency already exceeds the global average and access to technology and financial resources far exceeds the global average, there are fewer opportunities for improving efficiency in some of the world's most extensive areas for growing monoculture crops such as soy and corn.

Climate Change and Sustainable Intensification

One of the main arguments for sustainable intensification is the potential for reduction of greenhouse gas emissions.[49] However, it turns out that the use of nitrogen to produce food and feed has a major climate impact.

LAND USE AND ITS CONSEQUENCES   161

Let's start with the familiar fact that agriculture overall is one of the main drivers of climate change, recently estimated by the IPCC to be responsible for as much as 23% of all greenhouse gas emissions. Moreover, among the many adverse consequences of global warming is its role in fueling still greater land degradation. Warming leads to weather pattern disruptions—too little rain, too much rain, intense rainfall events, or rain in the wrong stage of the growing cycle and excessive heat that produces desertification, soil erosion, or nutrient loss. In other words, agriculture leads to more warming, and more warming leads to greater loss of productive land. It seems to follow that reducing the agricultural footprint of land will at the very least help us adapt to global warming and, hopefully, generate fewer emissions if fewer carbon-sequestering acres are cleared for cultivation. However, two points are worth noting.

First, the IPPC observes that climate change is often "a secondary driver subordinated to other overwhelming human pressures" that on their own lead to land changes such as desertification, erosion, and soil nutrient loss.[50] In less complicated language, climate change is driven by choice of agricultural techniques that contribute to land degradation that fuels climate change. Thus, it is important to consider which aspects of agricultural production contribute most to climate change.

The single most important contribution of agriculture to greenhouse gas emissions is due to the production and application of nitrogen fertilizers, and the second most significant contribution is from livestock production through enteric fermentation and manure.[51] The specific greenhouse gas associated primarily with the use of nitrogen fertilizers—and secondarily with livestock manure—is nitrous oxide (N_2O). It is the third-largest contributor to climate change after CO_2 and methane—the more well-known byproduct of ruminant livestock. Moreover, it is a long-lived greenhouse gas, and it is almost 300 times more potent than CO_2 over a 100-year period.

162   A LIVABLE PLANET

New research suggests that the climate impact associated with the pace of uptake of nitrogen fertilizers is on track to match the N_2O impact projected by the high emissions scenario (RCP8.5) used in earlier IPPC reports.[52] Given the large contribution of nitrogen fertilizer to agricultural emissions, the expanded use of nitrogen fertilizers is not a sustainable solution. It undermines efforts to control the rise of global warming.

Moreover, issues of unsustainable emissions due to nitrogen fertilizer use and the N_2O emissions from the production of farm animals are tightly linked. Not only is livestock manure the second largest cause of N_2O emissions—the third-largest contributor to climate change—but livestock also is one of the major reasons for expanded use of nitrogen fertilizers in the first place. Absent the expansion of production of animal feed, both the land footprint of agriculture and the production of climate damaging N_2O from fertilizers and livestock would be far less.

In short, agriculture's contribution to climate change would not be what it is but for the added emissions from fertilizer required to devote more land to feed instead of food, and we end up with more direct harmful emissions from livestock than would be produced by most food crops. Although land scarcity and climate are important and intertwined concerns, the solution is not as simple as an intensification plan that requires more chemicals to grow more feed to raise more livestock on less land. The optimal path forward is to grow more food and less feed, thereby reducing the two biggest agricultural contributors to greenhouse gases while also using less land.

Intensification and extensification therefore are not the only choices. What matters from the perspective of climate change impact and the size of the agricultural land footprint is what is grown on agricultural lands. And perhaps most importantly, the conversion of agricultural land from feed to food takes the pressure off the food security challenge, freeing up more land to meet human needs and securing human rights to food.

Urbanization and Cropland

Perhaps there is a socially and economically less disruptive way to tackle the twin problems of agriculture's outsized land footprint and its contribution to climate change. Where, then, might we look for more space suitable for agriculture and, in the process of making the change, reduce its greenhouse gas footprint, still grow lots of feed and raise livestock, and not encroach forests?

One option for offsetting the added climate impacts due to the chemical intensification of farming—and simultaneously reduce forest conversion—would be to bring food production closer to densely populated areas. This change would reduce "food miles" and curb the heavy carbon footprint of elongated supply chains and food transportation.[53] Also, it would re-deploy land already dedicated to some human purposes rather than expand into forests and other environmentally sensitive zones. The relocalization of food production is attractive also as a way of expanding consumer options for food that might be both healthier and potentially beneficial from a food security perspective given the logistical difficulties illustrated by supply chain failures arising during the peak of the COVID-19 pandemic. In fact, supply chain problems could become even worse as the world's urban population grows and more people become more distant from the sites of food production.

The relocalization of food production is a great idea for so many reasons. However, bringing food closer to cities is not that easily achieved in many places. Because the land footprint of cities is expected to triple in the same period as their population doubles, there will be even more pressure on agricultural uses from competing uses of peri-urban land.[54] Also, urban expansion takes place on the same highly fertile cropland typically found in the river valleys and deltas where humans tend to settle. The net effect of this competition between agricultural land use and other human uses for the same land is an increase in the costs of peri-urban land, and, ultimately, that means increases in the costs of food if it is grown on

164 A LIVABLE PLANET

more expensive land. In affluent countries, competing high-value uses for such land make it unlikely that agricultural production on repurposed lands can be ramped up at a scale sufficient to change the climate impact calculus.

The prospects for re-deploying existing peri-urban land, thereby reducing the carbon footprint of food transportation, are even worse in many less economically developed countries. Although the overall expected effect of urbanization on the available area of cropland is relatively modest, accounting for only 2% of future global cropland loss, the negative effects of urbanization on agricultural yields is far greater in "hotspots" in Africa and Asia, where the expected global loss in yields due to growth in urbanization is concentrated.[55] For example, urbanization in Nigeria could result in a 17% reduction of rice production and 12% of maize production, a more than 40% reduction of rice and more than 60% of maize in Egypt, and a 26% continent-wide loss of wheat in Africa, and a 9% global decline of rice, predominantly in Asia.[56]

To make matters worse, sea level rise from climate change will further diminish the availability of prime farmland located in river delta settlements, adding more to the costs of food produced near urban centers. These are costs that very few residents of these rapidly urbanizing cities can afford. As we saw in Chapter 5, commodity price spikes and other events show that even small changes in food costs exacerbate the risk of hunger and food insecurity for the roughly 2 billion people who make less than $2 per day and spend over half of their household budgets on food.

In short, the competing uses for peri-urban land is especially keen in the low- and middle-income countries. These are the places most adversely affected by food insecurity, where most of the population growth is occurring in the outlying informal settlements, and where sea level rise will shrink existing land area even further. While the relocalization of food production may be a boon for both specialty growers and affluent shoppers at farmers' markets in New York or San Francisco, matters look very different when viewed from a planetary

LAND USE AND ITS CONSEQUENCES   165

perspective. Overall, it is highly unlikely that there will be enough fertile peri-urban land available at affordable prices to significantly reduce either the global land degradation caused by agriculture or the contribution of food production to climate change. While there are many good local ecological and public health reasons to change the way residents of affluent urban areas eat, significant reduction in food's impact on climate is not among them.

Biogeochemical Flows

This brings us to a third reason for caution about continuing with business as usual in our approach to fertilizer use, given the amount needed for producing livestock feed. In addition to the risks of breaching planetary boundaries that define a "safe operating space" for the climate system, continued reliance on nitrogen fertilizers and nitrogen-intensive livestock practices poses a threat to the stability of another vital Earth system. The planetary boundary for biogeochemical flows, specifically phosphorus (P) and nitrogen (N) cycling, also is at risk.

The issue is both complex and perhaps somewhat unfamiliar to many readers, but a highly simplified version of the scientific issue is sufficient to make a rather straightforward point. Earth scientists aim to quantity the safe boundaries for human contribution to both nitrogen and phosphorus in global circulation, not just how much is safe for a particular region (e.g., the Lake Erie basin). To that end they identified global-level boundaries for phosphorus, based on calculations of what is necessary to prevent a large-scale ocean anoxic event (e.g., dead zone), as well as a regional-level P boundary, designed to avert widespread eutrophication of freshwater systems caused by fertilizers applied in the world's croplands. They performed a calculation for safe levels of nitrogen produced from industrial-scale agricultural nitrogen fixation using stringent water quality criteria as their guide.

166   A LIVABLE PLANET

The scientific details and some of the debates about methods of quantification are beyond what we need here (or my expertise to assess). The relevant point is two-fold: first, the anthropogenic perturbation of the nitrogen and phosphorus cycles arises from the excessive global level of fertilizer application, and second, levels of flow for both nitrogen and phosphorus as early as 2015 were already in the range Earth scientists classify as the high-risk zone.[57] Concretely, that means nitrogen and phosphorus flows transgress currently established safe boundaries for maintaining planetary stability. More recent attempts to forecast the nitrogen and phosphorus contributions for 2050 project that the continuation of current practices would lead the world to further exceed the lower planetary boundary for nitrogen by 125% and exceed the lower boundary for phosphorus application by 75%.[58]

Perhaps we might reduce our inefficient use of fertilizers that end up as runoff. That would help, assuming the market impediments described earlier are overcome, but recent research also suggests that the imbalance of nitrogen caused by livestock production alone exceeds the lower limit of the planetary safe zone.[59] In fact, the overwhelming bulk of that nitrogen imbalance—68%—is from crops grown to feed animals. The researchers' conclusion is that technical fixes alone are unlikely to keep agriculture within the planetary boundaries for nitrogen pollution. Their findings offer one more reason why the world—especially the world's most affluent consumers—will need to produce and consume less meat and dairy products.

The upshot of this section is that humanity faces some important and highly complex choices about the future of food production. Factors relevant to decision-making cannot be examined in isolation, for example, simply by comparing alternative ways of reducing the land footprint of the type of agriculture we already have. There is only one pathway that reduces the impact of water pollution within local ecosystems, knocks out the two biggest sources of agricultural greenhouse gas emissions, reduces the outsized land

LAND USE AND ITS CONSEQUENCES 167

footprint of feed, and halts and reverses the disruption of planetary biogeochemical flows. The only ecologically sustainable pathway involves a major shift from the "fertilizer for feed" model that underpins industrial-scale livestock production. Of course, such a transformation will not satisfy the appetites of carnivores and capitalists whose established pathways to pleasure and profit would be disrupted.

Forests and Biosphere Integrity

Deforestation

If the land footprint of agriculture expands, it will mean the further conversion of forests rather than significant incursion into expensive peri-urban locations. Deforestation—defined as the long-term or permanent loss of forest cover—is widely recognized as an important ecological problem that goes far beyond ordinary tree loss. For example, much public attention is focused on the need to preserve tropical forests because of their role as carbon sinks. They are vital for counteracting the emissions that drive climate change. They absorb greenhouse gases that would otherwise end up in the atmosphere, and, in addition, forest clearing generates new emissions.

There is a global consensus on the urgency of halting deforestation, and among the major reasons for that agreement are the climate consequences of land degradation and loss of carbon sequestration capacity. Forest preservation is a key component of the aim of achieving global land degradation neutrality established in SDG 15.3 (Life on Land). More specifically, the widely endorsed aim of the New York Declaration on Forests (NYDF), launched at the 2014 UN climate summit, is to cut deforestation in half by 2020 and halt it by 2030. More than 200 governments, companies, civil society organizations, and indigenous communities signed on

168   A LIVABLE PLANET

to the initiative. However, the trend is going in the wrong direction. A United Nations Environment Programme (UNEP) assessment, published in 2021, concluded that the world is not on course to achieve its general goal of land degradation neutrality.[60] Specific targets for forest preservation also appear further out of reach. A recent NYDF progress report shows that very few signatory countries have taken significant steps toward fulfilling their pledges, most countries have not incorporated forest plans into their climate change goals at all, and several countries most at risk rolled back enforcement efforts, thus accelerating forest clearing for agriculture and extractive industries.[61]

Agriculture figures centrally in global deforestation trends. More than half of the increase in agricultural activity since 1980 has been at the expense of intact forests, especially resulting from the increased consumption of meat, now accounting for 70% of agricultural production in many newly deforested tropical areas.[62] By some estimates, tropical forest loss accounts for more than 90% of global deforestation, with the hotspots being located in Amazon Basin nations of Bolivia, Brazil, Colombia, and Peru, where agriculture is responsible for as much as 70–80% of the loss.[63] Empirical evidence for specific countries is especially discouraging. For example, the Institute for Satellite Deforestation Monitoring Project in Brazil shows a 30% increase in 2019, resulting in the largest increase since 2008.[64] Equally disturbing is satellite-based evidence showing that forest degradation in the Amazon may be as much as 44–60% more than previously realized.[65]

The ecological significance of deforestation extends beyond localized ecosystem damage and its contribution to climate change. One of the nine critical planetary boundaries developed as markers of a safe operating space for Earth systems is pegged to land use changes, specifically, the conversion of forests to other uses. The safe zone preserves at least 75% of original global forest cover, but the current estimate is that only 62% is preserved, putting the planetary threat of deforestation squarely into the

LAND USE AND ITS CONSEQUENCES   169

high-risk "red zone."[66] Although breach of a planetary boundary is not equivalent to passing a threshold or tipping point where irreversible harm occurs, the transgression of any of the nine boundaries carries substantial risks for the continued functioning of the Earth systems.[67]

Other scientists have suggested alternative metrics, some more closely tied to specific regions, ecosystem types, or specific land uses.[68] However, the overarching point for non-specialists is that there is widespread scientific agreement that operating within safe limits on anthropogenic deforestation is central to preserving the functioning of the Earth systems and that we are operating with a slim margin of safety. More specifically, it means "reserving space most suited to agriculture, maintaining high conservation-value forests, and keeping carbon-rich soils and ecosystems in either a totally undisturbed or at least carefully managed condition."[69] By any metric, we are far from a sustainable use of forests.

Biodiversity and Biosphere Integrity

Deforestation is closely linked to habitat destruction and biodiversity loss. Forests are home to roughly 80% of the world's terrestrial biodiversity. The most biologically diverse forest ecosystems are the tropical rainforests found in equatorial regions of Central and South America, western and central Africa, western India, and southeast Asia. These are the same ecosystems most heavily subjected to deforestation. The biggest driver of biodiversity loss and the loss of species habitats has been the human transformation of forest land, primarily for the sake of producing food for a global population that has doubled in less than 50 years. The proliferation of industrial-scale production of fewer crops and species and the destruction of natural forests to make way for plantation agriculture and the production of other export commodities (e.g., palm oil, minerals) are the main examples.

170   A LIVABLE PLANET

The most attention to biodiversity loss in the popular press is given to the risk of extinction of the iconic species—lions, tigers, and rhinoceros—whose images adorn the brochures and web pages of conservationist organizations. The statistics are both familiar and staggering, but a growing body of expert panels, including the Intergovernmental Platform on Biodiversity and Ecosystem Services (IPBES), express their greatest concerns about levels or types of biodiversity loss that might trigger irreversible changes to the Earth system. The recent renaming of the relevant boundary pertaining to biodiversity—now known as biosphere integrity—signals the urgency of concerns beyond preservation of the variety of species, their numbers, and/or genetic diversity within species. Biosphere integrity emphasizes the importance of guarding against the basic causes of biodiversity loss in all its forms. For example, habitat destruction and fragmentation are the primary threats to 85% of the threatened and endangered species catalogued in the "Red List" compiled by the International Union for Conservation of Nature (IUCN).[70]

Progress, however, has been elusive. For example, a recent study shows progress for only 7% of the biodiversity conservation and other environmental goals, targets, and indicators embedded in the SDG framework, in contrast to progress for 41% of the socioeconomic development indicators.[71] Similarly dire findings are contained in the 2021 review of research informing the findings of the IPBES, IPCC, and other environmental assessment panels. The report, *Making Peace with Nature*, observes that nearly a third of the SDGs directly related to biodiversity are not being met, and, in some cases, they are even becoming further out of reach. They noted that none of the targets agreed upon in 2010 (the "Aichi Biodiversity Targets") was fully met by the target deadline of 2020, and only partial progress has been made in just four of the 20 targets.[72]

Robert Watson, the chair of the IPBES panel, has made it a part of the panel's public mission to explain that the loss of biodiversity

LAND USE AND ITS CONSEQUENCES   171

(and biosphere integrity) is just as catastrophic for humanity as climate change.[73] The report emphasizes the scientific consensus that biosphere integrity and climate change are "core boundaries," meaning that preserving a safe operating space for both should have the highest priority. Transgressions of the boundaries for these two systems are particularly worrisome because large changes in either, on their own, are sufficient to cause serious adverse effect on human well-being, and they have the potential to alter and predispose other systems to boundary transgression because of their high levels of system integration.

A second set of reasons to be concerned about biosphere integrity—apart from the very great long-term importance of biosphere integrity for the stability of Earth systems—points to more immediate impacts on human well-being. Forests offer an irreplaceable source of livelihood for many people. Forests contain the organisms that are the building blocks of potential medicines. They provide the means of containment of the organisms that have the potential for the spread of zoonotic disease. Without buffers between forests and human settlements, human health is put at increased risk.

Moreover, maintaining genetic diversity in wild plant species offers a kind of insurance policy against the potential consequences of our growing reliance on fewer and fewer species to feed ourselves. Between 1900 and 2000, there has been a 75% loss of world's crop diversity.[74] Of some 6,000 or more plant species cultivated for food, less than 200 contribute substantially to global food output, and only nine account for 66% of total crop production.[75] One widely cited estimate is that 75% of the world's food supply comes from only 12 plants and 5 animals.[76] Even more striking is the fact that over 40% of the world's food supply, as a percentage of calories, comes from just three crops—wheat, maize, and rice.[77] The FAO estimates that the world's livestock production is based on about 40 animal species, with only a handful providing the vast majority of meat, milk, and eggs, and, of the remaining 7,745 local

172   A LIVABLE PLANET

(i.e., occurring in one country) breeds of livestock, 26% are at risk of extinction.[78]

The loss of genetic crop diversity makes preservation of genetic diversity of all species of plants even more urgent. The reason is that, over the longer term, the loss of variety in wild plant species could make it harder to breed new crops better adapted to survive the added heat and drought produced by climate change. Human well-being is thus highly dependent on biological diversity, and, given the concentration of diversity in forests, we have yet another crucial reason to prioritize forest protection.

Crop biodiversity also depends on biodiversity in another way. The preservation of all the plants, animals (wild and domesticated), and an unknown number of microorganisms (such as soil-dwelling fungi and bacteria) is vital because they keep soils fertile, pollinate plants, purify water and air, keep fish and trees healthy, and fight crop and livestock pests and diseases.[79] For example, pollinator species are critical to more than 75% of global food crop types, including fruits and vegetables and some of the most important cash crops, such as coffee, cocoa, and almonds.[80] As E. O. Wilson famously put it, "If we were to wipe out insects alone, just that group alone, on this planet—which we are trying hard to do—the rest of life and humanity with it would mostly disappear from the land. And within a few months."[81] Forest preservation is critical in the preservation of the hard-working pollinators and, in turn, crucial to the food that sustains human well-being. Without the lowliest creatures, the entire food chain and whole ecosystems would collapse.

High-Risk Commodity Production

What explains how we have reached this point, and what are the implications for the pathway forward? There is a consensus on five empirically supported conclusions.

LAND USE AND ITS CONSEQUENCES 173

First, one reason that the diversity of the global food supply has contracted so dramatically in such a short period of time is the nature of global market organization. As explained in Chapter 5, the profitability of the agricultural and other production systems depends on a concentrated market led by small number of purchasers who, in turn, do business with a small number of large-scale producers. The overwhelming business incentive for growers, as we saw, is to produce a limited number of commodities to meet the purchasers' demands, and a dominant incentive for purchasers is to search for these same globally marketable commodity crops in as many locations as financial and environmental conditions permit. Concretely, that means more pressure to find land that is cheap (by the standards of transnational corporations) and to utilize that land to produce export commodity crops or livestock feed, even if it requires substantial chemical inputs and forest clearing to produce them. Neither of these options is sustainable.

Second, many of the ecologically most significant consequences of forest conversion and habitat destruction are due to the expansion of pasture for beef or large-scale monocropping plantations—especially palm oil, soya, and other livestock feed—all heavily concentrated in the Indonesian, South Asian, South American, and African tropical forests.[82] These products have earned the label of "high-risk commodities" because of the pace and scale of deforestation and other adverse ecological effects such as habitat and watershed destruction. For example, in less than 10 years, just since 2010, the area planted with soy in Brazil has increased by 45%, and Indonesian palm oil production went up 75%.[83]

Third, high-risk commodity production is almost entirely for export purposes. Consumption is largely by residents of wealthier nations while the burdens of ecological devastation are heavily concentrated within tropical producer nations.[84] Recent calculations of the "deforestation footprints" of consumption of forest-based goods (e.g., coffee, chocolate, cattle, soy, palm oil, and timber) illustrate the unequal global ecological impact of trade.[85] The

174 A LIVABLE PLANET

deforestation footprints of some of the world's largest economies provide good examples of how much of that footprint is due to global outsourcing.

A country's deforestation footprint is made up of two components: the domestic deforestation footprint of consumption and the "imported" deforestation footprint from consumption of foreign-made products. For 2015, for example, in Japan, Germany, France, the United Kingdom, and Italy imported products accounting for 91–99% of their total contribution to deforestation, of which 46–57% was from tropical forests.[86] The expansion of global supply chains has enabled these countries and others—including countries that have slowed or reversed deforestation at home—to decouple consumption of forest-based products from domestic environmental damage. Residents of the importing countries not only outsourced the localized environmental damage of consumption to poorer equatorial countries that grow the crops and strip their forests. The "imported deforestation" footprint from tropical forests also damages some of the planet's most important sites for carbon storage and the richest biodiverse ecosystems that house the overwhelming majority of terrestrial species.

Fourth, in the words of the UNEP, "Given the interconnected nature of climate change, loss of biodiversity, land degradation, and air and water pollution, it is essential that these problems are tackled together."[87] The interconnected nature of the elements that comprise our ecological predicament is a major theme of this book, and no lens better reveals how ecological problems—and their solutions—are intertwined than the human transformation of the land.

Fifth, the UNEP's assessment report sums up a second major theme of this book. "Decades of incremental efforts have not stemmed the environmental decline resulting from an expansive development model because vested and short-term interests often prevail. Only a system-wide transformation will achieve well-being for all within the Earth's capacity to support life, provide resources

LAND USE AND ITS CONSEQUENCES 175

and absorb waste."[88] The authors elaborated by noting that "transformation involves a fundamental, system-wide shift in world views and values and in the technological, economic and social organization of society."[89]

Nature-Based Solutions

Some proponents of "nature-based" climate solutions suggest that many of the interrelated ecological and economic problems could be tackled together using strategies already widely known. Ecosystem conservation efforts, such as protection of forests and other natural carbon storage biomes, is one of three types of nature-based solutions most often discussed. The other two solutions are restoration or rehabilitation of degraded biomes and better management of cropland, for example, by increasing soil carbon content through use of cover crops.[90]

One of the advantages that puts prevention of deforestation at the top of the list of priorities is the multiple benefits it offers. Climate change, biodiversity loss, and the destruction of the basis for subsistence rights of forest dwellers can be addressed at the same time. Many threats to climate, biodiversity, and subsistence rights also result from the same root causes, such as converting forests for industrial-scale export agriculture or the extraction of minerals or forest products.

However, some proposed solutions fall far short of the transformative change required, and, in some instances, they make existing problems worse. For example, several studies have shown that large-scale tree planting projects do little to improve tree cover, biodiversity, or peoples' livelihoods.[91] And yet one of the most widely discussed proposals is a massive global campaign of tree planting—afforestation—as a way of increasing carbon sinks, with most of the discussion focusing on the Global North rather than where it really counts, in the Global South, where vast stores of carbon and biodiversity are concentrated.

176   A LIVABLE PLANET

The basic argument behind the push for afforestation everywhere is that more trees would absorb more of the emissions from fossil fuels during a period of transition to a fully decarbonized economy.[92] Such proposals are politically popular, and they require no change in consumption patterns. However, such proposals rest on the false assumption that enough land—including marginal and otherwise unproductive land—is available for this purpose and that widespread planting of trees will have the desired impact. There are ample reasons for skepticism on both counts.

A major problem is the lack of suitable land. For example, a Shell Oil Company scenario—known as Sky1.5—calls for planting trees to slow the pace of climate change. The company anticipates that it could reduce net emissions by 30%, but, by their own estimation, it would require a land area the size of Brazil.[93] In addition, the best available evidence demonstrates that existing intact forests generally absorb more carbon than newly planted trees, leading many researchers to conclude that a strategy more heavily weighted toward a combination of emissions reductions and forest preservation would be a far superior plan.

An emerging body of evidence also shows that not all trees provide equal carbon sequestration benefits. There are considerable differences in the carbon absorption capacities of different species of trees, and many trees in mature forests are shown to have superior capacities.[94] Some afforestation policies fail to recognize these differences. In Chile, for example, the government subsidized tree plantations. With 25 years of afforestation payments to the private sector, plantation growers expanded the areas covered by new trees. But because growers replaced native forests with the profitable, subsidized trees, they decreased the area of carbon-dense and biodiverse native forests.[95] The subsidies had the perverse effect of decreasing rather than increasing carbon storage, while accelerating biodiversity losses and displacement of human residents.

A related limitation of afforestation as a strategy for absorbing excess emissions is the fact that some trees lose their ability to absorb carbon as global temperatures rise.[96] Moreover, there is evidence that even some existing tropical forests counted as emissions offsetting carbon sinks can become net carbon emitters under conditions of higher-than-average temperatures.[97] Also, newly planted species of trees are intended to function as carbon sinks, but there is uncertainty about the durability of the carbon absorption benefits. For example, when proponents claim climate benefits for these projects, they often overlook the fact that forests are subject to wildfires and diseases and are at risk from future expansion of logging activities.[98]

The upshot is that there are many good reasons to plant more trees, adopt better farming practices, and so on. Trees can improve soil quality, prevent erosion, remediate damaged watersheds, and provide relief from the urban heat island effects of climate change. However, if these strategies are viewed as scalable alternatives to ambitious decarbonization efforts, they are likely to provide false assurance that enough is being done, fast enough to slow the damage from climate disruption. Forest preservation, and in the most ecologically sensitive areas—not more trees overall—is what crucially matters most, not only for efficient carbon sequestration, but for biodiversity goals and the human rights of those who depend upon forests for subsistence.[99]

Another problematic aspect of the current enthusiasm for nature-based solutions is the elasticity of the definition and the risk that the label will be stretched to give green cover to seriously flawed decarbonization strategies. Biofuel proposals are particularly problematic. They divert scarce crop land from production of food to the production of fuel.[100] Even more problematic is the suggestion that biofuels can offer a large-scale alternative to fossil fuels. Most IPCC scenarios project the need to increase the current 15–30 million hectares of land used for growing biofuel crops by 10–30 times to slow the pace of warming by 2050, but the higher end estimate means conversion of a total of more than 724 million hectares, an area almost the size of Australia.[101]

178   A LIVABLE PLANET

Moreover, a further risk is that biofuel plantations will have the same effects as the Chilean tree planation schemes. They can crowd out existing carbon-absorbing forests and generate massive quantities of new emissions. For example, a report commissioned by Rainforest Foundation Norway concluded that current ambitions for using biofuels are likely to lead to a massive increase in demand for palm oil and soy by 2030, causing an estimated 7 million hectares of deforestation.[102] To put that figure into perspective, it would result in additional emissions greater than China's current annual emissions from burning fossil fuels. However short-sighted such undertakings are from an ecological perspective, they make sound financial sense to wealthy foreign investors. Land in the Global South is relatively cheap, and the inclusion of alternatives to fossil fuels in their energy investment portfolios burnishes their green credentials.

In short, the planet has no spare land mass the size of Brazil or Australia, and the world's investors have both the economic means and financial incentives to treat land as assets that can be converted to any profitable use, no matter the ecological or economic costs imposed on others. And it is the forest ecosystem we have most reason to care about, not the global tree census. Forest preservation, especially in the tropics, is vital to sustaining the ecological basis of overall human well-being. Ending deforestation attributable to the production of high-risk commodities that benefit primarily the global affluent is a priority, thereby stopping the destruction of both the livelihoods and healthful environment of the inhabitants. It is a matter of basic justice as well as an ecological imperative.

Proposals to set aside 30% or even half of nature free from human imprint have a better chance of protecting against deforestation and preserving biodiversity.[103] However, that strategy also carries risk of injustice. The exact percentage to set aside and choice of location is a matter that requires recognition of the potential for displacing populations, thus replicating the errors of an earlier generation of conservationists who adopted the "fortress" approach to

LAND USE AND ITS CONSEQUENCES 179

ecological protection and imposed it upon indigenous peoples of the Global South.[104]

Land and Human Rights

The implications of massive land conversion for agriculture and high-risk commodities, especially in the extractive hotspots of the Global South, are sobering. As Johan Rockström and colleagues observe, "Humanity may be reaching a point where further agricultural land expansion at a global scale may seriously threaten biodiversity and undermine regulatory capacities of the Earth System (by affecting the climate system and the hydrological cycle)."[105] Moreover, the risks created by some of the worst global agricultural and commodity extraction practices are universal, but they are not undertaken for the sake of universal benefit. The conversion of intact forests and ecosystems for agricultural purposes and other types of export-driven commodity production—as well as some of the proposed market-based solutions—illustrate how global market practices benefit some corporations and consumers to the detriment of other communities. They enable some countries to extend and preserve their available natural resource base by capturing the economic value of foreign land resources, offload the ecological burdens of extractive practices, and increase their own citizens' opportunities for profits from non-productive or predatory investments in land and land-based commodities. No real progress is possible so long as these practices go unchecked.

Coalitions of indigenous communities have proposed rights-based strategies for countering these practices. The Kari-Oca 2 Declaration and the Geneva Declaration are important examples. The Kari-Oca 2 Declaration was issued by a coalition of more than 500 indigenous peoples meeting in parallel with the United Nations Conference on Sustainable Development Rio+20 in 2012. Its underlying message was straightforward. "Our rights

180   A LIVABLE PLANET

to self-determination, to our own governance and own self-determined development, our inherent rights to our lands, territories and resources are increasingly and alarmingly under attack by the collaboration of governments and transnational corporations."[106] The primary focus, therefore, was not advocacy for better compliance with voluntary guidelines for responsible foreign investment, a demand for more humanitarian assistance from developed nations, or even calls for reparations for colonialism and ecological damage. Their emphasis was on the strategic importance of rights that confer control over land and its resources, thereby protecting themselves against predatory economic activity.

Moreover, the coalition makes their case for local control based on its implications for ecological stewardship. For example, signatories subsequently noted that, in 2021, indigenous peoples were responsible for protecting an estimated 22% of the planet's surface and 80% of biodiversity.[107] The assumption is that those whose lives and livelihoods directly depend upon preservation of local environmental conditions have more at stake in what happens than do transient investors. Recent research supports their position. A review of more than 300 studies concluded that the area of intact forest under indigenous community control in the Amazon Basin declined by only 5% between 2000 and 2016, compared to non-indigenous areas, where it fell by 11%.[108]

In 2022, similar concerns about the importance of rights that confer control over environmental conditions were articulated in the Geneva Declaration issued by La Via Campesina on behalf of 200 million peasants, indigenous peoples, migrant workers, and pastoralists from organizations based in 81 countries. The Declaration's core proposals for action are prefaced by diagnostic premises, including claims that "the global crises that confront our world today—namely, the corporate control and concentration in the international food systems; global warming aggravated by industrial farming techniques; large-scale deforestation; the dispossession of rural communities through forceful and violent

LAND USE AND ITS CONSEQUENCES 181

eviction from territories; . . . soil destruction due to extensive use of agrochemicals, etc.—are a result of an unchecked and unregulated expansion of global financial capital."[109]

One of the main globally significant proposals in the Declaration is a demand for "the overhaul of the current international trade system and steps toward the creation of a Global Multilateral Framework based on Peoples' Food Sovereignty principles and . . . human rights instruments, such as the UN Declaration on the Rights of Indigenous Peoples (UNDRIP)." Moreover, the Declaration emphasized the centrality of its human rights approach. "An essential pre-condition for these changes to take root would be the urgent implementation of the Articles of the UN Declaration on the Rights of Peasants and Other People Working in Rural Areas (UNDROP)." One of the first steps toward the overhaul is that the UN Human Rights Council should "create a special procedure on the UNDROP, which would allow for effective implementation, especially UNDROP mainstreaming and monitoring at the international level."

Equally important, however, are the proposals for state-level implementation, also based on a rights agenda. For example, they endorse concrete "national and multilateral policies that promote the right to land, build public food stocks procured from peasants and small-scale food producers, implement and enforce strong anti-dumping legislation, and forbid the use of agriculture to produce bio-fuel."

Both declarations reflect considerable practical agreement among activists in many of the communities most heavily affected by the current ways of organizing land resources in the global political economy. Their diagnosis and proposed remedies correspond closely to many of the central points developed in this book, for example, an understanding of the fundamental causes of our ecological predicament and the centrality of a human rights approach as a guide to first steps toward a more just and sustainable organization of the global political economy.

7

Water and Social Organization

Freshwater is a resource that is essential for life. Moreover, it is a resource for which there are no substitutes. Access to clean drinking water and sanitation is now widely regarded as a human right, and water is indispensable for the secure realization of other human rights, such as rights to health, food, and subsistence. Although water is a replenishable resource, it is subject to scarcity. It is vulnerable to threats due to (intermittent or persistent) physical scarcity, which requires management through complex systems of social organization and cooperation. It is vulnerable also to threats created or exacerbated by the structure of social organization.

The first section surveys some leading estimates of current and projected freshwater scarcity and its various causes and consequences. It then explains why responsibilities for fulfilling the human rights to water within highly interdependent, densely concentrated human settlements are wide-ranging and difficult to carry out in the absence of centralized institutional coordination.

The second section examines the global political economy of water resource acquisition and use. It first looks at the adverse global effects of national policies designed to decouple economic growth from domestic water consumption. It then surveys differing explanations for the prevalence of unsustainable, water-intensive agricultural production and export policies, along with incentives for and consequences of the global acquisition of water and water-adjacent land to be used for production of water-intensive crops and consumer items.

The third section examines the push for privatization of water delivery and sanitation services, the political objectives and market

A Livable Planet. Madison Powers, Oxford University Press. © Oxford University Press 2024.
DOI: 10.1093/oso/9780197756003.003.0007

WATER AND SOCIAL ORGANIZATION 183

dynamics behind it, and the problems that have ensued. It critiques the normative foundations of market allocation policies, and it assesses the political and ecological implications of placing highly consequential water resource decisions in the hands of private institutions.

The Management of Scarcity

In research and policy contexts, water scarcity definitions and related terms (e.g., water stress, high water stress) typically refer to the shortage of renewable freshwater relative to demand.[1] For example, the UN-Water approach designates a geographic territory as "water-stressed" when 25% or more of its renewable freshwater resources are withdrawn annually. Sustainable Development Goal (SDG) 6 incorporates this approach, establishing a 25% annual rate of depletion as its benchmark of unsustainable water use.[2] Although water use has remained relatively stable at the global level, with an average of 17.3% of available water resources being withdrawn annually, the average global rate hides large regional variations. In total, 2.3 billion people live in regions where the annual rate of depletion exceeds 25%. This figure includes high water-stress regions that withdraw 40–80% of their available annual supply and extremely high water-stress regions that either withdraw more than 80% of their renewable water resources annually or rely on non-renewable resources that eventually will run dry.

Assessments and projections differ in methodology and their definitions of scarcity, but they concur that unsustainable levels of water stress are experienced by at least one-quarter of the world's population, and they agree that the problem is almost certain to worsen.[3] For example, a recent study estimates that 500,000 people in the world currently face "severe water scarcity" all year round, but two-thirds of the global population (more than 4 billion people) live under conditions of severe water scarcity at least 1 month of

184 A LIVABLE PLANET

the year, with nearly half of the affected people living in India and China.[4] The number of people living in such conditions is likely to increase to 4.8–5.7 billion in 2050, with almost 70% of the affected people expected to live in Asia.[5]

Although many of the most water-stressed regions are arid and desert areas, demand is an essential component of the scarcity equation. The 2030 Water Resources Group forecasts that under business-as-usual conditions, total global water demand will rise 50% by 2030, with agriculture driving nearly half of the increase.[6] As a consequence, the shortfall in global water supply could be as much as 40% by 2030 if no changes are made in how demand is managed.

Moreover, the growth in overall demand for water will not be uniform throughout the world. Water consumption per person tends to increase with affluence, and many of the high-demand users are concentrated in urban areas where physical availability of water cannot sustain these higher demand levels.[7] Developing nations can expect demand to increase at a much sharper pace because their rates of urbanization and economic growth are higher. For example, by 2030, annual demand for water could increase 283% in sub-Saharan Africa, compared to 42% in North America.[8]

The impact of urbanization and income growth illustrates how importantly demand figures in the water scarcity equation, as well as the reason to expect many of the large population centers of the developing world to be disproportionately affected. However, concerns about physical scarcity—the decrease in volumetric abundance of the water supply within a geographic area—have gained prominence in global policy discussions since the 1977 United Nations conference in Mar del Plata, Argentina. Hydrologists observed that historical patterns of physical availability are changing, sometimes rapidly, with physically available freshwater in global decline almost everywhere, not only in the world's arid regions.[9]

WATER AND SOCIAL ORGANIZATION   185

The causes of increased physical scarcity are multiple and inter-active, and climate change, of course, contributes to or magnifies the effects of existing causes, such as land use decisions affecting absorption and runoff, water-intensive consumption and production patterns, and the rapid drawdown of water in densely populated areas.[10] The net result is that both surface water and groundwater sources are diminishing, and they are mutually reinforcing phenomena.

Surface Water

More than 40% of the world's great cities supplied primarily by surface water are expected to be highly vulnerable to severe shortages and drought by 2040.[11] In many parts of the world, the primary sources of surface water are glacier-fed rivers, which contain nearly 70% of the world's accessible freshwater. However, satellite data show that glaciers worldwide are in steep decline and that the rate of loss is accelerating sharply in nearly all regions of the world.[12]

Decline in glacier ice has an outsized impact on many developing countries. For example, glacier loss has doubled in 40 years in the Tibetan Plateau and surrounding regions which contain the largest reserve of freshwater outside the polar regions.[13] One widely cited study projects that glaciers in the densely populated and intensively irrigated basin areas in Pakistan, India, and China could lose between 70% and 99% of their volume by 2100, primarily because of climate change, if temperatures continue to rise at current levels.[14] The region likely will reach peak water availability sometime between 2030 and 2050.[15] The consequences of subsequent decline would be devastating. Runoff from snow cover, permafrost, and glaciers in the Himalayan and neighboring mountain ranges provides up to 45% of the total river flow that nearly 2 billion people depend upon for drinking, irrigation, and hydroelectric power.[16]

186   A LIVABLE PLANET

Changes in glacier ice mass and snowpack that feed rivers are complex and interactive. Because temperatures rise faster at high altitudes, glaciers begin to lose mass, leaving less initially available freshwater upstream. Warmer temperatures also cause snowpack to shrink and melt earlier.[17] When snowmelt timing is disrupted by early warming, downstream water availability is reduced when it is most needed over the summer and dry periods. Loss of initial glacier mass also means less heat from the sun that is reflected, creating a feedback loop (known as the *albedo effect*), setting in motion conditions for further increases in higher altitude temperatures and leading to an increase in the rate and magnitude of glacier ice mass loss.

Research also shows that, with higher temperatures, soil dries faster and plants require more water. Drier soil means that farmers require more water to grow their crops, again leaving less water for other immediate uses and less water left over to replenish lakes and rivers where it can be stored for later.[18] The result is a self-perpetuating cycle of depletion of available surface water driven initially by global warming, but magnified in its impact by efforts to adapt.

Groundwater

As surface water supplies diminish, either from unsustainable withdrawals, climate change, or some combination, water-stressed communities turn to groundwater reserves to meet the needs of growing urban centers and water-intensive agricultural production. Deep underground aquifers contain about 30% of Earth's freshwater. However, it is being extracted at dangerously unsustainable rates.[19] More than half of the world's population is experiencing groundwater depletion below recharge rates. Satellite studies show that 13 of the world's 37 largest aquifers are being drained faster than they are being replenished, and the main impact is in the poor, densely populated regions of northwestern India, Pakistan, and northern Africa.[20] These aquifers are heavily concentrated in food-producing regions that support up to 2 billion people. The problem is expected to worsen. Aquifer withdrawals are predicted to increase by 50% by 2025 in developing countries and 18% in developed countries.[21] This trend is significant because aquifers already account for 35% of human water use worldwide and considerably more in arid territories and elsewhere experiencing prolonged periods of drought.[22]

Water withdrawal for agricultural irrigation is the primary driver of groundwater depletion. Millions of farmers depend on groundwater irrigation to help produce 40% of the world's agricultural output, including a large proportion of staple crops like rice and wheat.[23] Because intermittent rainfall limits the scale of agricultural production, irrigation is preferred to rainfed production.[24] But many large-scale state-funded irrigation schemes rely on tapping directly into groundwater for large quantities of water, and it is often wasted in the process of application to crops, putting unsustainable pressure on non-renewable resources from underground aquifers.[25]

India is a pertinent example of the dynamics of groundwater depletion. It now has more irrigated land than any other country in the world. The World Bank estimates that groundwater extraction provides 85% of India's drinking water and more than 60% of its irrigation water.[26] The best estimates from India indicate that its water demand will be twice the available supply by 2030.[27] The situation in India's Ganges Basin is compounded by farmers drilling deeper, hoping to tap new aquifers to make up for the lack of surface water and the exhaustion of older shallow wells that have run dry.[28] As the water table goes down, aquifers become less able to store water in the future. Those who can afford it drill even deeper wells, while surrounding communities, neighboring farms, and growers who are unable to bear the high costs of drilling are deprived of water they once depended upon.

188   A LIVABLE PLANET

The intensified pace of groundwater extraction also produces a cascade of environmental knock-on effects. As aquifers are depleted, the ground sinks. The technical name is *subsidence*. It occurs when aquifers are drained and the land collapses down to where the water used to be. Subsidence due to groundwater extraction for irrigation is a problem in Indian agricultural regions and elsewhere, including in California's agricultural heartland, the Central Valley, where water tables have dropped 50 feet or more in just a few years.[29]

Subsidence is a big environmental problem, not only because it causes the collapse of roads, bridges, and other infrastructure. Water quality also deteriorates as farmers turn to deep well extraction. Water from deeper wells in India contains greater levels of arsenic and fluoride.[30] A study of 11,000 California public wells shows that 20% of the groundwater extracted for household use contains high concentrations of arsenic, uranium, and nitrate.[31]

Subsidence caused by the over-pumping of aquifers also exacerbates ecological conditions in coastal zones. These areas are already prone to flooding due to sea level rise caused by the combination of glacier melting and thermal expansion of water volume as temperatures rise. Approximately 58% of the world's coastal citizens live on soil and bedrock that is already collapsing beneath their feet, in significant part due to over-pumping of groundwater together with coastline development that destroys tidal marshes, coastal wetlands, and barrier islands that serve as buffer zones for coastal-dwelling communities, preventing saltwater infusion of freshwater systems.[32] The combination of sinking coastlines caused by unsustainable land and water use practices and rising sea levels due to climate change results in what is known as *relative sea level rise*, sometimes rising at three and four times the global average.[33] In other words, the anticipated problem of flooding in the world's coastal cities will not be uniform in their effects. Nor will they be caused by climate change alone.

WATER AND SOCIAL ORGANIZATION 189

In sum, resort to deep aquifers to compensate for losses from other freshwater sources exhausts the reserves necessary for the long term and triggers a cascade of other socioeconomic and environmental problems. Climate change often figures importantly (but not uniquely) in initiating the chain of events by diminishing surface water availability. The ultimate ecological impact is a function of the interaction among a plurality of anthropogenic causes, including climate disruption, water resource withdrawal policies, and land use decisions affecting both surface and groundwater sources.

Water and Human Settlements

One thing that's clear from the discussion so far is that water management is technically complex. It also raises a host of normative issues. Under typical circumstances of contemporary human settlements, individuals depend upon extensive social mechanisms for the provision of services for the satisfaction of their basic needs. Because freshwater is subject to depletion, diversion, and degradation by the activities of other users, the water management task necessarily includes adjudication among competing uses and users. The satisfaction of competing needs for water depends on extensive social coordination, leaving fewer decisions to individual judgment and discretion.

Even in the most rural regions of the world today where freshwater gathering for personal use is primarily an individual household task, the quantity and quality of available water—along with the mechanisms for and burdens of access—are heavily determined by a web of background social conditions largely beyond individual control. Individual options are constrained by the fact that rivers are diverted, water is polluted, and forests, watersheds, and wetlands are transformed, often for the benefit of large landowners, urban elites, and commercial enterprises.

190 A LIVABLE PLANET

In one sense, the basic shape of the problem is not new. Ancient civilizations in Egypt, Rome, and China developed complex systems for harvesting, transporting, and distributing potable water, built in conjunction with systems for flood control, irrigation, and wastewater management.[34] Modern social organization has merely upped the ante. Humans have more extensively transformed river basins and watersheds, replaced traditional social and economic mechanisms through which water is available, and altered and expanded the purposes it serves.

The complexity of the freshwater management task argues for a comprehensive, basin-level approach, known as *integrated water resources management* (IWRM). IWRM is standardly defined as "a process for coordinating the development of water, land, and related resources, in order to maximize the resultant economic social and welfare in an equitable manner without compromising the sustainability of vital ecosystems."[35] Concretely, that means regulating suburban sprawl and other land uses, balancing competing claims on water from agricultural and industrial activities, controlling pollution, adjudicating between the interests of upstream and downstream users, protecting biodiversity, wetlands, and aquatic systems, and more.[36]

The reason for the breathtaking scope of the basin-level management task is the sheer number and extent of anthropogenic disruptions of the hydrologic cycle due to radically transformative changes in the configuration of human settlements.[37] Here are a few features of the management task. Start with fact that urbanization depends on deforestation, which results in watershed destruction and the proliferation of impermeable surfaces. Land now covered in impermeable asphalt and concrete reduces the natural capacity for replenishment of surface water sources by increasing runoff. Runoff, due to changes in the composition of urban surfaces, is no longer efficiently reabsorbed into the ground to recharge aquifers or diffused in reservoirs and lakes that store water for later use.

WATER AND SOCIAL ORGANIZATION 191

Runoff also leads to erosion, which further exacerbates the soil's decreased ability to absorb water essential to recharging aquifers and replenishing bodies of surface water. Moreover, disruptions in surface water replenishment and aquifer recharge capacity are interactive. Decreased capture of rainwater in surface water bodies contributes to slower recharge rates for aquifers, and declining aquifers in turn alter the replacement rates of surface waters, thereby reducing both sources of available freshwater.[38]

In addition, the concentration of toxic substances typically found in urban watershed areas leads to more soil degradation and water pollution. When the toxicity of both water and soil is further elevated, water is less likely to be reabsorbed into the ground or diffused in reservoirs and lakes. Reduced absorption triggers still greater concentrations of toxicity, further reducing the quantity of usable, high-quality water available.

Such examples illustrate the daunting management task ahead for watersheds in a rapidly urbanizing world. A 2016 World Bank report expects that reduced physical availability of freshwater will combine with increased water use for energy and agriculture, potentially resulting in reduction of overall water availability in the world's cities by as much as two-thirds by 2050, compared to 2015 levels.[39] Given the interactive effects of multiple human activities and policy choices, there is a need for coordinated and centralized basin-level decisions about removal of forest cover, construction of impermeable surfaces, geographic concentration of industrial and agricultural sources of pollution, options for power generation, the design of transportation systems, the disposal and treatment of wastes, and infrastructure for flood control.

The relevant policy choices for water managers touch on nearly every major aspect of shared life within organized society. These are inherently moral and political decisions, not merely technological problems or narrowly economic questions that might be resolved based on cost-benefit analyses or comparative assessments of technical efficiency. Their resolution turns on judgments about

192   A LIVABLE PLANET

the social arrangements best suited to securing a bundle of basic social and economic human rights, not only to water and sanitation, but also, secondarily, rights to food, subsistence, and protection of health and environment.

Water Management and Human Rights

To evaluate how well current institutions are discharging their human rights responsibilities, at least with respect to water and sanitation, some indicators of the extent and distribution of unmet needs are required. Water stress metrics, such ones developed according to the UN-Water definition, reveal only the gap between supply and demand, not whether there is a shortfall in meeting human needs. Demand could exceed supply in circumstances in which basic needs are met or, more likely, the burden of shortfall is borne by the poor. Progress reports for the targets set for UN SDG 6 shed light on this question.

Target 6.1 calls for universal and equitable access to safe and affordable drinking water for all by 2030. However, 29% of the world's population—2.2 billion people—lack access to safely managed drinking water services, defined as an improved drinking water source that is accessible on the premises, available when needed, and free of fecal and priority chemical contamination.[40] Freshwater may be available in sufficient quantities and affordable but of poor quality, for example, because of inadequate sanitation leading to contamination. Target 6.2 therefore calls for access to adequate and equitable sanitation and hygiene for all and the end of open defecation by 2030. However, 55% of the global population—4.2 billion people—still lack access to such services.[41]

Targets 6.1 and 6.2 therefore are tightly linked, with progress on one tied to progress on the other. A recent World Health Organization (WHO) report estimates that 3.6 billion people lack access to both safely managed household drinking water and

WATER AND SOCIAL ORGANIZATION   193

sanitation and hygiene services, and they project that the 2030 target date for universal access to both will not be met unless the current rate of progress in the least-developed countries increases almost 10-fold.[42]

Three facts illustrate further troublesome aspects of the truly daunting global water quality challenge. First, over 80% of the world's wastewater—and over 95% in some least-developed countries—is discharged without treatment into rivers and other water bodies, and, ultimately, it flows into aquifers.[43] Second, water used for industrial purposes and large-scale agriculture can be so heavily polluted that it becomes unsuitable for drinking or bathing, and some of these types of pollution are less amenable to conventional treatment processes.[44] Third, Target 6.3 aims for the reduction of water pollution by eliminating dumping and minimizing release of hazardous chemicals and materials, but a whopping 70% of global industrial waste is dumped untreated into surface waters.[45]

Finances are another problem. In less-developed countries and poorer regions within developed countries, poverty, and inadequate institutional capital investment rank high among the most important factors contributing to the lack of clean water and sanitation. Achieving universal access to safe drinking water and sanitation in 140 low- and middle-income countries could cost approximately US$114 billion per year.[46] However, to put this figure into proper context, governments across the world (excluding China and India) currently spend around US$320 billion a year on water and sanitation subsidies. The problem in many instances is not lack of financial resources, but the fact that funding does not reach those who need it most. For example, a recent World Bank study of 10 low- and middle-income countries found that 56% of the subsidies benefit the richest 20% and only 6% of subsidies are directed to the poorest 20%.[47] Such findings confirm the conclusion of the 2006 UN Human Development Report: "[t]he scarcity at the heart of the global water crisis is rooted in power, poverty and inequality."[48]

194   A LIVABLE PLANET

The arguments for the indispensable role of social organization and institutional mechanisms in creating and maintaining the conditions for satisfaction of needs for water and sanitation underscore a central claim from Chapter 4. The central function of and justification for human rights is their role in meeting basic human needs that are routinely subject to threats not otherwise manageable. More specifically, the secure fulfillment of a human right involves the institutionalization of social rules that provide the right-holder with a high degree of durable insulation from predictable sources of deprivation. Human rights therefore set a high bar for justification for public policies that have serious adverse impact on the satisfaction of basic water-related needs. The next two sections illustrate ways in which current market practices and political institutions fail to meet that burden of justification.

The Political Economy of Water Resources

Target 6.4 of SDG 6 aims for increase in global water-use efficiency. The goal can be furthered in two commonly recommended ways. Efficiency within a country is increased when countries switch to less water-intensive domestic production techniques. In addition, a more efficient global allocation of scarce water resources can be achieved when water-stressed regions import water-intensive crops (and goods) rather than growing (or producing) them domestically.[49]

Decoupling

Technical efficiency (i.e., productive efficiency) is achieved by producing the same material output from a smaller amount of water. The technical efficiency of production can be improved, for example, by developing crops that require less water or by switching

WATER AND SOCIAL ORGANIZATION   195

to manufacturing processes that use less water. In principle, were more countries to switch to less water-intensive domestic production techniques, greater global efficiency could be achieved.

Indeed, the overall global trend is toward relative decoupling, that is, using less water per unit of productive output. For example, between 1900 and 2000, the global economy expanded 30-fold, while global water consumption grew by only 6-fold.[50] Relative decoupling has been most dramatic in the developed world, where the ratio of domestic water use to gross domestic product (GDP) has been declining much faster.[51] An obvious attraction of relative decoupling is that water conservation does not necessarily require a reduction in material standard of living.

However, greater productive efficiency does not guarantee an absolute reduction in global water use. Total global water consumption can—and typically does—continue to rise as total economic output rises. This is an instance of the rebound effect discussed initially in Chapter 2. The water footprint for each unit of production goes down, but not enough to offset the overall increase in total water consumption. Even if the number of countries that make progress in relative decoupling increases dramatically, the global consumption of water will not decline unless the consumption of blue jeans, for example, at least remains constant. But the evidence to date suggests that we can expect a rebound effect, especially as the world becomes more affluent.

In addition, the production of less water-intensive consumer goods, even if overall water use remains constant, does not necessarily result in a fairer or more efficient allocation among competing uses. Water saved at soda bottling plants and blue jeans factories does not automatically lead to greater availability of water for vital uses such as agriculture or drinking and hygiene. Productive efficiency, of course, is a good thing, but, on its own, it does not address questions about the distribution of water resources.

Moreover, nations that do manage to achieve greater productive efficiency can and often do reduce their domestic (internal)

196   A LIVABLE PLANET

water footprint of production simply by outsourcing their water-intensive production. By importing water-intensive crops and consumer goods from other countries these nations can maintain their high standard of living while using fewer of their own domestic resources. In other words, they can reduce their own national water footprint of production, but they do so without reducing their aggregate water footprint of consumption.

The practice of importing water-intensive products is sometimes referred to as "virtual water." Water that is physically used in one county (or region) of production is effectively transferred through the trade of water-intensive goods to the consumption country (or region). In principle, the virtual water trade could be efficient and mutually beneficial, as conventional economic wisdom claims. Affluent countries that can pay for water-intensive imports can maintain their lifestyles without depleting scarce domestic water resources, while water-rich countries can reap the benefits of accelerated economic development. However, international water trade does not conform to what economists recommend.

For example, per capita water consumption in the United States and many European nations is roughly double the global average, and their external water footprint (i.e., their water consumption footprint from imported commodities) also tends to be much higher than the global average.[52] At the higher end, as much as 95% of the total water consumption footprint in the Netherlands is attributable to imported goods, and in Italy, Germany, and the United Kingdom, the external water consumption footprints constitute 50–80% of their gross water footprint.[53]

By contrast, the domestic (or internal) per capita water consumption footprint for some countries is quite low, as it is generally in less industrially advanced countries, but often their gross water footprint is among the world's highest. For example, India and China are among the world's top three nations in terms of their gross water footprints, but much of that footprint is due to the production of water-intensive export commodities. India and China, as we have seen, are water-stressed countries, and many of the virtual water-importing European countries that rely heavily upon these external water resources have ample domestic supplies of water and land. The result is neither efficient nor sustainable. Nor does it promote the secure realization of human rights.

In fact, the inefficient and unsustainable practices of water transfer are a significant component of the global agricultural system. Approximately 25% of the world's agriculture is grown in areas defined as high water-stress regions.[54] Worse yet, more than 40% of wheat is grown in areas facing high or extremely high levels of water stress, and more than half of global cotton production is undertaken in regions of high or extremely high stress.[55]

The explanation of this upside-down pattern of virtual water trade is complex—in fact, far more complicated than some models of globalization might suggest. For example, the traditional "dependency thesis" holds that developed countries maintain their high standard of living at the expense of colonies, former colonies, or economically dependent countries that squander their natural resources and fall further behind in development by restricting themselves to production of export commodities.[56] Of course, there are plenty of examples of the persistence of this neocolonial trade pattern, but both highly developed and less-developed economies are unsustainable net exporters of water-intensive crops.[57]

Countries as diverse as the United States, Mexico, Iran, and China both export and import food produced on land irrigated by rapidly depleting aquifers, including many of the crops that contribute most to the non-renewable groundwater trade, such as rice, wheat, cotton, maize, and soybeans.[58] Moreover, a majority of the world's population now lives in countries sourcing nearly all their staple crop imports from trading partners that deplete their groundwater to produce them.[59]

198   A LIVABLE PLANET

Water-Intensive Agricultural Production

What explains the fact that water-stressed regions, in both affluent and developing countries, are engaged in such clearly unstainable water-intensive agricultural production practices—policies that undermine their capacity to meet the long-term needs of their residents? Patterns in four countries illustrate the diversity of explanations.

Iran exemplifies how one element of the global political economy leads to a short-sighted economic development strategy. Iran is one of the most water-stressed countries in the world, but it urges farmers to plant water-intensive crops like wheat, subsidizes electricity costs of its production, and maintains price supports for those crops. Roughly 90% of Iran's total water consumption is used for agricultural purposes, with around 80% of that drawn from aquifers.[60] The policy has resulted in aquifer depletion in a country where some of its provinces expect as little as 50 years of remaining groundwater, and, with increased heat in the region, rainfall is expected to decline, further undermining the ability to replenish its aquifers.[61]

Self-sufficiency of their domestic food supply, however, not the expansion of global exports is the rationale for Iran's policies. The key incentive for their decision is their geopolitical precariousness, as reflected in the recent history of international sanctions and regional hostilities with its neighboring states. However, the policies designed to ensure food security in the face of potential geopolitical pressures are self-undermining. They are rapidly eroding the resource base upon which the food security of its people depends.

India offers a contemporary example with a different historical trajectory. It, too, is one of the planet's most water-stressed regions.[62] And yet it produces 26% of the world's cotton, one of the least suitable crops for such a water-starved region. A kilogram of cotton requires between 1,800 and 7,660 gallons of water to produce.[63] The production of a kilogram of denim fabric for a pair of

WATER AND SOCIAL ORGANIZATION 199

jeans requires about 2,625 gallons (10,000 liters) of water.[64] The explanation of its production policy is quite different from Iran's. Today's vast acreage of land devoted to the production of cotton is a holdover from the colonial era, when the British introduced a massive program of irrigation for growing cotton for export to its mills. India is an example of path-dependent economic development, where it becomes difficult for a country to abandon existing revenue streams even when its economic activities are undermining the very basis of its economic and ecological future.

China, another very highly water-stressed region, now rivals the United States as the world's largest grain producer, and, as a result, it has one of the three largest gross water footprints in the world. But falling water tables are adversely affecting their harvests in the North China Plain, an area that produces half of the country's wheat and maize.[65] Over-pumping has largely depleted the shallow aquifers, forcing well drillers to turn to the region's deep aquifers, which are not replenishable.[66] The implications of the rapid water withdrawals in China's agricultural heartland are brought into context by the fact that its water resources per capita are only about 25% of the world average, and, more specifically, its heartland contains 51% of the country's cropped land, where only 20% of its water resources reside.[67]

Moreover, the North China Plain suffers from severe groundwater pollution with, more than 70% of overall groundwater quality classified as unfit for human contact.[68] Even so, farmers rely upon it to irrigate their crops. But, over the long term, water pollution is so widely seen as a limiting factor to sustainable agriculture and economic development that Chinese "experts have given it a special term, *shui zhi xing que shui*, or literally 'water-quality-driven water shortage.'"[69] China's unsustainable policy is an artifact of an aggressive pro-growth policy, designed for near-term alleviation of poverty, whatever the long-term ecological consequences.

The same pattern of aquifer over-pumping for irrigation of crops produced for consumption elsewhere is found in the United States,

200   A LIVABLE PLANET

for example, in the Western Great Plains. The Ogallala-High Plains Aquifer is one of the world's largest groundwater sources, extending through portions of eight states. It provides drinking water to 82% of the people who live within the region.[70] However, approximately 90% of the withdrawals are for irrigation.[71] In fact, the High Plains is one of the most intensively irrigated areas in the United States, accounting for about 30% of all US groundwater withdrawn for irrigation.[72] However, production is not for their own local markets. The region supplies approximately one-fourth of the nation's agricultural production, including the feed for 40% of US feedlot beef output.[73] The consequence is that 30% of the groundwater has been depleted, and another 39% will be depleted over the next 50 years if existing trends continue.[74]

The specific explanation for the unsustainable Western states agricultural model lies in the confluence of several factors. The problem is not the lack of efficient technology. The region is in the forefront of adoption of some of the most advanced irrigation technologies that have led to substantial increases in the productive efficiency of water—more crop per drop—and yet overall groundwater withdrawal continues to rise because the area of irrigated land also expands. One reason for the expansion of acreage is the fact that irrigation technology allows farmers to expand production of commodities with higher market values. For example, crops with higher market value include irrigated corn and feed crops instead of dryland (non-irrigated) wheat. Farmers therefore have reinforcing incentives to invest in irrigation technology, buy or lease more acres, and switch production to higher market value commodity crops. All that leads to more acreage of irrigated land, growing more water-intensive crops, and more over-pumping.

In addition, farmers can take advantage of state and federal subsidies for adoption of efficient water technologies and other subsidies in the form of price supports. The rationales for these subsidies mirror some of the reasons subsidies are utilized in Iran and India. Food security and economic development are

WATER AND SOCIAL ORGANIZATION 201

paramount concerns. Because of the thin profit margins in farming, a system of federal subsidies was created to support farmers in lean years, thereby keeping production capacity intact. The subsidies effectively guarantee a minimum level of income for farmers by setting a price floor on the main agricultural commodities. That floor generates further incentive to ramp up production and invest in more expensive efficient technology, knowing that their income will increase if they place more subsidized acres under production.

Growing larger quantities, however, floods the market, further reducing crop prices and farm incomes, but doing so triggers more federal subsidies to make up the difference. In good years or bad, the dominant incentive is to put more acreage into production, even though it depletes water resources necessary for sustaining production over the longer term.[75]

For quite different reasons, the leaders of all four countries might say that they have little choice but to continue with business as usual, knowing the longer-term risks, but also knowing the challenges of embarking on a new path. Some countries maintain unsustainable water-intensive agricultural policies primarily for geopolitical reasons, others due mainly to lack of readily available better economic development opportunities. China and India are mindful of the urgency of poverty relief, while the United States overextends its water resources so that its citizens can continue to eat beef, preserve existing jobs in cattle and meat-packing industries, and, of course, please the region's major financial contributors to political campaigns.

These four examples demonstrate the mix of market and nonmarket reasons for water-stressed countries and regions to adopt unsustainable agricultural practices; become locked into existing economic trajectories that are difficult to change, especially when the lure of high market value commodity crops (often for export) over the short-term is so difficult to resist; and governmental policies prop up existing market arrangements.

202 A LIVABLE PLANET

Economics of Extraction

Another aspect of the global system of trade in water resources is the acquisition of water and water-adjacent land for production of water-intensive consumer items, such as bottled water, soda, and blue jeans. For example, water for production of "packaged water"—bottled water and sachet water—and soda is an increasingly valuable commodity in a highly competitive, water-stressed world. Sites of water extraction are not necessarily chosen because of local abundance. In many places—in both domestic and foreign arenas—soda and bottled water companies are attracted mainly by opportunities to extract massive quantities of water for very little cost beyond purchase price for acquiring the adjacent land or the payment of a nominal governmental fee. Some of the world's largest bottled water conglomerates obtain water from water-starved places such as Arizona and California. In California's San Bernardino National Forest, one company pays an annual rate of $524 to utilize its high-capacity wells to extract about 30 million gallons, even during its long periods of severe drought.[76]

The volume of water extracted under such conditions, domestically or globally, is not the core of the problem. In fact, the volume of the virtual water transferred as a result of foreign direct investments by transnational companies is a small percentage of the total virtual water transfers, and the virtual water transfer specifically due to foreign land acquisitions is only a small fraction of the international trade in virtual water.[77] The normative significance of water extraction practices, however, lies in its "hidden socio-environmental costs," including reduced water access for poor residents and small-holder farms, displacement, and environmental pollution from production or extractive activities.[78]

Unlimited extraction or an unlimited rate of extraction has particularly serious consequences for those communities where operations are legally unconstrained. Unregulated extraction imperils the reliability of local municipal supplies, undermines

WATER AND SOCIAL ORGANIZATION 203

the long-term ability of aquifers to recharge, disrupts stream flow thereby affecting water quality and biodiversity, and interferes with the water filtering capacity of watersheds.[79]

These adverse effects are facilitated by archaic legal frameworks, often set in place for the benefit of politically powerful, large landowners.[80] Many jurisdictions around the world impose few or inadequate restrictions on the quantity of water used or the impact on other users. Of particular importance is the fact that water ownership rights throughout much of the world are established according to permissive rules, such as the "law of capture" that allows unlimited withdrawal regardless of purpose, or the "rule of prior appropriation" that allows appropriation so long as the water is put to some (expansively interpreted) beneficial use. Even stricter legal rules that set limits to "reasonable appropriation" are often permissive in granting legal rights to surface water, groundwater, or both to whomever is first to divert it for their own use, so long as their use does not unreasonably affect other wells or the aquifer system.[81] Lax rules on acquisition of water and other resources are among the core elements of the permissive regulatory legal environments described in Chapter 5 as a key factor in many global investment decisions.

In addition, proliferation of bottled water has been implicated in a broader set of water policy failures beyond the localized adverse effects on municipal supply, watersheds, and the functioning of aquifers. An emerging concern is the normalization of bottled water as an alternative to systems of public provision of safe, reliable drinking water in developing nations. In particular, the worry is that industry marketing efforts, designed to expand global bottled water sales, contribute to the delegitimation and further underfunding of public systems of piped water. They promote the misleading claim that "bottled water provides at least a partial solution to the problem of often-unsafe water found in economically developing countries."[82] Its promotion, which is largely for the convenience of affluent consumers, undermines the social solidarity

204   A LIVABLE PLANET

upon which the achievement of universal access depends. In fact, no country has—or can—make real progress toward the first target of SDG 6 to achieve universal and equitable access to safe and affordable drinking water for all by 2030 without broad community support.

In addition, many other well-known economic and environmental problems have been created by the growth of the bottled water and soda industry, including exorbitant costs; consumer misunderstanding of quality and safety; the excessive amount of water that is wasted in the bottling process; the carbon footprint of extraction, processing, and transport; and the industry's contribution to the massive global build-up of non-biodegradable plastic wastes in landfills and oceans.[83]

The main point of this section, however, is that shortage anywhere is now a problem with global economic and ecological consequences. Businesses search for new locations for water-intensive production, not only where water is in abundance, but also where legal and economic barriers to resource acquisition are low or regulation of their impact on water quality is minimal. Intensified global competition for scarce resources, including water, makes it difficult for governments of economically vulnerable jurisdictions to resist opportunities that provide short-term benefit, even when it means greater longer-term risk of resource depletion and ecological destruction. However, these global practices allow residents of global affluent jurisdictions to conserve their own resources, offload the negative social and environmental risks of extraction, and preserve or improve their standard of material well-being.

The Privatization of Essential Services

The first section of this chapter shows that management of water involves a complex array of tasks that dovetail with state

WATER AND SOCIAL ORGANIZATION 205

responsibilities for securing human rights to water and sanitation, food, and subsistence, and protection of health and environment. The second section reveals further layers of complexity generated by global trade dynamics and the political priorities of individual states. This section expands the discussion by examining institutional arrangements for delivering water and sanitation services.

The privatization of public water systems and drinking water supplies and infrastructure is widely proposed as a vehicle for implementing market-based approaches to the problem of water scarcity. Most privatization arrangements have many common features.[84] They employ long-term contracts (e.g., 20–40 years) and rarely provide for outright legal transfer of water resources. Typically, such contracts involve the outsourcing of management of treatment and delivery services; assign responsibilities for specific aspects of infrastructure construction, maintenance, or basin management under public-private partnership (PPP) agreements; and contain revenue stream guarantees and clauses protecting private investment.

The Push for Privatization

The World Bank maintains that it is officially neutral on the choice between public and private systems of municipal provision.[85] However, critics have been led to believe that the deck is stacked against public systems. The widely cited preface to the Bank's 1993 water policy memo claims that "[g]overnments have often misallocated and wasted water, as well as permitted damage to the environment, as a result of institutional weaknesses, market failures, distorted policies, and misguided investments."[86] More specifically, the Bank's management guidance shows a decided preference for market-based solutions, whatever the mode or ownership and control that might be employed. It says that a "key component of the reforms to be supported by the Bank will thus

206   A LIVABLE PLANET

be greater reliance on incentives for efficiency and financial discipline . . . [in particular], the importance of pricing and financial accountability by using estimated opportunity costs as a guide in setting water charges."[87]

The basic principle behind any market-based approach is captured by the slogan "full-cost recovery." The assumption is that unless water is treated strictly as a market commodity, with market-based pricing that captures the full cost of extraction, treatment, and delivery, water systems will be inefficient and wasteful. Moreover, sensitivity to price is assumed to be the key to ensuring that water is not wasted, thereby leaving insufficient resources for the satisfaction of basic human needs or vital social objectives, such as food security and watershed health.

The heart of the problem of inefficiency is described by the Bank as "a 'vicious cycle' of poor-quality and unreliable services that do not meet consumers' needs and for which they are unwilling to pay, often leading the poor to pay more for water elsewhere, which, in turn, generates inadequate operating funds and a further deterioration in services."[88] This diagnosis points to the role of markets as a potential solution for the problems the Bank sees as endemic to public systems. Having to pay the true cost of water treatment and delivery incentivizes people to conserve it. It also enables individuals to decide for themselves how to reduce wasteful consumption without resort to coercive rationing schemes.

In addition, the anticipated uptick in consumer-driven demand—and willingness to pay—for higher-quality water is expected to attract private capital or command higher user fees, thereby providing the much-needed funds for upgrading systems and service delivery. Most importantly, the Bank highlights the prospect that the infusion of capital—whether from user fees, private investment, or both—will lead to the expansion of services into underserved areas, thereby promoting poverty alleviation, which it describes as its overarching objective for involvement in the water sector.[89]

WATER AND SOCIAL ORGANIZATION 207

Of course, privatized systems are not necessary to achieve full-cost recovery. Public systems could be run on the same principles. But the Bank's skepticism about the track records of governments, together with growing faith in the efficiency-generating capacities of for-profit entities, has made privatization the default option in the global development community. Also, management service–exporting nations and transnational institutions created specifically for the advancement of privatization utilize their ties to the Bank and the International Monetary Fund (IMF) to promote the private sector's technical expertise and capacity for new capital infusion.[90]

The motivations of local municipalities and governments for adopting privatization contracts are another factor in the uptake of privatized delivery mechanisms. Motivations differ somewhat across communities, but the usual case involves a combination of government officials' desire to upgrade aging facilities, concern about inadequate tax revenues, the lure of immediate infusion of capital, and the elimination of future municipal service and infra-structure investment obligations in exchange for payment of long-term private management fees. Also, because investments in PPPs typically do not appear on their balance sheets as governmental expenditures or debts, municipalities improve their creditworthi-ness, borrowing capacity, and eligibility for lower costs of credit.[91]

Moreover, the burden of complying with the full-cost recovery conditions imposed by lending institutions, the aggressive pro-motional efforts of influential private sector organizations, and the financial burdens experienced by government entities explains why so many countries and municipalities have seen few feasible alternatives to privatization.

Privatization and Its Problems

Systematic studies, however, reveal a mixed record, raising se-rious questions about the value of privatized systems. They

208 A LIVABLE PLANET

show wide variation in water quality and service across public and private systems, with no decisive efficiency or service advantage gained from privatization; a lack of clear benefit to the communities, especially the poor; and the added financial risks privatization creates for developing nations.[92] Even a World Bank internal analysis concluded that "there is no statistically significant difference between the efficiency performance of public and private operators in this sector."[93]

Some spectacularly disappointing privatization experiments, such as the one in Cochabamba, Bolivia, saw rates go up substantially, no expansion of service areas, and no improvement in quality.[94] In the United States and elsewhere, service rates generally have gone up substantially after privatization, often well beyond the overall cost of living.[95] A World Bank review of the outcomes of 15 years of water PPPs around the world also found that corporations often "failed to invest the amount of private funding they had originally committed and did not always meet their original contractual targets for coverage."[96]

The results in Bolivia and elsewhere added impetus to the international water rights movement, whose objectives are embodied in the Cochabamba Declaration. It asserts that "water is a fundamental human right and a public trust to be guarded by all levels of government, therefore, it should not be commodified, privatized or traded for commercial purposes."[97]

The dismal outcomes that prompted the popular uprising in Bolivia are generally cited as the primary reasons that many other communities have chosen to end their long-term management contracts, even in the face of contractual obligations requiring payment of steep early termination fees. Atlanta, Georgia; Allentown, Pennsylvania; Stockton, California; and Bayonne, New Jersey are high-visibility examples of successful termination efforts in the United States. Problems that these municipalities faced are replicated around the world, motivating more than 1,400 communities in less than 20 years since 2000 to demand cancelation

WATER AND SOCIAL ORGANIZATION 209

of long-term contracts and "remunicipalize" water and other traditionally publicly managed utility services.[98]

Moreover, fundamental problems are inherent in the business model embodied in standard PPP contracts. For example, guarantees of rates of return for the concessionaire create a layer of expense that is added to the operational costs of a previously government-run water system. Food and Water Watch estimates that corporate profits, dividends, and income taxes can add 20–30% extra to the operation and maintenance costs, plus another 25% extra to cover the costs of contract monitoring and administration and transaction costs of public-to-private conversion.[99]

Another problem is the higher cost of private financing compared to the costs of municipal borrowing.[100] The same pattern of more expensive private finance, without compensating public benefit, occurs in other sectors and in various countries in which PPPs or direct long-term outsourcing of governmental services have been tried.[101] In short, the one-sided terms of the contracts and the underlying business model of privatization schemes provide great low-risk opportunities for private business without the responsibility for addressing long-term economic and ecological consequences. In other words, the business model often conforms to what we have been calling economically predatory market practices.

More generally, the basic principle of full-cost recovery is in deep tension with other well-established social policies pertaining to the poor. Concretely, implementation typically means the elimination of public-sector subsidies, which are viewed as market-distorting because they undermine price-sensitive utilization. Of course, in theory, some subsidies could remain in place in a full-cost recovery system, but only if something like a tiered water rate scheme were adopted. In essence, that would mean charging larger users a premium sufficient to make up for the costs not covered by rates charged to low-income residential users or rebated through subsidies. Alternatively, a bloc rate scheme would set below-market

210 A LIVABLE PLANET

low rates for a certain amount of water for everyone, with steeply increasing per unit rates for water above the initial subsidized allotment. However, these options are perennial targets of pro-market champions of privatization simply because they are price-distorting policies, and they perpetuate a cadre of consumers whose utilization is not price-sensitive.

As a practical matter, modified pricing solutions are unlikely to appeal to potential management contractors. Expansion of services to low-income communities is not a profitable venture to begin with because of fee collection problems and fixed costs of hookups for customers whose bills are lower than average. Taking on more reduced-fee customers while charging more to their large customers to make up the difference is not an attractive business proposition. Private managers have stronger reasons for catering to large customers, in part because they are more politically powerful, but, more fundamentally, it is more cost-effective to focus the business on large customers whose per cubic foot cost of provision tends to be cheaper. In short, the aim of profit maximization runs counter to various ways of carrying out the governmental mission of providing basic water and sanitation services to its entire populace, regardless of ability to pay.

Privatization also raises issues beyond considerations of economic justice for the poor. Private managers assigned the discrete task of supplying treated water to the public lack a clear business purpose or institutional mandate to consider broader impacts on the natural environment, and they have powerful economic incentive to shift the environmental costs of water extraction to society.[102] PPP contracts are typically limited to service delivery, not broader environmental responsibilities. Integrated public systems, by contrast, are charged with environmental management tasks that are absent from fee-for-service delivery contracts. Such tasks include maintenance of minimum instream flows, protection of wetlands, preservation of watershed functioning and biodiversity, and integrated management of groundwater and surface water sources to promote aquifer health. In other words, PPPs that only take on the task of delivery service fragment the wide-ranging authority recommended by IWRM principles.

Also, private management arrangements are in tension with ecological sustainability goals. First, efforts to monitor and evaluate the environmental impacts of customer usage or impose conservation policies are contrary to the aim of profit maximization simply because they would reduce the volume of water sold.[103] Second, private contractors have little economic incentive to attend to risks of resource depletion or invest in public water systems' improvements or maintenance activities produced beyond the end of the contract term.[104] In short, private managers of treatment and delivery services have neither the economic incentives nor institutional authority to implement long-term, environmentally sustainable policies. In fact, the remunicipalization movement is often driven by the twin goals of more equitable access to services and a redirection of the funds that would have gone to private profits to public investment in green infrastructure, which private entities lack incentive to undertake.

Of course, public authorities can fail to pursue long-term goals of ensuring the availability of water resources and preserving the environmental integrity of watershed systems.[105] They, too, may be driven by concerns about short-term political benefits and costs. However, cross-sector responsibilities according to IWMR principles are absent altogether under fragmented PPP arrangements. They assign responsibilities for discrete facets of water policy to private entities, and their performance is driven by purely private economic incentives that are in tension with both expanded access for the poor and environmental goals.

Public systems and private systems also differ in another normatively important respect. Private systems, by design, often suffer from a lack of accountability. There are two distinct aspects of the problem. First, according to many pro-market advocates, the governing body of a privatized system has a strict fiduciary duty

212   A LIVABLE PLANET

to shareholders. To the extent that private water concessions contractually embrace that truncated understanding of the social responsibilities of private enterprise, historical norms of accountability to consumers and voters no longer apply. Second, private management firms routinely insist on contract language that limits accountability to ratepayers, giving them wide policy discretion without the usual mechanisms of review of public utility oversight boards.

By contrast, proponents of privatization often count insulation from political pressure as an institutional virtue rather than a deficit of democracy. However, when multinational corporations assume authority over vital resources, they make the kinds of decisions that should be subject to collective democratic decision-making. A narrowly profit-driven decision-making body preempts the moral judgments of those communities affected by such policies, for example, decisions about fees, subsidies for the poor, and long-term investment for the sake of future generations.

Importantly, PPPs and other private water management concessions are emblematic of a larger global trend toward de-democratization, where the self-interested financial judgments made by owners of hypermobile capital foreclose opportunities for democratically accountable collective decision-making.[106] As demonstrated in Chapter 3, the democratic deficit is neither an unintended nor unforeseen consequence of privatization arrangements. Market fundamentalists were explicit in their desire to limit what they sometimes called "excesses of democracy."

There are many strands of the anti-privatization argument surveyed thus far, but the unique risks it poses to the human rights to water and sanitation is summed up by Léo Heller, former United Nations Special Rapporteur on the human rights to water and sanitation. He notes that the heightened risks are due to "a combination of three factors: profit maximization, the natural monopoly that characterizes water and sanitation provision, and power asymmetry."[107] The first factor highlights the inherent tension between

WATER AND SOCIAL ORGANIZATION 213

the profit motives of a private entity and the responsibilities of public entities to ensure access regardless of ability to pay. The second factor identifies the lack of feasible alternatives for individuals to meet their own basic needs in circumstances in which public provision is their only realistic option. The third factor is in part due to the combination of the first and second factors. A service delivery system that has no incentives to meet basic needs for those who cannot pay, together with no feasible alternatives, leaves consumers powerless. But powerlessness is a consequence also of the contractual arrangements that foreclose democratic accountability, leaving citizens without the political mechanisms for demanding satisfaction of their rights.

The Infrastructure Deficit Argument

In the face of various shortcomings of privatization, its champions now mount an additional line of defense. They claim that there is no feasible alternative, given the current economic realities in which there is a global problem of infrastructure deficit. As we have seen, many cash-strapped local municipalities have found this argument convincing. The argument gains traction also among global development experts who worry that many national (and provincial) governments have too much sovereign (or public) debt and not enough foreseeable tax revenue to fund the necessary infrastructure improvements. Cost estimates for achieving Target 4 of SDG 6, which aims for greater efficiency in water use and treatment systems, range between US$74 billion to US$116 billion annually.[108] Estimates of funding required for implementing all 17 SDGs are between US$3.3 trillion and US$4.5 trillion a year.[109] However, the infrastructure deficit argument masks three important objections.

First, reliance upon outsourcing as a solution to structural budgetary woes can be a self-defeating strategy. Using metrics created by the IMF, the World Bank identified serious economic and

214   A LIVABLE PLANET

environmental risks associated with PPPs when created under conditions of elevated fiscal stress. In line with other studies previously cited, they concluded that the "development, bidding and ongoing costs in PPP projects are likely to be greater than for traditional government procurement processes."[110] That same report acknowledged the deleterious effects of a lack of private-sector incentive to promote economically or environmentally sustainable delivery systems, noting that the "[p]rivate sector will do what it is paid to do and no more than that."[111]

Second, the infrastructure deficit argument ignores morally salient factors that contribute to the infrastructural shortfall in the first place. Decades of onerous austerity conditions imposed by the IMF, World Bank, regional development banks, and private lenders precipitated massive tax cuts, leaving debtor states and municipalities without sufficient revenue to fund many of these projects, thereby forcing them to choose between privatization of essential services or the risk of elimination.[112]

Third, budgetary shortfalls, exacerbated by austerity and tax cut measures, are compounded by tax competition discussed in Chapter 5. In response to competitive pressures, nations cut corporate taxes dramatically, further depriving themselves of the revenues necessary to fund essential services. The threat of flight to a lower-tax jurisdiction not only allows capital owners to benefit from public goods and infrastructure without paying their fair share. It also erodes democracy and government budgetary autonomy, and it fuels inequality, given that there are few alternatives for making up for lost revenue other than by hiking taxes on poorer sections of society. Inequality then rises along with the reduction of tax revenue.[113]

There is something deeply disturbing about arguments that take private-sector replacement of democratic institutions as a given and then build a case for handing over still more profits to the very entities that contributed so much to the origins of the infrastructure deficit problem. And yet the power of the privatization movement persists within international development circles.[114]

This section and the chapter overall can be summarized by recalling a few key points. First, the global water crisis has regionally variable impacts, but it is truly global in nature. Scarcity in one place drives resource extraction and predatory investments in distant places. Second, although climate change will be—and already is—a very big factor in the water crisis going forward, other anthropogenic causes have been in play for a long time. Third, global trade in water can be both efficient and mutually beneficial under the right conditions, but domestic incentive structures and the organization of the global political economy often undermine both aims. Fourth, the pursuit of technical efficiency is not a solution to the problem of rising water consumption or its fair and efficient allocation. Nor is it a sufficient reason to allow private gain or geopolitical dominance to subvert democratic aspirations for collective control over the most basic terms of a sustainable human existence. Finally, the main water policy decisions faced by nations are not strictly economic. They are moral and political decisions that should be guided by empirically informed judgments about social arrangements that secure a bundle of basic social and economic human rights and preserve democratic institutions.

8

Energy Transition Pathways

Historians observe that a major social transition occurs when "business as usual becomes untenable and divergent pathways emerge."[1] The evidence suggests that the world has reached such a point with climate-altering greenhouse gas emissions. For example, the 2022 UN Climate Change Synthesis Report estimates that emissions reductions pledged by 193 states under the Paris Agreement would still put the world on track for 2.5°C of global warming.[2] The *Emissions Gap Report* by the United Nations Environment Program (UNEP), also released in 2022, projects that the world is on track for around 2.6°C warming above pre-industrial levels under policies in place today, with an upper bound of uncertainty at 3.9°C.[3] Projections will change, but the UNEP report emphasizes two key points that crystalize the contours of the decarbonization challenge. First, because damages accumulate as warming increases, long before any critical tipping points are reached, every fraction of a degree matters; and, second, a "wide-ranging, large-scale, rapid and systemic transformation" will be required if humanity is to avoid the most dangerous levels of warming.[4]

The energy resources that produced industrial civilization must be discarded, but new energy transition pathways will generate new ecological and economic risks, introduce uncertainties into social relationships, and disrupt established expectations. Hence the appeal of incrementally transformative pathways and the lure of sacrifice-free solutions.

The first section considers incrementally transformational pathways driven by false hopes. Solutions rooted in false hopes are unlikely to result in timely, necessary changes, primarily because

A Livable Planet. Madison Powers, Oxford University Press. © Oxford University Press 2024.
DOI: 10.1093/oso/9780197756003.003.0008

ENERGY TRANSITION PATHWAYS 217

they depend on unrealistic assumptions regarding human behavior or the operation of markets. The second section examines proposed solutions that involve *false starts*. False starts are partial and non-durable solutions. They produce some positive results, but they also create problems within another sphere of activity, shift problems onto other persons or communities, or merely postpone or magnify risk of long-term harm. The third section considers a variety of path dependencies, constraints on the feasible options for the future created by institutions or practices that lock in existing social and economic relations. The point of examining these various energy transition options and the obstacles they present is to demonstrate the need for a more decisive break from existing social practices and entrenched power relations.

The chapter concludes with examples demonstrating the normative alignment of key arguments in this book with policy proposals and strategies developed by indigenous and other advocacy groups that put a human rights agenda at the center of their work.

False Hopes

Solutions that are rooted in false hopes are unlikely to result in timely, necessary changes. Examples include faith in the power of conscientious consumer-driven solutions, trust in the enlightened international leadership originating from within high-consumption nations, and confidence in market-driven technological innovation.

Consumer-Driven Change

The pathway toward a more sustainable economy will require substantial recalibration of expectations, especially for the global affluent and those who aspire to a more resource-intensive,

218   A LIVABLE PLANET

ecologically impactful way of life. Typical suggestions include admonitions to consume less, recycle more, switch to renewable energy sources and biodegradable, non-petroleum-based materials, and utilize more efficient modes of transport.

It is undeniable that reduction of individual consumption, especially by the global affluent, is an essential component of any transitional pathway. The most affluent 20% of the global population generates roughly three-quarters of the global gross domestic product (GDP), the majority of that in the form of consumer spending.[5] The climate impacts of these unequal and resource-intensive patterns of consumption are wide-ranging. The richest 10% of households generate more than half of the global carbon dioxide emissions, the richest 1% are responsible for 15% of emissions, and the poorest half of humanity generates only 7%.[6] To put these differences into perspective, the average carbon footprint in the top 1% of emitters is more than 75 times higher than that in the bottom 50%.[7]

Skeptics will ask whether individual decisions to reduce ecologically destructive consumption will make a difference. The answer is complicated. On the one hand, many environmental harms are not caused in a way that adding a single drop of water to a full glass causes it to overflow. If you ask yourself what the odds are that your weekend drive in a gas guzzler will tip the climate scales, the answer is that it's virtually certain that your actions, in that sense, are harmless.

However, not all ecological problems arise only when the harmful effects reach some threshold or tipping point, thereby bringing about large-scale, long-term catastrophic consequences. A congested highway offers a better analogy than a full water glass in most cases. Total traffic gridlock, where a road becomes impassible, might not result from the addition of one more car on the road. However, with each additional vehicle, harmful consequences for travel accrue gradually. Passage becomes progressively more difficult, and roads no longer perform their intended function at the same level. In similar fashion, additional pollutants in streams make matters measurably worse as water quality deteriorates and adverse human health consequences increase.

The same analogy illustrates the dynamics of climate change that the UNEP report emphasizes. Although much of the discussion of global warming focuses on the potential for propelling Earth systems beyond irreversible tipping points, the harms begin far earlier in the process. Increments of warming result in more heat-related illnesses and deaths. Disrupted weather patterns lead to more frequent and prolonged droughts, crop losses, coastal and river basin flooding, and soil erosion and nutrient runoff. However, as many philosophers argue, because it is uncertain how much, if any, difference an individual's carbon-intensive action is likely to make to the overall outcome, individual behavioral change can seem futile.[8] Even if it is true that individuals have sufficient reason to keep one more car off the road, add fewer chemical pollutants to the water supply, or emit less carbon, simply because every little bit matters, it is unclear how much they can expect their choices to contribute to the scale and pace of change needed. Apart from the influential impact of celebrities with a large social media following, individual decisions to travel fewer miles, eat less meat, or buy less non-degradable plastic, if intended to change the behavior of producers and other consumers, may not have the desired effect, at least not quickly enough. Critics of a consumer change model therefore argue that only political action, not consumer choices, reasonably can be expected to lead to change in the background structural conditions.[9]

Critics are correct that consumers, acting on their own, face an uphill battle on several fronts. One problem is that production decisions are not always as sensitive to changes in consumer demand as we might assume. Because producers often are aware of the risk of overproducing relative to demand, they make production decisions that build in a buffer to accommodate slack in sales, and they adjust their pricing to reflect the prospect that some excess

220 A LIVABLE PLANET

will simply be wasted, given away, or sold at deep discount.[10] Even when the decisions of manufacturers and retailers are highly sensitive to price signals, their strongest incentive is to respond to the preferences of the most affluent consumers who spend more and have greater environmental impact. Moreover, a perverse consequence of widespread adoption of less carbon-intensive practices among the affluent is a global price decline in fossil fuels, leading to an uptake in consumption elsewhere as energy generation becomes more affordable in new locations.

Another problem is that pinning hope on the cumulative decisions of ecologically conscientious consumers overestimates both the extent of consumer awareness and their willingness to act on that knowledge. There are serious limits to what consumers can be expected to know. The harm-causing processes often are largely invisible and the chain linking cause and effect is not readily legible. We may be sure that frequent transatlantic flights produce lots of greenhouse gases, but the carbon footprint of our seemingly innocuous daily activities often elude us.

Moreover, consumer knowledge is compromised by deliberate efforts to obfuscate scientific findings and undermine the credibility of science. Such strategies, familiar in the tobacco industry, are widespread in other commercial sectors. The aim of these "merchants of doubt" is to generate misinformation, thereby helping to postpone or head off regulatory action by preempting or tamping down public demands for testing, risk monitoring, disclosure, and mitigation.[11] When information relevant to informed decision is deliberately made more difficult to obtain and understand, the "let-the-consumer-decide" solution becomes even less plausible.

Also, the free market, free-for-all approach can only work if two conditions are satisfied. First, there must be good reasons to believe that letting individuals make their choices for themselves in the marketplace will lead to improvements in their well-being. That happy coincidence, of course, is undercut when the relevant

ENERGY TRANSITION PATHWAYS 221

information for prudent choice is withheld, misrepresented, or simply too complex for most consumers to assess. Second, the consumer choice model only works when the well-being of each consumer is strictly a function of individual choices. Of course, informed individuals can control some of their health risks (e.g., by choosing among dietary options or pharmaceuticals), assuming they have access to relevant information. However, for many other threats, only the management of risk through collective action will suffice. For example, no matter how much information individuals have, they cannot use the marketplace to select their own personal air quality. Climate change is no different. What matters is what we all do together, not what individuals choose for themselves, according to their own preferences. In these instances, market choice offers no adequate solution.

A consumer-driven approach also depends heavily on the prospect that greater public awareness of the disproportionate burdens of hazardous extraction, production, or disposal falling on residents of other countries or communities will motivate behavioral change among the affluent. However, at least in the near-term, increased awareness can overwhelm individuals and foster ecological quietism, a calm acceptance of things as they are, rather than increase motivation to resist or change things.[12] More generally, consumer culture as it currently exists would be unimaginable without the reinforcement of behavior by patterns of denial, indifference, or deliberate disregard for the fate of other people and the ecological limits of the planet.

Moreover, too often the consumer-driven approach seems to rest on the belief that behavioral change is largely an organic, spontaneous response to better information, including the effects that individual consumption imposes on others. However, it is now generally understood that comprehensive behavioral change does not occur without government policies that facilitate ecologically sustainable choices or eliminate otherwise avoidable demand for ecologically destructive products.[13] For example, the scope and scale

222 A LIVABLE PLANET

of transition from private passenger vehicles to public transport is very limited in the absence of public infrastructure investment, and avoidable emissions are not controlled without policies that tamp down demand for ecologically harmful goods and services, for example, by eliminating subsidies for meat production, banning short-distance domestic aviation routes, or restricting sales of inefficient appliances.[14]

The upshot is that success of a consumer choice model of social change depends on scientific knowledge that is often lacking or compromised, and, even when it filters into greater public awareness, it is unlikely be sufficient to drive behavioral change at the scale and pace required to avert our predicament, especially in the absence of a mixture of public policies that support green choices and remove other choices from the marketplace. Of course, individuals should change their consumption behaviors and encourage others to do so, but it is not a stand-alone pathway forward.

Enlightened Global Leadership

Perhaps the force of elite opinion can overcome obstacles that ordinary consumers cannot as easily surmount. Optimism of this sort fills the headlines when delegates to the UN's conference of parties (COP) meet to update their commitments under the framework for international agreement for cooperation on climate change. A familiar theme there and at annual gatherings of the World Economic Forum at Davos is the importance of leadership by the 20 or so nations responsible for roughly 80% of annual greenhouse emissions. However, history shows how soon hopes for leadership from the high-consumption nations are dashed.

Here are a few illustrative examples of the impediments to progress. Many of the roadblocks to timely decarbonization were engineered by developed nations, beginning at the 1992 Earth Summit, when the United Nations Framework Convention on

Climate Change (UNFCCC) was established. At the insistence of the United States and other developed nations, the Convention included no binding decarbonization commitments or timetable for action.

At the 2009 climate conference in Copenhagen, rich nations pledged US$100 billion a year by 2020 to help developing nations adapt to climate change and mitigate further temperature rises. However, the self-reports of donor countries reveal a significant shortfall, with actual contributions averaging 70–80% over each of the past few years.[15] Moreover, the reported contributions are widely viewed as inflated and unreliable. The donor country reports include a mix of market-rate loans for profitable private-sector mitigation projects, private-sector funds they take credit for having mobilized, and double-counted funds already appropriated for other foreign aid programs.[16] By some estimates, outright assistance grants—that the lowest-income countries most urgently need for adaptation projects—account for perhaps as little as one-third of the funds that donor nations report as their contribution to their annual pledges.[17] United Nations officials also conclude that an accurate accounting method, one based on "realistic scenarios," shows that contributions fall far short of the promised amounts, with no prospects for getting on track.[18]

Two examples of climate change politics put the 100-billion-dollar annual commitment into context. First, the 100-billion-dollar pledge, even if fully honored, pales in comparison to the roughly US$2 trillion needed annually by developing nations just to meet their Paris Agreement commitments for mitigation and adaptation.[19] Second, the top priorities of the economically developed countries are revealed by their energy subsidies. The estimated total of annual fossil fuel subsidies by the 52 countries that account for 90% of global supply is more than US$555 billion per year.[20]

Some observers of the UNFCC process see encouraging signs in the statement issued at the close of COP27 in 2022. A group of 134 developing countries known as the G-77+China successfully

224 A LIVABLE PLANET

negotiated a deal for the creation of a "loss and damage mechanism." The purpose is to establish a fund from which countries harmed by climate change could obtain financial relief for the impacts of the climate crisis that are too severe for countries to adapt to and are not prevented by mitigation efforts under the Paris Agreement. The agreement has been described as a breakthrough achievement insofar as it elevates issues of climate justice to the top of the agenda. However, victory is tempered by two considerations. First, the text and public statements by representatives of developed nations reaffirm Article 51 of the Paris Agreement, stating that the mechanism does not provide the basis for legal liability and that the funds it distributes are not intended as compensation based on historical emissions. Second, the agreement postponed resolution of central issues such as the mechanisms for collection and distribution of funds, its eligible recipients, and the amount and sources of funding. In other words, there was no admission of responsibility and no tangible commitment to action. In advance of COP28, host country representatives and news reports indicate progress in the creation of mechanisms for distributing voluntary contributions. But the true measure of progress will be the size of the financial commitment and how much of that commitment is fulfilled.

The reluctance of developed countries to extend meaningful assistance to nations most affected by climate disruption, coupled with the perpetuation of domestic fossil fuel subsidies, is part and parcel of a more general pattern of economic nationalism that has stifled other global initiatives for expanding assistance for economic development and poverty relief. For example, many developed countries that signed on to the Doha Declaration on Financing for Development and subsequent reaffirmations committed to dedicating 0.7% per annum of their gross national income to development assistance. But most countries fall far short. The percentage recently donated by the United States is a mere 0.217%, and the overall percentage for all donor countries in recent years has averaged approximately half of the promised contribution.[21]

ENERGY TRANSITION PATHWAYS 225

Moreover, a limitation inherent in assistance programs generally is the practice known as "tied aid." Developmental aid provided by the United States, United Kingdom, many of the EU countries, Japan, and China routinely come with strings attached. Some strings commit recipient nations to policy positions, such as birth control initiatives or economic liberalization of some sector of the economy, but the hallmark of tied aid is the requirement that recipient nations procure services and goods from companies based in donor nations. Instead of using aid to ramp up and solidify the domestic economic capacities of recipient nations, procurement restrictions advance the economic competitiveness objectives of donor countries. For example, legislative authorization for one of the main US food aid programs provides healthy subsidies to domestic farmers and mandates that 50% of the cargo ships that transport the food must be US-flagged vessels (employing 75% American labor). The result is shipping delay, food spoilage, and an estimated 60–175% additional cost to food, which could have been used to feed more people.[22]

Moreover, the disparity between international climate assistance and domestically subsidized emissions is mirrored in economic foreign policy generally. In the United States and elsewhere, foreign development aid is eclipsed by domestic industry subsidies. For example, agricultural subsidies in countries of the Organisation for Economic Cooperation and Development (OECD) alone are over three times the total foreign aid to developing nations.[23]

In short, the fierce economic nationalism that drives the foreign policies of developed nations is readily explicable and unlikely to abate. Political leaders are keenly aware of the electoral costs of any proposal that might result in sacrifices in standard of living or even the imposition of modest costs on consumer goods. Politicians act at their peril if they acknowledge that a more just and sustainable pathway to the future might disrupt ways of life that the global affluent often take for granted. Lasting progress on all fronts is stymied so long as the economically powerful entities and their

226 A LIVABLE PLANET

principal beneficiaries can maintain their way of life by turning their own problems into other people's problems or by simply ignoring the global consequences of their own actions. More generally, imagine the economic and political upheaval likely to ensue in developed nations—and major exporting nations—if the most affluent 20% of the global population, generating roughly three-quarters of the global GDP, adopted climate policies that reduce consumer spending. Hence, the enduring appeal of no-sacrifice solutions touted by both pro-market boosters and "green new deal" advocates.

Market-Driven Technological Innovation

An alternative view is that market dynamics can provide technological solutions to sustainability problems that neither enlightened politicians nor conscientious individual consumers can resolve. It combines two ingredients. The first is the market fundamentalists' belief that the real engine of social change is the profit motive. The second element is technological utopianism. It counts on the boundless nature of human ingenuity, believed to be sufficient incentive for finding new technologies that can cure any problem that might have been created by old technologies. They also argue that there is no socially viable alternative. Modern societies will not accept a decline in their material standard of living, especially if it means a return to a romanticized, pre-industrial existence.

Moreover, proponents of a market-driven approach to technological innovation also point to history in support of their case. Whatever problems humanity now faces, the history of progress over the past three centuries of capitalist social organization demonstrates the dynamism of markets and their capacity to improve the human condition. They point to the steady downward trend in the portion of world plagued by poverty, hunger, premature death, and numerous debilitating diseases, and even (by some

ENERGY TRANSITION PATHWAYS   227

metrics) the casualties of warfare.[24] History shows that human inventiveness has overcome seemingly insurmountable challenges, such as feeding an expanding world population. Time and again, they say, the technological pessimists, from Malthus to more recent exponents of the "limits to growth" thesis, have been proved wrong.

Probably everyone agrees on the importance of technological innovation. Even critics who reject the equation of a high material standard of living with human well-being, as well as those who rightly worry that the benefits of technology will not be widely shared or achieved at the expense of others, will agree on the need to explore an array of technological solutions. Examples are numerous. Desalination technology, if made less energy intensive and the infrastructure becomes less costly, would be a welcome addition to the toolkit for responding simultaneously to the planet's water crisis and climate crisis. Protein alternatives to meat could cut emissions and also reduce ecological pressures on soil, forests, and water. Phasing out hydrofluorocarbons in air conditioning and refrigeration devices could buy a lot of precious time in slowing the increase in atmospheric accumulation of greenhouse gases.

Many other potential technological options could be mentioned, but faith in markets to deliver these technologies in a timely manner is an entirely different matter. Even some proponents of sustainable capitalism argue that technological fixes generated by market incentives can liberate humanity from material poverty without sacrificing the rest of nature, but only if institutional guardrails are provided by well-functioning governments. Technological solutions require both economic support and direction from governments to get going, avoid the prospect that their benefits will come too late and help too few, and ensure that innovation does not shift ecological and economic burdens to other production sectors or societies.

Reasons for doubting that markets alone, without massive institutional support and regulation, can deliver a just and sustainable energy transition are based on an understanding of the ways

228 A LIVABLE PLANET

in which technology is diffused by market processes. As a rule, history shows that we can expect no widespread change in technology until new substitutes become more profitable and that the transition can be far slower than often supposed. For example, alternatives to coal as a source of electricity have been available for decades, but the share of global electricity generated by coal has remained constant, at just below 40%.[25] There are several marketplace reasons for its persistence. Often, there is no compelling business case for abandoning coal-fired electrical generating plants even if, as the evidence suggests, the price per kilowatt of new energy produced by solar has dropped—and is likely to drop even further—to less than half of the price of coal in many regions of the world.[26] As long as existing coal facilities have a useful life, and continued use allows the operator—whether public or private—to recoup "sunk" costs, a wholesale shift will not come about until the last marginal unit of economic value is extracted from old technology.

Of course, as demand for more electricity increases, reduced costs of operation, materials, and financing for solar will tilt new investment away from new coal-fired plants. The lower marginal cost of solar-generated electricity means that coal will be phased out by market forces, but it is not likely to go away fast enough if total energy demand continues to rise, as every plausible scenario predicts. Rising demand, together with the sunk costs problem, ensures a lag in the transition as new technology merely adds to rather than replaces the old.

Moreover, news headlines announcing that renewables are now the fastest growing share of new energy production ignore rebound effects described here and in earlier chapters. The positive effects of efficiency gains are often diminished or erased by a rebound in overall resource utilization. Coal production is one example, but there are many more. Because the total level of consumption determines ecological impact, it is essential to reduce overall consumption, not just make each unit of consumption greener.

ENERGY TRANSITION PATHWAYS 229

The transition to more efficient technologies generates new energy demands in the processes of production, along with additional material requirements, mostly in metals, minerals, concrete, and land. Even though new products may be more energy efficient for the consumer to operate, a full accounting of net ecological benefits must incorporate these behind-the-scenes impacts of new technology on emission levels and material use that occur much further back in the supply chains.[27] Building the new energy grid needed for renewable electricity to replace coal and oil will require more energy and more materials before net ecological benefits accrue.

In some instances, the rebound occurs in new locations. Even as coal generation facilities are retired from service in places where it no longer makes economic sense for the operator, it does not yet mean the end of coal globally. Both industry associations and independent experts assume that coal will help drive economic development in emerging nations for decades to come because their aggregate energy demand is expected to soar. Some countries will continue to rely on coal because it is a plentiful, cheap, and locally available resource that offers the added benefit of energy security. Pakistan and Poland are geopolitically relevant examples. Also, countries pursuing an aggressive export-led industrial policy rely heavily on the cheapest, most polluting forms of coal that some countries have shunned. And, until recently at least, countries that have begun phasing out their oldest coal burning facilities still finance the sale of their retired coal and processing equipment for foreign purchasers.[28] In short, one of the ironies of the downward pressure on demand for coal in some places is that it results in a global price drop that makes coal more attractive elsewhere in a world in which total energy demand is still rising. Coal is likely to die a slow death.

To sum up this section, there are lots of false hopes for solutions that simply won't do enough fast enough. Conscientious affluent consumers are not numerous enough and too slow in the pace of change that they can mobilize to make the timely difference we

230 A LIVABLE PLANET

need to save the planet from the incrementally rising harmful effects of climate disruption. The most enlightened political leaders of affluent nations are boxed in, unable to step much beyond what their least conscientious consumers and most powerful corporate interests will tolerate. Green capitalism is far less green than often assumed, and the reality of innovation is far from the romanticized ideal of what is achievable by nimble market maneuverers driven by profit motivations.

False Starts

New technologies also carry the risk of false starts. False starts are partial and non-durable solutions. They produce some positive results but only by shifting problems to another sphere of production or other communities or by postponing or perhaps magnifying the damage that later reappears. Technologists often refer to this phenomenon as technological "whack-a-mole." The phrase is derived from a North American arcade game. The object of the game is to use a wooden mallet to knock back mechanical animals as they pop up out of holes on the game board, only to reappear randomly from other holes. The metaphor points to recurring problems that arise in unexpected ways after implementing a fix for an initial problem, yielding only piecemeal or temporary results. The upshot is that genuinely sustainable solutions to one part of the cluster of ecological problems must be addressed in tandem with solutions to other ecological problems.

Renewable Energy Alternatives

A false start might involve a reduction in fossil fuel use achieved by alternate technologies that require higher water consumption, lead to more deforestation, destroy biosphere integrity, or even increase

ENERGY TRANSITION PATHWAYS   231

net atmospheric carbon. For example, recent research findings estimate that carbon capture technology sufficient to keep the climate crisis in check would double humanity's water footprint.[29] Another example is the Indonesian government's plan to introduce "co-firing" of coal plants using 10% biomass. An estimated 1 million hectares of forest would have to be cleared to provide wood pellets, and, at the outer bounds of the estimate, the new technology would result in vastly greater overall emissions.[30]

Dams provide a wide-ranging case in point. The construction of large dams and water diversion projects has been a strongly favored solution to unmet energy needs and freshwater shortages due to intermittent rainfall and the seasonal demand to store and conserve quantities of water sufficient for irrigation and other purposes, especially in countries reliant on freshwater for agriculture.

Large dams thus offer especially attractive energy solutions because they enable development of large-scale agricultural production, and they create the conditions for economic modernization. Run-of-the-river dams can provide both stable supplies of water and electricity necessary to meet the growing demands from rapidly expanding municipalities. They use hydroelectric plants to harness the natural flow of water to produce electrical power, typically with initial construction costs considerably less than many other comparably sized electricity generating facilities. It is thus no wonder that large dams became a symbol of civilizational achievement and a source of national pride in the late 20th century. Journalists and politicians routinely compare the size of newly constructed dams and reservoirs to the Hoover Dam built during the Great Depression.

Moreover, the attractiveness of large dams is enhanced by the fact that hydropower is currently viewed by many of its proponents as the largest renewable source of electricity (71% of global production of renewable energy).[31] A further advantage of hydropower is that, with proper reservoir management, it is not subject to intermittency, thus enabling utilities to balance load variations in the

232 A LIVABLE PLANET

electric distribution system. Moreover, it is estimated that less than a quarter of the global hydropower potential is exploited.[32]

However, at the moment of explosive growth in large dam construction in the Global South, many industrialized countries are decommissioning old dams because of their undesirable side effects. Dams often do great damage to both land-based agricultural production and harvesting of aquatic life for food.[33] Intact rivers support aquatic life and carry tons of silt containing nutrients needed for growing plants downstream, but dams result in river fragmentation, thereby reducing downstream soil fertility.

Dams not only block the movement of nutrients and sediment, but they result in poor water quality, deforestation, and biodiversity loss.[34] Dams destroy fish and wildlife habitats and damage coastal estuaries by changing the temperature, chemical composition, and dissolved oxygen levels of the water.[35] For example, 60% of the sediment needed to nourish Vietnam's rice paddies in the Mekong Delta could be blocked by a single dam in Cambodia and "would create a complete barrier to migratory fish."[36] One analysis found that if all the dams planned for the Mekong network are built, 97% of the sediment that once flowed to the river's mouth could be blocked by 2040, depriving massive quantities of land of nutrients needed for agriculture.[37]

In addition, the longer-term prospects for sustainable hydropower generation are clouded by climate change. For example, researchers say that many of the dams in Brazil are likely to produce far less electricity than anticipated. The Amazon Basin is predicted to receive less rainfall and face higher temperatures because of climate disruption, which in turn leads to further reduction of available water because of increased evaporation. Reduction in rainfall and water retention leads to deforestation, which is expected to exacerbate the water shortage problems for hydropower plants in the Amazon region.[38] As a result of extensive tree removal for construction, the forest's water recycling mechanism is undercut and rendered more vulnerable to the ill effects of drought.

ENERGY TRANSITION PATHWAYS   233

The more trees die, the less rain falls, which in turn makes tree die-offs worse.[39] Similar concerns have been raised about hydroelectric power generating dams in the Volta River Basin in Africa. Climate researchers anticipate that temperature rise over the next century could lead to a 20% decrease in rainfall, along with increased water loss from evaporation, resulting in a net 45% reduction in water flows needed to run the turbines.[40]

In short, dams are a classic case showing the potential for creating whack-a-mole problems. Dams often fail to achieve their intended goals in a sustainable manner, sometimes work at cross purposes to other environmental and food security goals, and routinely produce benefits for some communities at the expense of others. Moreover, enthusiasm for new dam construction ignores the extent of difference in their expected economic benefits around the world. A recent analysis of the impacts of 631 hydropower dams ($\geq$1-megawatt capacity) constructed since 2001 found that newly constructed dams were associated with increased GDP in North America as well as other environmental and economic benefits for urban areas in Europe but with decreased GDP and greater costs due to environmental impacts in the Global South.[41]

The point of this discussion is not that the case against dams is conclusive in all instances. Far from it. The example merely illustrates the importance of avoiding the risks of exacerbating the initial problem and other crises by attempting to solve problems in isolation or without full accounting of potential spillover effects. The lesson is that we must remain attuned to the fact that our ecological predicament is a cluster of concurrent, causally intertwined, mutually reinforcing crises.

Looking forward, the potential for generating similarly troublesome whack-a-mole problems is illustrated by the shift to electric vehicles. The transition might reduce reliance on fossil fuels to power automobiles and trucks, but it does require massive quantities of scarce minerals that have to come from new and expanded sites of extraction. The new material requirements mean new sources of

234　A LIVABLE PLANET

water, air, and soil pollution; more deforestation; more human dislocation; and, initially at least, more emissions from the fossil fuels used for extraction and production.[42] In addition, electric vehicle use perpetuates land use patterns that are unsustainable, first because of the extended land footprint of the highways and, second, due to the expanded land footprint of human settlements created by urban sprawl.[43] In short, solutions that maintain existing residential patterns and preserve jobs have much appeal, but there is a risk of ignoring the environmental problems it leaves in place as well as the ones it generates in new places.

Offshoring Emissions and Trading Carbon Offsets

False starts also include solutions that are non-durable and incomplete in a somewhat different sense. Some attempted solutions merely geographically relocate the problems to other groups of people, rather than mitigating problems on a planetary scale. Similar examples in Chapters 6 and 7 show how nations achieve a high degree of decoupling of consumption from environmentally destructive or resource intensive domestic production by offshoring those activities. For example, while emissions produced within the United Kingdom's borders declined by 41% between 1990 and 2016, a whopping 46% of the emissions attributable to UK consumption were produced overseas in 2016, compared with 14% in 1990.[44]

Offshoring of emissions is merely a recent example of an old and more general pattern of international economic interaction. Industrial nations are able to obtain what has been called "ecological relief," or as it is also called "environmental load displacement." Ecological relief for one country is based on its ability to displace the environmental load (i.e., burden) that would have accompanied home country extraction, production, or waste disposal. One of the things that gave Britain a great head start as it industrialized was its

ENERGY TRANSITION PATHWAYS   235

ability to remove large parts of its own land from the production of food (grains, livestock), energy (firewood, charcoal), and fiber (wool, cotton) by importing these goods from its colonies.[45] The specifics change over time, but the phenomenon of environmental load displacement continues today.

Indeed, there is a considerable body of evidence suggesting that no nation has been successful in achieving a substantial degree of decoupling without the negative consequences of consumption or production showing up on the environmental accounting ledger of other nations.[46] Industrial nations have reduced their own domestic carbon footprint, water footprint, and materials footprint by transferring the ecological consequences of their consumption to other countries. From a planetary perspective, the implication is clear. Given the likelihood that environmental burdens of consumption have been offloaded to other less-affluent communities, the global affluent have precautionary reasons to consume less, not just consume products that are greener in one way or another for their own communities. Such reasons are reinforced by a point made earlier, that consumers have very little power over (or understanding of) the environmentally damaging decisions made along spatially extended supply chains.[47]

Similar problems are inherent in the global trade in *carbon offsets*. Carbon offsets—the purchase of carbon sinks as a way of decreasing the net carbon footprint of a country or corporation—purport to help both industrialized countries and less-developed countries and further global emissions goals. Many national net-zero pledges pursuant to the Paris Climate Agreement depend on extraterritorial contributions of carbon offsets to compensate for otherwise unabated domestic emissions. Article 6.2 of the Agreement establishes a market mechanism. Countries that have excess carbon sinks, defined as carbon sequestering resources that reduce their net emissions below the targets in their climate pledges, can sell their surplus to countries failing to meet their own domestic climate goals.

236 A LIVABLE PLANET

Businesses, like countries trying to meet their Paris Agreement commitments, can offset their high emissions by purchasing or leasing overseas land that sequesters carbon, thereby reducing their net emissions.[48] The carbon offset could be achieved by various sequestration mechanisms, including preservation of existing forest cover, peat bogs, or mangroves; undertaking regeneration projects for degraded land; or implementing improved management of cropland.

One objection to offset markets is sometimes referred to as *carbon colonialism*. In essence, the claim is that this trading mechanism is unfair, constituting a form of ecological relief obtained at the expense of poor nations. Nations that got rich by generating climate altering emissions now want nations that are typically hurt first and worst by climate disruption to preserve their carbon sequestering land, thus foregoing industrialization and resource extraction so that the wealthy nations can continue with business as usual. The unfairness objection focuses on the fact the sellers assume the ecological burdens of other countries' production, undertaken largely for the benefit of the global affluent who make no sacrifice in lifestyle beyond the marginal costs of offsets added to the price of consumer goods.

In addition to objections to the unfairness of offset markets, there are reasons for doubt about the integrity of claims made for carbon sequestration at nearly every stage of the process. Examples include offset credits for not harvesting forests that would not have been cleared anyway and inflated estimates of carbon sequestered by forests or cropland management techniques. Purchasers can make valid claims of offsetting only if they remove carbon dioxide that otherwise would have been absorbed into the atmosphere, but the lack of technical and logistic abilities to measure and monitor the results makes it inherently prone to abuse, not to mention the increased potential for wishful thinking and greenwashing.[49]

Even if there were solutions to problems in verifying how much carbon is removed, the success of any underlying scheme of carbon

ENERGY TRANSITION PATHWAYS   237

sequestration depends on how long the croplands are maintained or how long the forests are protected from clearing or remain free from depletion by natural causes. Moreover, recent analyses of pledges of countries eager to sell their extra carbon sinks to foreign buyers searching for offsets for their high-emissions activities reveal some remarkable—indeed, incredible—claims regarding the size of their surplus. For example, the Central African Republic reported 1.8 billion tons of carbon absorbed by its forests annually, which analysts at the *Washington Post* describe as "an immense and improbable amount that would effectively offset the annual emissions of Russia."[50] In addition, the growth of a global market for carbon offsets has wider ecological implications. Because the market value is based on the presumed capacity for carbon sequestration, the dominant incentive for potential purchasers is to opt for the lowest-priced offsets, which tend to be the least reliable options.

Working Group 3 of the Intergovernmental Panel on Climate Change (IPCC)'s Sixth Assessment Report amplifies concerns about the potential consequences of overreliance on both nature-based carbon sequestration techniques and a suite of carbon dioxide removal (CDR) technologies more generally. Although the authors assume that there are no scenarios where warming can remain below 2°C without CDR technologies and carbon offsets— for dealing with hard-to-abate emissions from industries such as concrete and steel production—large-scale deployments "could obstruct near-term emission reduction efforts, mask insufficient policy interventions, might lead to an overreliance on technologies that are still in their infancy, could overburden future generations, might evoke new conflicts over equitable burden-sharing, [and] could impact food security, biodiversity or land rights."[51]

To sum up: less overall consumption becomes a moral imperative in a world in which there are more people buying more goods (the rebound effect), often creating new environmental problems in other productive sectors of the economy (the whack-a-mole problem), and routinely relying on other countries and

238 A LIVABLE PLANET

communities to offload the ecological consequences of their heavy consumption or offset their high emissions from production (environmental load displacement).

Path Dependencies

A sustainable energy transition faces multiple problems of path dependencies, patterns of behavior or institutional organization that lock in existing social and economic relations and constrain options for the future.[52] Some obstacles to change are largely a function of private business decisions about the most profitable market opportunities, while other obstacles are rooted in fiscal and political incentives that drive governmental decisions.

Market Obstacles to Change

Three sets of examples illustrate some of the many market-based reasons that incumbent technologies of all kinds are difficult to displace from their prominent marketplace position.

In the first set of examples, products that have been banned or are no longer marketable in highly regulated economies are not removed from the global market if profitable sales opportunities remain in place elsewhere. Environmentally hazardous products routinely end up in lower-income jurisdictions due to the combined effect of weak regulatory systems in both exporter and importer nations. Pesticides are a classic example. EU and UK manufacturers take advantage of regulatory gaps—in reality, carefully crafted concessions to manufacturers—that permit them to export highly toxic pesticides that are illegal to sell or use in the countries of origin but legally permitted in less stringently regulated countries.[53] An example relevant to decarbonization pathways is the production of low-quality, highly toxic diesel fuel, unabashedly labeled as

"African quality" by global commodity traders. The fuel is specially formulated by companies based in European countries, where it is banned; often produced at offshore locations; and intended solely for export to Africa and other countries lacking adequate regulations on its harmful impacts.[54] It is high in carbon emissions and a major source of local air pollution.

In a second set of examples, efforts to replace wasteful, unsustainable, or non-durable consumer products are thwarted by corporate strategies that perpetuate older, ecologically damaging technologies. Planned obsolescence is one corporate strategy, for example, shown in the widely cited decision to decrease the strength of fibers in nylon stockings to prompt consumers to buy more and in a collusive agreement among manufacturers to increase sales by shortening the life span of incandescent lightbulbs from 2,500 hours to 1,000 hours. Although genuine instances of planned obsolescence are not always distinguishable from more straightforward cases in which products are superseded by ones having superior or more highly valued design features, market incentives for keeping consumers eager to buy more and newer goods are strong. Whether or not obsolescence is a consequence of deliberate product churning—new product designs solely for the sake of generating profits from new sales—businesses have multiple reasons for manufacturing products with shortened lifecycles. Non-durable materials lower production costs, make products cheaper and available to more customers, raise profit margins, and generate repeat sales.

Plastic, made from petrochemicals, is an example of another way the proliferation of non-durable consumer goods perpetuates ecologically unsustainable business models. Indeed, plastics are expected to provide a lifeline to petrochemicals and the future of the fossil fuel industry. For those who already view plastic as an important environmental problem, the connection to fossil fuels may not be among the first things that come to mind. More often, news coverage features the giant garbage patch in the Pacific Ocean or the

240　A LIVABLE PLANET

non-biodegradable waste that clogs landfills and litters coastlines and even remote mountain peaks.[55] However, a potentially bigger long-term problem is due to the fact that plastics are made primarily from petrochemical stocks, and petrochemical demand is expected to account for a third of the growth in global oil demand by 2030 and rise to half by 2050.[56] If these projections are anywhere near accurate, it means that plastics and other petrochemical products will keep the fossil fuel industry alive, ensuring that hydrologic fracking and the greenhouse gases it adds to the atmosphere will continue beyond the likely phase-out period for the combustion engine in automobiles. Simply put, there can be no carbon-neutral economy without eliminating production of plastics that are responsible for the "practically irreversible" adverse changes to carbon and nutrient cycles and the contamination of soils, sediments, and aquatic ecosystems.[57]

Examples showing how ecologically unsustainable market practices are perpetuated, whether through changes in marketing, artificially shortening the useful life of products, or preserving a flawed business model by expanding the product line, also show the extent to which consumer options depend on the somewhat opaque market incentive structure of producers. The producers make the big social decisions which define the parameters within which the decisions of everyone else are made. They use a range of market strategies to steer consumer preferences in the direction of greater profitability. And they choose technology with an eye to the advantages that accrue from significant global discrepancies in purchasing power. They select their markets for sale of high tech-products based on who has the means to pay. For these reasons, the diffusion of technology for the benefit of humankind tends to lag and the older, ecologically damaging technologies live on.

These first two sets of examples also offer guidance for thinking about the future. We are not only locked into existing, costly, difficult to replace technologies, but our choice of transitional technologies in the near term also will dictate the pathway forward.

ENERGY TRANSITION PATHWAYS   241

Any miscalculation or well-meaning but flawed strategy for solving problems, such as phasing out fossil fuels by substituting slightly less dirty fuels, risks locking in a new bundle of technologies that can make further transition that much more difficult and protracted.

In a third set of examples, corporations routinely manage market risks by using general legal rules or contractual provisions, such as those shielding them from economic loss from regulation or legal liability for "consequential damages"—the label lawyers attach to the harms caused by products. In some cases, these legal rules extend immunity from liability during a product phase-out period or guarantee that any losses triggered by lawsuits or government regulation are reimbursed from public funds.

Other little-known elements of the legal architecture of the global economy also give businesses a way to lessen the sting of the well-known problem of "stranded assets." The stranded assets problem refers to the long-term risk that oil and gas fields, coal mines, and other components of the fossil fuel energy production infrastructure will become corporate liabilities once renewables overtake them. Fears of declining revenues and devaluated assets are genuine business concerns, but their potential for motivating timely change is offset somewhat by the variety of available legal solutions that allow corporations to continue with business as usual.

For example, businesses often lobby on legislation that affects their ability to extend the life of their environmentally destructive operations. Efforts to pass new legislation imposing legal liability for damages due to local environmental harm or climate disruption have been vigorously opposed by industry trade associations around the world. Moreover, investors have plenty of existing legal rules that protect them against losses caused by emissions regulations that might jeopardize the profitability of their operations or force an early closure. National laws regulating extractive industries often require leaseholders to keep producing for the

242 A LIVABLE PLANET

benefit of owners of royalty rights or have a financial stake under license agreements. Mineral or oil rights leases often contain similar contractual provisions, and the effect in both cases is to extend the life span of production even when it involves short-term financial loss to the operator. For example, when the price of natural gas fell in the United States, fracking continued on economically unproductive lease sites and profitability rebounded as global energy supplies dwindled.

Alternatively, companies can invoke investor–state dispute settlement clauses to blunt the threat of governmental regulations that they are not able to stop by reliance on new or existing legislation. For example, bilateral trade agreements described in Chapter 5, as well as provisions of the multilateral Energy Charter Treaty, give investors access to special courts, using legal rules highly beneficial to foreign corporations, to sue governments for losses caused by regulatory policies adopted after the investment.[58]

Business-friendly provisions contained in bilateral trade agreements, the Energy Charter Treaty, and existing domestic laws, together with the ability to craft favorable (or defeat unfavorable) new laws are neither unusual in global markets nor matters of marginal ecological significance. Legal mechanisms are routinely used to tie the hands of governments, protect investors from economic losses due to prospective regulation, and help prolong the life span of environmentally destructive technologies.

A study by the International Institute for Environment and Development found that, of 257 foreign-owned coal power plants worldwide, at least three-quarters enjoy some kind of investor–state dispute settlement provision.[59] Also, a non-governmental organization (NGO) study tracking the scale and pace of pending litigation shows that the potential sums at stake could exceed current transfers of climate adaptation funds pledged by developed nations.[60] In fact, the threat of litigation or exit from the jurisdiction, given the advantages possessed by the cadre of specialty lawyers who litigate and often draft the key provisions of international and

ENERGY TRANSITION PATHWAYS 243

bilateral treaties, is usually sufficient to force the hand of would-be regulators.

The upshot is that transnational businesses and their lawyers have very many not widely recognized legal advantages allowing them to perpetuate profitable but ecologically harmful business activities. They can sell their products in markets not legally foreclosed, utilize new or existing legislation or invoke provisions of treaty agreements to protect themselves against stranded assets or avoid liability for ecologically harmful activities, or move their operations to escape legal liability that courts might impose for climate or other environmental harms.

Governmental Obstacles to Change

States often have their own direct incentives for preserving the status quo in energy markets. Tax revenues and the overall health of the economy are tied to the fate of oil, gas, and coal industries in countries that engage in high levels of exploration, production, and operation of wells and mines. Fossil fuel energy also figures prominently in the portfolios of many sovereign wealth funds, as well as in the investments of private employer-based pensions that many governments depend on to top up perennially underfunded state-sponsored retirement funds.

Moreover, states themselves are major players in the oil and gas sector. Nineteen of the 26 top oil and gas companies are partly or fully nationalized.[61] More importantly, they respond to a somewhat different set of incentives than their private-sector competitors. While multinational companies are under pressure from lenders, shareholders, and activists to speed up their transition to clean energy, the giant state-owned companies in the Middle East, Africa, and Latin America do not answer to shareholders. In hierarchically ordered political regimes, they are not accountable to voters. Often, they are not beholden to banks for financing new operations

244   A LIVABLE PLANET

because they can tap into cheaper, government-issued bonds. In many instances, state-owned energy enterprises are responsive primarily to internal fiscal pressures to increase production to raise revenue for paying down sovereign debt or financing government operations.[62] Their strongest incentive is to keep on pumping and mining, and there is not much countervailing pressure to change course.

National security interests also figure in the calculus of national energy policies, especially in countries that invest heavily in the military. Estimates of military emissions are subject to some guesswork because they have been shielded from scrutiny. The "national security provision" in the original 1998 Kyoto Protocol (adopted at the insistence of the United States) provided for a blanket exemption of military emissions from inclusion in national carbon dioxide reduction targets and reporting requirements. Although the loophole was partially closed in the 2015 Paris Climate Agreement, governments are not required to provide full data on greenhouse gases emitted by their armed forces. Nevertheless, it is indisputable that big military spenders like the United States, China, Russia, Saudi Arabia, and France have a substantial carbon footprint. For example, the US armed forces—the largest institutional source of greenhouse gases in the world—would rank somewhere between the 47th and 55th worst emitter in the world if it were a country.[63] Even without going to war, the constant readiness for warfare generates massive emissions. The US Pentagon, for example, maintains buildings on more than a half million bases around the world; uses fossil fuels to power its armored vehicles, helicopters, jet fighters, and fleets of vessels; and it manages an extensive network of container ships and cargo planes to supply its operations.

When looked at from another perspective, the Pentagon accounts for only a small percentage of greenhouse gas emissions in the United States.[64] However, the raw numbers do not tell the whole story. It has "locked itself into hydrocarbon-based weapons systems for years to come by depending on existing aircraft and warships for open-ended operations."[65] The military's path-dependent, carbon-based energy policy also narrows the feasible energy options for other productive sectors of the economy. The military is an economic behemoth that entrenches the technology used by a global network of suppliers and contractors. They must align their own systems if they are to provide services, fuels, and compatible components.

Some media reports suggest a somewhat rosier picture of how both public and private entities might escape the grip of path dependencies. For example, much is made of the fact that funding for sustainable energy alternatives is not financially out of reach. A widely cited report calculated that $570 billion will be spent on new oil and gas development and exploration annually between 2020 and 2030. Some observers noted that if these funds were invested in wind and solar energy, it would be sufficient to bridge the US$450 billion annual funding gap to displace oil and gas production in line with the 1.5°C goal.[66] For now, at least, the trend is moving in the opposite direction. The United States is in the forefront of this investment boom. Energy expert Gus Speth estimates that the United States "is expanding oil and gas extraction on a scale at least four times faster and greater than any other nation and is currently on track to account for 60% of global growth in oil and gas production."[67]

Even if states and private businesses were to redirect all those development funds, there is another obstacle hidden behind the headlines. Replacing our current fossil-fuel–based industrial system will require a massive quantity of energy, mostly from existing fossil fuels that account for 83% of current global energy needs. For the foreseeable future, we will rely heavily on these existing energy sources "to mine materials; transport and transform them through industrial processes like smelting; turn them into [and install] solar panels, wind turbines, batteries, vehicles, infrastructure, and industrial machinery."[68]

This section illustrates some of the many path-dependent obstacles to a sustainable energy transition. Incumbent technologies

246   A LIVABLE PLANET

are difficult to displace because of the sunk costs of producers, the ability of companies to perpetuate the use of old technologies or offload them to other jurisdictions, the ubiquity of components in a range of products that make substitutions unfeasible, the legal options for protecting against liability for ecological harm and the risk of stranded assets, and the geopolitical motivations of states and other stakeholders for maintaining existing technologies. These examples also reinforce points from earlier sections. Individual consumers have limited capacity to bring about necessary changes in political and legal culture through the marketplace. Financial incentives work against an enlightened business response, and the range for diplomatic maneuvering among states is highly restricted. Moreover, the kinds of purely technological solutions proposed for escaping our ecological predicament risk creating or compounding other ecological crises or shifting problems to other communities.

Human Rights and Alternative Pathways

This chapter thus far has surveyed the extent to which an energy transition is stymied by a combination of entrenched market practices, economic self-interest, and national priorities, all underwritten by ideological commitments that favor continuation of business as usual. It does not inspire optimism. Or, more accurately, it casts doubt on the ability and willingness of global affluent individuals, countries, and corporations to take the necessary and timely steps toward decarbonization. In other words, the prospects of change initiated from the top down are tempered by the existence of vested interests, entrenched power, settled expectations for a way of life among the global affluent, and institutional inertia.

The case for a fundamental, advocacy-driven change of course, as recommended by the human rights approach, is reflected in an open letter to the Secretariat of the United Nations Framework Convention on Climate Change (UNFCCC). On October 12, 2022,

ENERGY TRANSITION PATHWAYS 247

the Business & Human Rights Resource Centre & Indigenous Peoples' Rights International (IPRI) submitted comments on behalf of more than 200 signatories from a wide range of movements and organizations working for climate justice, human rights, labor rights, and corporate accountability. The letter called for a just energy transition that centers on human rights as an alternative to a "neoliberal climate agenda that maintains existing industrial models . . . and expects communities that contributed the least to the climate crisis to bear the brunt of the transition, without benefiting from it and without being able to shape it."[69]

For real progress, according to the letter, we need a broader recognition "that human rights are central to the climate response," and it argues that "the profit driven extractive model has entrenched and exacerbated inequality, and contributed to driving conflict, environmental damage, attacks on communities and defenders, while simultaneously playing a significant role in emissions."

Specifically, the letter emphasizes several policy implications of its human rights agenda: protecting "the individual and collective rights of customary land rights holders"; priority for ensuring "the safety of human rights, labor and environmental defenders"; enactment of legislation "to put an end to the most egregious corporate abuses"; the urgency of "mov[ing] away from the extraction-to-exhaustion model of production"; and "centering the human rights of Indigenous Peoples, frontline communities, and workers throughout the renewable energy value chain."

In the words of one of the letter's signatories, the International Federation for Human Rights (FIDH), "the core message . . . is that the energy transition needs to be just, in particular for Indigenous and other frontline communities, otherwise it will continue to be resisted, delayed, and will ultimately fail." Their conclusion mirrors the argument from Chapter 4. Although the implementation of a human rights approach faces many steep obstacles and offers no guarantee of success, a pathway out of our ecological predicament is unimaginable without it.

248   A LIVABLE PLANET

Perhaps most importantly, the human rights agenda proposed in the open letter has an additional merit. It does not depend on the generosity of institutions and individuals or the virtue of other countries and corporations. Their demand is for what I described in Chapter 4 as an institutional framework for ecological self-defense, a bulwark that communities can use against the worst forms of economically predatory market practices that subvert the ecological conditions essential for the secure realization of human rights. The aim of institutionalization will not be achieved overnight, and it will happen only if instigated from the grassroots.

9

Control over the Future

Throughout this book, I have argued that a transition to a more just and sustainable global political economy requires reconfiguration of the roles of states and markets in shaping the terms of collective social life. The goal of transformational change is enhancement of the ability of states, individually and collectively, to secure the high-priority, dual-purpose human rights that protect the ecological conditions that sustain human life and make possible the satisfaction of basic needs. When implemented through an effective institutional enforcement scheme, these rights form a bulwark against economically predatory, ecologically destructive market practices. An enforceable human rights agenda enables states to counteract corporations and other entities seeking to undermine sovereignty over natural resources, interfere with environmental and social welfare policies, derive profit from extractive activities and speculative investments, and game the fragmented system of states for private advantage.

Human rights also confer upon individuals more power over their ecological futures. They constrain policy tradeoffs that compromise prospects for survival or sacrifice basic human needs, reduce the opportunities for governmental complicity with extractive enterprises, and impose wide-ranging duties on states to protect human welfare interests at risk from ecologically consequential investment, production, and waste disposal decisions.

Even in the absence of robust enforcement mechanisms and diligent efforts by governments to fulfil their duties to protect, a human rights perspective provides citizens and activists with moral criteria for diagnosing and campaigning against unjust and

A Livable Planet. Madison Powers, Oxford University Press. © Oxford University Press 2024.
DOI: 10.1093/oso/9780197756003.003.0009

250 A LIVABLE PLANET

unsustainable market practices and public policies, especially those pertaining to the acquisition, control, and use of land, energy, and water resources.

More generally, a human rights agenda differs from proposed solutions to our ecological predicament that leave existing social relations and patterns of power in place. Rights generate justifiably enforceable demands for institutional mechanisms that check concentrated market power and entrenched political power. The enhanced level of human rights protection for the ecological conditions that sustain life and well-being matters crucially because humanity can no longer continue with business as usual. There is no time for indulging in false hopes, betting on solutions that depend on citizens of the world's largest economies voluntarily foregoing the near-term benefits derived from long-term ecological destruction. And there is no pathway to progress through false starts, solutions that provide some benefits but only by transferring problems from one sphere of economic activity to another, typically impinging on human rights in a different way or transferring ecological problems to other communities whose rights are sacrificed for the benefit of the powerful and the fortunate.

We conclude by arguing that the targeted human rights approach is superior to many alternatives, but two features that commend it also pose obstacles to its success: its direct confrontation with entrenched economic power and the indispensability of political transformation within states.

Wealth and Power

The root of our ecological predicament is not simply that the affluent consume too much, but that they control too much. Concentrated wealth shapes private investment and production decisions that determine our collective ecological fate. Human rights, by contrast, redistribute power away from concentrated

CONTROL OVER THE FUTURE 251

capital held by corporations or accumulated disproportionately in some countries. An effectively implemented human rights agenda not only establishes a social welfare floor that the powerful may not encroach for the sake of other goals. It also expands the scope of state responsibility for protecting the human rights of its residents.

More specifically, the fulfilment of these expanded responsibilities requires states to make two transformational changes in the institutional basis of their economies. First, it requires states to re-regulate or, in some instances, prohibit market practices having the potential for outsized ecological impact and dissolve concentrations of economic power that fuel predatory advantage-seeking market behavior. Second, it requires states to remove some key ecologically impactful decisions from the discretionary judgment of private entities, for example, because of the outsized effect of concentrated wealth on public investment and tax policy, channeling resources toward some economic beneficiaries and clustering ecological burdens elsewhere.

Concentrated wealth locks into place international and intergenerational power relations, leaving control over the future in the hands of many of those who seek to flee the regulatory reach of state jurisdictions. They rely upon tax havens and other legal mechanisms to preserve wealth and escape democratic accountability for the activities that have increasingly global impact.

Concentrated wealth gives too much decisional power to philanthropies and dynastic foundations that may do good work at the margins of big problems. However, their control over extensive resources gives them power to block structural transformation. They exercise outsized control over the public conversation about social change, perhaps inadvertently preserving the power of those who often did the most to create—and benefited the most from—the economic and ecological problems humanity faces.[1] The assertion of human rights, not more generous charitable giving or international assistance, is the only reliable way to alter patterns of control.

252 A LIVABLE PLANET

Concentrated wealth shapes seemingly ordinary patterns of social organization that have large and durable ecological impact on the rights of the least well-off, which often go unnoticed or unchallenged by affluent beneficiaries. For example, the environmental influence of socioeconomic stratification is reflected in the grids of human settlements in rich and poor countries alike. Costly and ecologically damaging conveniences enjoyed by the affluent routinely take priority over the necessities of the poor. The informal settlements of the Global South lack the essential services provided to their affluent urban neighbors. The social investments in infrastructure for transportation and water treatment and sanitation predominantly track the preferences of the most affluent political constituents rather than the needs of the least well-off. In both the Global South and Global North, the ecological burdens of material well-being are clustered in heavily polluted and impoverished frontline communities abutting coal fields, oil and gas production facilities, and chemical processing plants. Suburban flight of middle classes in affluent countries leads to investment of scarce resources in extensive systems of highways and connector roads used for private transport, thereby draining resources that could have been spent for broadly beneficial railways and public transportation.

Even rather mundane public utility decisions in the Global North are relevant to the capacities of states to fulfil their human rights responsibilities. Three examples are illustrative. Vast quantities of water are diverted for building and maintaining golf courses in the desert, just miles from tribal reservations without the basic infrastructure for supplying households with running water and sanitation services. Residential lawns are the most heavily irrigated crop in the United States, requiring more water than corn, wheat, and fruit orchards combined, and keeping all that turf alive can account for 50–75% of residential water bills; ultimately, they are hidden subsidies for the affluent and they result in high infrastructure costs that could have been directed to meeting basic water and sanitation needs.[2] Direct farm subsidies disproportionately benefit

CONTROL OVER THE FUTURE   253

large landowners, incentivize the expansion of the land footprint of food production, and promote ecologically destructive agricultural practices that tend to undermine societal goals of food security for all.

Many other specific examples of the unequal ecological burdens built into the fabric of daily life are manifested throughout the world are surveyed in earlier chapters, but the overall lesson is clear. Protection of strategically important, dual-purpose human rights is essential for the environmental self-defense of economically disempowered communities everywhere. A higher priority for securing these rights would help put an end to unsustainable market decisions that stem from and reinforce the divergence between the recipients of economic benefits and the communities that bear the ecological burdens.

In some respects, lessons from the study of political economy, once widely understood in the earliest days of the explosive growth of capitalism, need to be relearned. Even its venerable champion, Adam Smith, offers a damning explanation of the dark origins and stubborn persistence of its differentially advantaging institutions. "Civil government, so far as it is instituted for the security of property," he claimed, "is instituted for the defence of the rich against the poor, or of those who have some property against those who have none at all."[3] In other words, Smith is reminding us that the institutions of the state are often designed for and, at the very least, easily converted into instruments through which both privilege and privation are created and sustained side by side. Because state institutions play such an important role in maintaining the status of powerful classes, a pathway to a more just and sustainable future depends on the ability of adversely affected communities to mobilize their own states to become the guarantors of the human rights of the less powerful economic classes.

A human rights perspective therefore brings to the forefront the question of who exercises control over the future. Robust implementation of social and economic rights not only requires

254 A LIVABLE PLANET

reversal of the power relations between states and markets. It also involves a transformation of power relations between the affluent and everyone else, as well as changes in who controls state power.

To be sure, many adverse ecological changes and localized environmental damages are, to some degree, unintended and unforeseen. However, accounts of the onset of the Anthropocene too often convey the misleading impression that our ecological predicament just crept up when no one was looking. That said, it is not necessary to definitively resolve the question of how much causal impact is attributable to a combination of hubris and lack of foresight and how much is due to deliberate, well-considered economic decisions designed to differentially benefit the affluent. Instead, we only need to take note of the continuing relevance of John Dewey's insight that "it is demonstrable that many of the obstacles to change which have been attributed to human nature are in fact due to the inertia of institutions and to the voluntary desire of powerful classes to maintain the existing status."[4] Power relations tend to remain in place, however they arose. They go unchallenged, and the holders of power strive to make sure it goes unquestioned. As corporate law theorist Adolf A. Berle famously observed, it is only on rare occasions that people ask, "Why should this man, or this group hold power?"[5]

Already, we have ceded an enormous amount of power to a few who hold the fate of the planet in their hands. Change will never come if we wait for the powerful to voluntarily relinquish power or exercise it for the benefit of the common good. Frederick Douglass was right: "Power concedes nothing without a demand. It never did and it never will."[6] His remark captures the essence of human rights: they make justifiably enforceable demands on the powerful.

Because human rights pose such a direct challenge to established power relations, this approach faces obstacles not encountered by more conciliatory alternatives. However, decisions regarding the basis of modern life and the fate of the planet carry too much risk or too much uncertainty to be left to a free market free-for-all, where the rule of the economically stronger routinely prevails.

Sovereign States and Global Problems

The recommendation to re-empower states is proposed as a first step in a transition to a more just and sustainable global political economy. For now, the state is an indispensable vehicle for change. Nothing more. Nevertheless, the arguments for and against giving more power to states are instructive. They provide guidance for taking advantage of their strengths, and they offer warnings for navigating the obstacles created by the internal organization of states and the overall structure of the system of sovereign states.

The first point to note is that states remain in existence not only because of entrenched power that supports them, but because of their potential usefulness. Indeed, state sovereignty is an ideal that has been widely endorsed across the political spectrum. At the end of World War I, for example, Woodrow Wilson placed great weight on national self-determination in crafting the League of Nations, but only for "great nations," while Lenin argued along similar lines on behalf of states emerging from colonial rule.[7] National self-determination generally and sovereign control over natural resources specifically were central elements of the political platforms of the next wave of newly decolonized states in the late 20th century. Nations in Africa and elsewhere in the Global South embraced national self-determination as central to "a new international economic order."[8]

Moreover, the diverse proponents of national self-determination often recite many of the same arguments. States provide an arena for democratic deliberation about matters of collective concern.[9] They facilitate a sense of solidarity that can encourage social cooperation and induce a willingness of co-nationals to make sacrifices for the common good and the least well-off.[10] National self-determination is instrumental for counteracting the predations of yet more powerful states and various transnational entities that possess asymmetric economic bargaining advantages and exercise state-like power over some aspects of the global order.

Proponents of national self-determination also seize upon the weaknesses of the alternatives. They reject arguments for the creation of supranational institutions that replace state sovereignty with global institutions or selectively supersede their authority on matters such as climate change. One the most powerful arguments against a world state, or even significant concessions of sovereignty, is the potential for entrenchment of governmental oppression more difficult to escape than the grip of unaccountable, self-perpetuating political hierarchies within states. Cosmopolitan theorists who favor replacement of the existing states system with some form of global democracy must reckon with added worries about the reduced potential for effective grassroots organization and advocacy in vastly larger-scale polities, especially if composed of more diverse members.

More significantly, the nature of our ecological predicament means that time is not on the side of proponents of any of the global governance alternatives. If there is any doubt on this point, one only needs to look at state resistance to modest demands for transparency and accountability in international climate policy negotiations and the rise of European skepticism about political and economic integration. Enhanced state power therefore remains the default option for change.

Nonetheless, any solution that assigns a central role to states, even as a transitional pathway, raises a multitude of concerns about their potential for perpetuating unjust power. States are limited in their willingness and ability to defend the rights of their citizens against threats, both internal and external. Chronic underfulfilment of human rights is due to lack of robust human rights norm internalization, deficiency in political will, limited economic means, disagreements about the comparative importance of developmental objectives, and a host of practical impediments that render legally institutionalized rights non-justiciable or unenforceable. When states do provide human rights protection, it is often highly unequal or selective, and, in the worst cases, the rights of women, religious minorities, immigrants, and others are systematically violated.

States routinely pursue goals of extreme economic nationalism, thereby undermining the human rights of non-nationals. They engage directly in predatory market activities in much the same way as private profit-seeking enterprises. They own ecologically destructive enterprises, and they have financial stakes in sovereign wealth funds and taxpayer-supported pension plans that engage in these activities. States contribute in other ways to the efforts of non-state entities to exploit other humans and the rest of nature. They act as agents of injustice by advancing the interests of domestic economic elites who use their access to state power to pave the way to enhanced profits and offload the environmental burdens of consumption on geographically distant communities or future generations.

A further risk of reliance on states as a source of global solutions is the prospect that nativist, anti-immigrant political parties will exacerbate the adverse consequences of nationalism, for example, by assigning blame for environmental crises to the global poor or employing populist rhetoric that casts migrants escaping from ecological disasters as potential competitors for the nation's resources and irresponsible stewards of the environment. This response to the global deterioration of ecological conditions is a current theme in recent dystopian fiction, such as John Lanchester's novel, *The Wall*, where citizen Defenders are conscripted to secure the wall that keeps out the increasingly desperate Others. However, such concerns are no longer the stuff of fiction. The marriage of economic nationalism and ecological survivalism is now evident in contemporary European politics, where authoritarian leaders rely on apocalyptic environmental narratives to bolster their case for

258 A LIVABLE PLANET

more exclusionary border policies and, literally, for building more walls.[11]

In addition, the ability of states to protect human rights is constrained by a combination of hyper-powerful states, regional trading blocs, globalized patterns of concentrated capital, and supranational financial institutions such as the World Bank, International Monetary Fund, and the World Trade Organization.

Most importantly, not all nation-states have comparable prospects for maintaining their independence from external interferences with domestic priorities. Some states fall below what has been referred to as a threshold of viability.[12] Although the terminology now seems dated, the persistence of differential state advantages and their implications are well-established. States may lack sufficient territory, population, resources, or bargaining power to establish resilient economies or gain access to highly lucrative opportunities within the central global supply chains that provide goods and services to affluent consumers. States may lack the ability to secure their borders without outside assistance or the forbearance of militarily and geopolitically stronger states. They may lack the tax base, infrastructure, access to patent-protected technology, or credit necessary to resist the regulatory and tax concessions demanded by potential investors. Often, economically less-developed states are no match for institutional entities in control of large sums of hypermobile capital, and heavily indebted states are in weak position to push back against loan conditionalities imposed by international banking and economic development institutions.

The disadvantages currently experienced by some states persist because of economic conditions deeply rooted in the history of the colonial powers from the 18th and 19th centuries and the "great powers" of the 20th century. Historically dominant economic powers often encouraged economic development, but only up to a point where it did not run counter to their own interests.[13] Current institutional rules governing the global political economy compound inherited disadvantages, cement the market power and political dominance of domestic and foreign elites, and perpetuate global patterns of deep inequality in the ecological conditions that sustain life and well-being.

Vast differences in purchasing power across nations alone—apart from institutional rules or the history of their creation—confer upon affluent countries environmental advantages not available to most low- and middle-income countries. Industrial countries can bypass ordinary competitive processes by hoarding green technologies and using state power to promote the outsourcing of ecologically destructive activities to foreign jurisdictions where the costs of operations are lower and regulatory regimes are weaker.[14] Economically weak states, by contrast, see little choice but to open their doors to the sale of their natural resources and submit to pressures of investors in search of permissive regulatory regimes.

In one way or another, even relatively strong states succumb to global pressures to retreat from oversight of competitive markets at home, and, very often, they respond to the "predatory inclinations of a transitory political elite" who encourage states to loosen the grip of democratic control over their own ecological futures.[15] With a globalized retreat from collective control over market decisions that affect the common good, private entities are then free to craft the economic rules in the regulatory void created in rich and poor states alike. A deregulated world is a politically contrived world, intentionally stripped of settled norms and enforceable expectations that help keep the powerful in check.

Future pathways out of our ecological predicament are thus constrained by the inertia of established institutions, the grip of political and economic ideas that underpin them, the durability of ingrained habits and traditions, the expectations generated by a way of life shaped by the built environment and incumbent technologies, the high social and personal costs of change, the deliberately engineered market strategies that artificially prolong the life of unsustainable products, and pernicious forms of nationalism that often accompany state power. As a consequence, the

260 A LIVABLE PLANET

continuation with business as usual, supplemented by reduction of wastes, a few technological fixes, improved governance, and the expansion of the reach and role of unregulated market mechanisms, is unlikely to provide a timely pathway out of our predicament.

Despite the obstacles—and there are many—the first steps toward a more just and sustainable global political economy will necessitate fundamental changes in the organization of global markets and the political institutions that support them. Such changes are likely only with an activist prosecution of an ecologically oriented human rights agenda, one that puts dual-purpose human rights at the top of its priority list because they secure basic elements of human well-being and advance sustainability goals.

Leaders of many social movements have reached similar conclusions for many of the same reasons already noted. Examples of an ecologically oriented human rights agenda include the Indigenous Peoples' Rights International (Chapter 8), the Geneva Declaration and Kari-Oca 2 Declaration (Chapter 6), the Bali Principles of Climate Justice, and the Indigenous People's Network's statement of principles (Chapter 4). In fact, members of these coalitions recognize that the only chance for success of a human rights approach depends upon the ability of activists to wrest power from corporate control of the governing apparatus of individual states.

However, sovereign states on their own cannot solve global problems. A human rights agenda is unlikely to be successful without collective action undertaken by politically subordinate and economically vulnerable states and subcommunities. Crucially important is the creation of international alliances capable of challenging economically and geopolitically powerful states and non-state entities that exercise a significant degree of state-like power. That is a tall order. Even a modest level of cross-border collaboration requires a degree of international solidarity that V. I. Lenin, J. A. Hobson, and others have seen as difficult to engender and still more difficult to sustain under the pressure of enhanced global

CONTROL OVER THE FUTURE 261

competition. For much the same reasons that there is no robust international workers' movement, mobilization of an international coalition of the ecologically dispossessed and disenfranchised is an uphill battle. Nevertheless, the best hope for success on a planetary scale—the only kind of success that counts—depends on the formation of cooperative alliances, especially among residents of states most susceptible to predation by the joint efforts of their own economic elites and their global partners.

Moreover, transformation of the global political economy requires reversal of two generations of ascendancy of market fundamentalist ideas and neoliberal legal norms. That, too, might seem unimaginable. But such pessimism ignores the relatively brief history of current legal systems that treat environmental costs as the evitable, morally tolerable side effects of progress. The onset of the Industrial Revolution, at the very point it emerged in each region of the world, coincided with a reversal of preindustrial traditions.[16] Those traditions gave priority to the protection of people and the property holdings upon which their basic livelihoods depend over improvement in overall standard of living and the aggregate material rewards of economic growth. The rules we have are difficult to dislodge, but they are not inevitable or immutable.

That said, the proposal for targeting economically predatory, ecologically destructive market practices and their supporting political institutions may not go far enough, fast enough. However, less ambitious options have virtually no chance of success simply because their targets are too far from the root causes of our ecological predicament. More ambitious alternatives that depend on the demise of capitalism or the elimination of the system of states seem even more unlikely to occur within the next few decades—or less—that we have left before large portions of the planet become radically inhospitable to human life and more deeply antagonistic to the rest of nature.

However, the difficulty of the task is insufficient reason to reject the targeted human rights approach. No realistic pathway will be

262   A LIVABLE PLANET

easy, uncontroversial, or sacrifice-free. Even the initial steps toward
the institutionalization of a robust human rights agenda would
up-end settled expectations of the global affluent and inaugurate a
seismic shift in the control over the machinery of states. As difficult
as it might be to imagine, without change within states, nothing else
will change.

Notes

Chapter 1

1. I use the term "ecology" as it is standardly defined, as the branch of science that studies how humans and other living organisms relate to each other and their shared physical environment.
2. Will Steffen et al., "Planetary Boundaries: Guiding Human Development on a Changing Planet," *Science* 347, no. 6223 (2015), http://dx.doi.org/10.1126/science.1259855.
3. Four planetary boundaries were considered as crossed in 2015. Will Steffen et al., "Planetary boundaries." More recent studies add freshwater resources to the list. See, e.g., Tom Gleeson et al., "The Water Planetary Boundary: Interrogation and Revision," *One Earth* 2, no. 3 (March 20, 2020): 223–234; and Lan Wang-Erlandsson et al., "A Planetary Boundary for Green Water," *Nature Reviews Earth and Environment* 3 (2022): 380–392, https://doi.org/10.1038/s43017-022-00287-8.
4. Johan Rockström et al., "Safe and Just Earth System Boundaries," *Nature* (31 May 2023), https://doi.org/10.1038/s41586-023-06083-8.
5. Samuel Moyn, "A Powerless Companion: Human Rights in the Age of Neoliberalism," *Law and Contemporary Problems* 77 (2015): 147–169.

Chapter 2

1. Madison Powers, "Sustainability and Resilience," in *Encyclopedia of the Anthropocene*, vol. 4, ed. Dominick Della Sala and Michael Goldstein (Oxford: Elsevier, 2018), 29–37, http://dx.doi.org/10.1016/B978-0-12-409548-9.10491-9.
2. Paul Warde, Libby Robin, and Sverker Sörlin, *The Environment: A History of the Idea* (Baltimore, MD: Johns Hopkins University Press, 2018), 134.
3. International Union for Conservation of Nature and Natural Resources, *World Conservation Strategy: Living Resource Conservation for Sustainable Development* (Gland, Switzerland, 1980).

264 NOTES

4. Warde et al., *The Environment*, 147.
5. World Commission on Environment and Development (WCED), *Our Common Future* (New York: Oxford University Press, 1987), 45.
6. UN General Assembly, "Report of the United Nations Conference on Environment and Development," A/Conf.151/26, Vol. I (August 12, 1992), https://www.un.org/en/development/desa/population/migration/generalassembly/docs/globalcompact/A_CONF.151_26_Vol.I_Declarat ion.pdf.
7. United Nations, "Transforming Our World: The 2030 Agenda for Sustainable Development," United Nations General Assembly resolution A/RES/70/1 October 21, 2015.
8. Wilfred Beckerman, "'Sustainable Development': Is It a Useful Concept?" *Environmental Values* 3, no. 3 (1994): 191–209; Dale Jamieson, "Sustainability and Beyond," *Ecological Economics* 24 (1998): 183–192.
9. Donella H. Meadows, Dennis L. Meadows, Jørgen Randers, and William W. Behrens III, *The Limits to Growth* (New York: Universe Books, 1972).
10. Robert Gilpin, *Global Political Economy: Understanding the International Economic Order* (Princeton and Oxford: Princeton University Press, 2001), 129. For more on the uniqueness of state rules, see Michael Blake, "Distributive Justice, State Coercion, and Autonomy," *Philosophy and Public Affairs* 30, no. 3 (2001): 257–296.
11. Gilpin, *Global Political Economy*, 17–18.
12. David Griggs et al., "Sustainable Development: Goals for People and Planet," *Nature* 495 (2013): 305–307, http://dx.doi.org/10.1038/495305a PMID: 23518546.
13. This globally applicable definition builds on some aspects of a National Research Council definition of a sustainable society: "one that can persist over generations; one that is far-seeing enough, flexible enough, and wise enough not to undermine either its physical or its social system of support." National Research Council, *Sustainability for the Nation: Resource Connections and Governance Linkages* (Washington, DC: National Academies Press, 2013), https://doi.org/10.17226/13471.
14. Nancy Fraser, "Behind Marx's Hidden Abode: For an Expanded Conception of Capitalism," in *Critical Theory in Critical Times*, ed. Penelope Deutscher and Christina Lafont (New York: Columbia University Press, 2017), 141–159.
15. James O'Connor, *Natural Causes: Essays in Ecological Marxism* (New York and London: Guilford Press, 1998).
16. Gus Speth, quoted by Ian Angus, *Facing the Anthropocene* (New York: Monthly Review Press, 2016), 189.

NOTES 265

17. Jason W. Moore, ed., *Anthropocene or Capitalocene? Nature, History, and the Crisis of Capitalism* (Oakland, CA: PM Press/Kairo, 2016).

18. Fred Magdoff and John Bellamy Foster, *What Every Environmentalist Needs to Know About Capitalism* (New York: Monthly Review Press, 2011), 30.

19. Fred Magdoff, "Ecological Civilization," *Monthly Review* 62, no. 8 (January 2011): 1–25, at 20.

20. Mathis Wackernagel and William Rees, *Our Ecological Footprint: Reducing Human Impact on the Earth* (Philadelphia: New Society Publishers, 1996); World Wildlife Fund for Nature, *Living Planet Report 2020: Bending the Curve of Biodiversity Loss*, https://www.footprintnetwork.org/living-pla net-report/.

21. Gar Alperovitz, "Sustainability and the System Problem: Address to the Executive Staff of the President's Council on Sustainable Development," *The Good Society* 5, no. 3 (Fall 1995): 1–10, http://www.jstor.org/ stable/ 20710696.

22. Vaclav Smil, *Growth: From Microorganisms to Megacities* (Cambridge, MA: MIT Press, 2019), 501.

23. Alfred Marshall claimed that "human wants and desires are count-less in number and very various in kind" and that with civilizational progress humans desire "a greater choice of things, and things that will satisfy new wants." Alfred Marshall, *Principles of Economics*, 8th ed. (London: Macmillan and Co., 1920), https://oll.libertyfund.org/titles/ 1676. Quoted in Kate Raworth, *Doughnut Economics: Seven Ways to Think Like a 21st-Century Economist* (White River, VT: Chelsea Green Publishing, 2017), 85.

24. Gillian Barker, *Beyond Biofatalism: Human Nature for an Evolving World* (New York: Columbia University Press, 2015).

25. Plato, *Republic*, in *Plato, Complete Works*, ed. and trans. John M. Cooper (Indianapolis and Cambridge: Hackett Publishing, 1997), 521a.

26. Plato, *Republic*, 551d.

27. Plato, *Republic*, 431b.

28. E.g., Aristotle, *Politics*, in *The Complete Works of Aristotle: The Revised Oxford Translation*, ed. and trans. Jonathan Barnes (Princeton, NJ: Princeton University Press, 1984), 1267a12–16.

29. This idea was evident in the memorable phrase, "All that is sacred becomes profane. All that is solid melts into air." Karl Marx and Frederick Engels, *Manifesto of the Communist Party*, in *The Marx-Engels Reader*, ed. Robert C. Tucker (London: W.W. Norton and Company, [1848] 1978). It was an animating concern in the works of Rosa Luxembourg and some critical

266 NOTES

theorists in the Frankfurt school. See Wendy Brown, "Neoliberalism and the Economization of Rights," in *Critical Theory in Critical Times*, ed. Penelope Deutscher and Christina Lafont (New York: Columbia University Press, 2017), 141–159.

30. Dan Callahan, *The Five Horsemen of the Modern World* (New York: Columbia University Press, 2016), 289–299.

31. Convention on the Organisation for Economic Co-operation and Development, 1961, Article 1 (a), https://www.oecd.org/general/conventionontheorganisationforeconomicco-operationanddevelopm ent.htm.

32. Joseph Stiglitz, Jean-Paul Fitouss, and Amartya Sen, *Mismeasuring Our Lives: Why GDP Doesn't Add Up* (New York: The New Press, 2010).

33. Quoted by Smil, *Growth*, 492–493.

34. Tim Jackson, *Prosperity Without Growth*, 2nd ed. (London and New York: Routledge, 2017).

35. Raworth, *Doughnut Economics*.

36. John Asafu-Adjaye et al., *An Ecomodernist Manifesto*, 2015, http://www.ecomodernism.org/manifesto.

37. Al Gore and David Blood, "A Manifesto for Sustainable Capitalism," *The Wall Street Journal*, December 14, 2011.

38. Mario Pezzini, "An Emerging Middle-Class," *OECD Observer*, 2015, https://oecdobserver.org/news/fullstory.php/aid/3681/An_emerging_m iddle_class.html.

39. Daniel W. O'Neil, Andrew L. Fanning, William F. Lamb, and Julia K. Steinberger, "A Good Life for All Within Planetary Boundaries," *Nature Sustainability* 1 (2018): 88–95, https://www.nature.com/articles/s41 893-018-0021-4.

40. Organisation for Economic Cooperation and Development (OECD), *Policy Challenges for the Next 50 Years*. OECD economic policy paper no. 9 (Paris OECD, 2014), 11.

41. Gene M. Grossman and Alan B. Krueger, "Economic Growth and the Environment," *Quarterly Journal of Economics* 110, no. 2 (1995): 353–377.

42. Ecological deterioration goes hand in hand with economic inequality within a country. See S. Nazrul Islam, *Inequality and Environmental Sustainability*. UN DESA working paper no. 145, 2015, https://www.un.org/esa/desa/papers/2015/wp145_2015.pdf.

43. For a discussion of how the distribution of the benefits of modern technology is often geographically decoupled from the distribution of its environmental impacts, see Thomas O. Wiedmann et al., "The Material

NOTES 267

Footprint of Nations," *Proceedings of the National Academies of Science* 112, no. 20 (2015): 6271–6276, http://dx.doi.org/10.1073/pnas.1220362110.

44. A recent UNEP report raises doubts about the possibility of decoupling given that the richest countries consume materials at a rate of as much as 10 times per capita as the poorest countries. International Resource Panel of the United Nations Environmental Programme, *Global Material Flows and Resource Productivity: Assessment Report for the UNEP* (Paris: United Nations Environmental Programme, 2016), 14–16.

45. International Resource Panel of the United Nations Environmental Programme, *Assessing Global Resource Use: A Systems Approach to Resource Efficiency and Pollution Reduction* (United Nations Environment Programme. Nairobi, Kenya, 2017), https://www.resourcepanel.org/repo rts/assessing-global-resource-use.

46. Jordi Teixidó-Figueras et al., "International Inequality of Environmental Pressures: Decomposition and Comparative Analysis," *Ecological Indicators* 62 (2016): 163–173.

47. Heinz Schandl et al., "Global Material Flows and Resource Productivity: Forty Years of Evidence," *Journal of International Industrial Ecology* 22, no. 4 (2018): 827–838, https://doi.org/10.1111/jiec.12626.

48. David Lin et al., "Ecological Footprint Accounting for Countries: Updates and Results of the National Footprint Accounts, 2012–2018," *Resources* 7, no. 3 (2018): 5858, https://doi.org/10.3390/resources7030058.

49. For more on the material footprints of consumption, see Wiedemann et al., "The material footprint of nations," and International Resource Panel of the United Nations Environmental Programme, Global material flows and resource productivity: assessment report for the UNEP (Paris: United Nations Environmental Programme, 2016), https://www.unep.org/resour ces/report/global-material-flows-and-resource-productivity-assessm ent-report-unep. Chapters 7 and 8 respectively examine water and carbon footprint differentials.

50. An influential survey of wide-ranging evidence is found in Danny Dorling, *The Equality Effect* (Oxford: New Internationalist Publications, 2017). Tables and charts illustrating many of the key claims are available on his website: http://www.dannydorling.org/books/equalityeffect/. For updates documenting the comprehensive environmental effects associated with economic inequality, see Maike Hamann et al., "Inequality and the Biosphere," *Annual Review of Environment and Resources* 43 (2018): 61–83, https://doi.org/10.1146/annurev-environ-102017-025949.

268 NOTES

51. James Boyce, "Is Inequality Bad for the Environment?" Working Papers, wp135, Political Economy Research Institute, University of Massachusetts at Amherst, 2007, https://ideas.repec.org/p/uma/periwp/wp135.html.

52. Lucas Chancel and Thomas Piketty, *Carbon and Inequality from Kyoto to Paris: Trends in the Global Inequality of Carbon Emissions (1998–2013) and Prospects for an Equitable Adaptation Fund* (Paris: Paris School of Economics, 2015), http://piketty.pse.ens.fr/files/ChancelPiketty2015.pdf.

53. Gregory M. Mikkelson, Andrew Gonzalez, and Garry D. Peterson, "Economic Inequality Predicts Biodiversity Loss," *PLoS One* 2, no. 5 (2007): e444, doi:10.1371/journal.pone.0000444.

54. Jungho Baek and Guankerwon Gweisah, "Does Income Inequality Harm the Environment? Empirical Evidence from the United States," *Energy Policy* 62 (2013): 1434–1437; Krister Andersson and Arun Agrawal, "Inequalities, Institutions, and Forest Commons," *Global Environmental Change* 21 (2011): 866–875; Renee Skelton and Vernice Miller, *The Environmental Justice Movement* (New York: Natural Resources Defense Council, 2017), https://www.nrdc.org/stories/environmental-justice-movement.

55. Judith Lichtenberg, *Distant Strangers: Ethics, Psychology, and Global Poverty* (Cambridge, UK: Cambridge University Press, 2013).

56. Elizabeth Currid-Halkett, *The Sum of Small Things: A Theory of the Aspirational Class* (Princeton, NJ: Princeton University Press, 2019).

57. See, e.g., Paul K. Piff et al., "Higher Social Class Predicts Increased Unethical Behavior," *Proceedings of the National Academies of Science* 109, no. 11 (March 13, 2012): 4086–4091, https://doi.org/10.1073/pnas.111 8373109; Jennifer Stellar et al., "Class and Compassion: Socioeconomic Factors Predict Responses to Suffering," *Emotion* 12, no. 3 (2012): 449–459, https://doi.org/10.1037/a0026508.

Chapter 3

1. John Williamson coined the phrase to designate specific elements of policy advice given by Washington-based institutions to Latin American countries in the 1980s. John Williamson, "What Should the World Bank Think About the Washington Consensus?" *World Bank Research Observer* 15, no. 2 (Washington, DC: The International Bank for Reconstruction and Development, 2000): 251–264. Critics appropriated the label to refer to socially destructive policies imposed on poor nations for the sake of the economic interests of developed nations.

NOTES 269

2. Gary Gerstle, *The Rise and Fall of the Neoliberal Order: America and the World in the Free Market Era* (New York: Oxford University Press, 2022). George Soros has likened market fundamentalists' faith in largely self-regulating or, at the very least, socially beneficial markets to the fervor characteristic of a religious movement. George Soros, *On Globalization* (New York: Public Affairs, 2002).

3. Joseph Stiglitz adopts the language of market fundamentalism in his acceptance essay for the Nobel Memorial Prize in Economic Sciences to criticize a bundle of global development policies that he describes as based on an incorrect understanding of economic theory and a flawed interpretation of historical empirical data. Joseph Stiglitz, "Biographical Essay, The Sveriges Riksbank Prize in Economic Sciences in Memory of Alfred Nobel 2001," http://www.nobelprize.org/nobel_prizes/economic-scien ces/laureates/2001/stiglitz-bio.html. For more of his comments on market fundamentalism, see Joseph Stiglitz, *Globalization and Its Discontents* (New York: W. W. Norton, 2003), xii, 35–36, 53–88, 259.

4. Quinn Slobodian, *Globalists: The End of Empire and the Birth of Neoliberalism* (Cambridge, MA: Harvard University Press, 2018); Thomas Biebricher, *The Political Theory of Neoliberalism* (Stanford, CA: Stanford University Press, 2018), 25–26; Jessica Whyte, *The Morals of the Market: Human Rights and the Rise of Neoliberalism* (London and New York: Verso, 2019), 60–62.

5. Wendy Brown, *The Ruins of Neoliberalism: The Rise of Anti-Democratic Politics in the West* (New York: Columbia University Press, 2019), 17–21; Michael Foucault, *The Birth of Biopolitics* (New York: Palgrave Macmillan, 2008); David Harvey, *A Brief History of Neoliberalism* (Oxford: Oxford University Press, 2005), 19, 43–54.

6. Joshua Cohen, "Editor's Note," in *Economics After Neoliberalism*, ed. Joshua Cohen (Cambridge, MA: Boston Review Forum, 2019), 6.

7. At times, Harvey appears to draw this distinction when he refers to neoliberalism as an orthodoxy in economic policy and having market fundamentalism as its intellectual basis. Harvey, *A Brief History*, 71–73.

8. See, e.g., Milton Friedman, *Capitalism and Freedom* (Chicago: University of Chicago Press, 2002), 177–195; Christopher Leonard, "Charles Koch's Big Bet on Barrett," *New York Times*, October 12, 2020.

9. Bruno Amable, *The Diversity of Modern Capitalism* (Oxford: Oxford University Press, 2003); Peter Hall and David Soskice, *Varieties of Capitalism: The Institutional Foundations of Comparative Advantage* (New York: Oxford University Press, 2001).

270 NOTES

10. Louison Cahen-Fourot, "Contemporary Capitalisms and Their Social Relation to the Environment," *Ecological Economics* 172 (2020): 106634, https://doi.org/10.1016/j.ecolecon.2020.106634.

11. Friedman, *Capitalism and Freedom*, 9.

12. Friedrich Hayek, *Law, Legislation, and Liberty, Vol. 2, The Mirage of Social Justice* (Chicago: University of Chicago Press, 1997), 25.

13. Hayek, *Law, Legislation*, 2.

14. Mont Pelerin Society, Statement of Aims, https://www.montpelerin.org/event/429dba23-fc64-4838-aea3-b847011022a4/websitePage:6950c74b-5d9b-41cc-8da1-3e1991c14ac5.

15. Hayek, *Law, Legislation*, 66–67.

16. Hayek, *Law, Legislation*, 68.

17. Friedman, *Capitalism and Freedom*, 15.

18. Isaiah Berlin, *Liberty*, ed. Henry Hardy (Oxford: Oxford University Press, 2002), 171.

19. Madison Powers and Ruth Faden, "Health Capabilities, Outcomes, and the Political Ends of Justice," *Journal of Human Development and Capabilities* 12 (2011): 565–570.

20. For the distinction between basic and non-basic liberties and reasons for not extending the categorical protection afforded to the basic liberties to non-basic liberties, which include various marketplace liberties, see John Rawls, *Political Liberalism* (New York: Columbia University Press, 1993), 291–299. For arguments based on similar distinctions in Mill's writings, see Madison Powers, Ruth Faden, and Yashar Saghai, "Liberty, Mill, and the Framework of Public Health Ethics," *Public Health Ethics* 5 (2012): 6–15.

21. Rawls, *Political Liberalism*, 7.

22. Friedrich Hayek, *The Constitution of Liberty* (London: Routledge and Kegan Paul, 1960), 166–167.

23. Karl Polanyi, *The Great Transformation* (New York: Amereon House, 1944), 130–132, 139–145.

24. Friedman, *Capitalism and Freedom*, 27.

25. For an elementary introduction to the first part of the Fundamental Theorem of Welfare Economics, see Amartya Sen, *On Ethics and Economics* (Oxford: Blackwell, 1987), 31–40.

26. Milton Friedman and Rose Friedman, *Free to Choose* (New York: Harcourt, 1980), 223.

27. Amartya Sen, *Choice, Welfare, and Measurement* (Oxford: Basil Blackwell, 1982), 41–106.

NOTES 271

28. Hal R. Varian, "Equity, Envy, and Efficiency," *Journal of Economic Theory* 9 (1974): 63–91.
29. E. J. Mishan, *Cost-Benefit Analysis*, 4th ed. (London: Unwin Hyman, 1988), 162.
30. Stiglitz, *Globalization and Its Discontents*, 218.
31. William Easterly, *The White Man's Burden* (London: Penguin Books, 2006), 75.
32. John Rawls, *Justice as Fairness: A Restatement* (Cambridge, MA: Harvard University Press, 2001), §§ 15 and 39.1; John Rawls, *A Theory of Justice*, rev. ed. (Cambridge, MA: Harvard University Press, 1999), 470, 478.
33. For example, Debra Satz claims that pro-market arguments are based on a conception of freedom which should be replaced by a more substantive conception of freedom. Debra Satz, "Markets Are Political," in *Economics After Neoliberalism*, ed. Joshua Cohen (Cambridge, MA: Boston Review Forum, 2019), 45–49. Harvey also remarks on "the astonishing lack of serious debate about the most appropriate conception of freedom." Harvey, *A Brief History*, 183–184.
34. According to Robert Dahl's classic definition of power, A has power over B to the extent that he can get B to do something that B would not otherwise do. Robert Dahl, "The Concept of Power," *Behavioral Science* 2 (1957): 201–215.
35. Hayek, like other market fundamentalists, is focally concerned with the problem of coercive state interference, but he offers a more encompassing definition. "Freedom refers solely to the relation of men to other men, and the only infringement on it is coercion by men." Hayek, *The Constitution of Liberty*, 12. His non-interference conception is commonly referred to as "negative freedom," signaling a concern for limiting external, human interferences with individual choice and action.
36. Elizabeth Anderson offers one example of a pluralist or multidimensional conception composed of at least three distinct concepts. "If you have negative freedom, no one is interfering with your actions. If you have positive freedom, you have a rich menu of options effectively available to you, given your resources. If you have republican freedom, no one is dominating you." Elizabeth Anderson, *Private Government: How Employers Rule Our Lives (and Why We Don't Talk About It)* (Princeton: Princeton University Press, 2017), 45.
37. A good survey is provided by Frank Lovett, *A General Theory of Domination and Justice* (Oxford: Oxford University Press, 2010).

272 NOTES

38. Cecile Laborde, "Republican Global Distributive Justice: A Sketch," *European Journal of Political Theory* 9, no.1 (2010): 54.
39. Rawls, *Justice as Fairness*, 130–131.
40. For arguments against the claim that state mechanisms of control are unique and that their effectiveness in securing and enforcing control is unmatched, see Michael Foucault, *Discipline and Punish: The Birth of the Prison* (New York: Vintage, 1979).
41. Judith N. Shklar, "The Liberalism of Fear," in *Liberalism and the Moral Life*, ed. Nancy Rosenblum (Cambridge, MA: Harvard University Press, 1989), 21–38.

Chapter 4

1. United Nations General Assembly, A/RES/76/300, "The Human Right to a Clean, Healthy and Sustainable Environment" (July 28, 2022), https://digitallibrary.un.org/record/3983329?ln=en.
2. E.g., James Nickel, *Making Sense of Human Rights*, 2nd ed. (Malden, MA: Blackwell, 2007), 137–153; UN General Assembly, *International Covenant on Economic, Social and Cultural Rights* (ICESCR) (United Nations, Treaty Series, vol. 993, December 16, 1966).
3. Henry Shue, *Basic Rights: Subsistence, Affluence, and U.S. Foreign Policy*, 2nd ed. (Princeton, NJ: Princeton University Press, 1996), 29, 32.
4. Shue, *Basic Rights*, 18.
5. Shue, *Basic Rights*, 18.
6. David Miller, *National Responsibility and Global Justice* (Oxford: Oxford University Press, 2007), 181.
7. James Nickel, "Moral Grounds for Economic and Social Rights," in *The Oxford Handbook of Economic and Social Rights*, ed. Malcolm Langford and Katharine G. Young (Oxford University Press, forthcoming).
8. E.g., Joshua Cohen, "Minimalism About Human Rights: The Most We Can Hope For?" *Journal of Political Philosophy* 12, no. 2 (2004): 190–213; John Rawls, *Law of Peoples* (Cambridge, MA: Harvard University Press, 1999), 65, 78–81.
9. James Griffin, *On Human Rights* (Oxford: Oxford University Press, 2008), 33.
10. Madison Powers and Ruth Faden, *Structural Injustice: Power, Advantage, and Human Rights* (New York: Oxford University Press, 2019).
11. Fourth Summit of the Americas, Declaration of Mar Del Plata: "Creating Jobs to Fight Poverty and Strengthen Democratic Governance" (Mar Del

NOTES 273

Plata, Argentina, November 5, 2005), https://www.summit-americas.org/iv_summit/iv_summit_poa_en.pdf.

12. Indigenous Environmental Network, "Indigenous Principles of Just Transition," http://www.ienearth.org/wp-content/uploads/2017/10/IENJ ustTransitionPrinciples.pdf.

13. International Climate Justice Network, "Bali Principles of Climate Justice, 2002." Reprinted in full at https://corpwatch.org/article/bali-principles-climate-justice.

14. Samuel Moyn, *Not Enough: Human Rights in an Unequal World* (Cambridge, MA: Belknap Press, 2018).

15. Jiewuh Song, "Human Rights and Inequality," *Philosophy and Public Affairs* 47, no. 4 (2019): 347–377.

16. Philip Alston, "Extreme Inequality as the Antithesis of Human Rights," *Open Global Rights*, 2015, https://www.openglobalrights.org/extreme-ine quality-as-the-antithesis-of-human-rights/.

17. This subsection is based on arguments central to the account of human rights in Powers and Faden, *Structural Injustice*. For a discussion of the potential for developing a structural approach to human rights, see Song, "Human Rights and Inequality," 366–372.

18. See, Powers and Faden, *Structural Injustice*, 3–4, 75–84, 141–145, 167–172.

19. Dinah Shelton, "Environmental Pollution: A Human Rights Perspective, in *Environmental Influences on the Immune System*, ed. C. Esser (Springer Wien, 2016), 359, doi:10.1007/978-3-7091-1890-0_15.

20. Daron Acemoglu and James A. Robinson, *Why Nations Fail: The Origins of Power, Prosperity, and Poverty* (New York: Crown Business, 2012).

21. The concept of opportunity hoarding is found in Charles Tilly, *Durable Inequality* (Berkeley: University of California Press, 1998).

22. Powers and Faden, *Structural Injustice*, 85–115.

23. See, e.g., Rob Nixon, *Slow Violence and the Environmentalism of the Poor* (Cambridge, MA: Harvard University Press, 2011); David Naguib Pellow, *What Is Critical Environmental Justice?* (Cambridge: Polity Press, 2018); Robert D. Bullard, *Dumping in Dixie: Race, Class, and Environmental Quality*, 3rd ed. (Westview Press, 2000).

24. Shue, *Basic Rights*, 30.

25. Joseph Raz, "Human Rights in the Emerging World Order," in *Philosophical Foundations of Human Rights*, ed. Rowen Cruft, Matthew Liao, and Massimo Renzo (Oxford: Oxford University Press, 2015), 217–231.

26. Powers and Faden, *Structural Injustice*, 131.

274 NOTES

27. Raymond Geuss, *History and Illusion in Politics* (Cambridge: Cambridge University Press, 2001), 146.

28. Andrew Dobson, *Justice and the Environment: Conceptions of Environmental Sustainability and Dimensions of Social Justice* (Oxford: Oxford University Press, 1998).

29. David Schlosberg, *Defining Environmental Justice: Theories, Movements, and Nature* (Oxford: Oxford University Press, 2007), 6.

30. Tim Hayward, *Constitutional Environmental Rights* (Oxford University Press, 2004), 34.

31. Charles Beitz, *The Idea of Human Rights* (Oxford: Oxford University Press, 2009), 48–72.

32. This overview is an inventory of the tenets of a naturalistic conception, adapted from Rowan Cruft, Matthew Liao, and Massimo Renzo, "The Philosophical Foundations of Human Rights: An Overview," in *Philosophical Foundations of Human Rights*, ed. Rowan Cruft, Matthew Liao, and Massimo Renzo. Oxford: Oxford University Press, 2015), 4.

33. Beitz, *The Idea of Human Rights*, 198.

34. For representative arguments for the dynamic nature of human rights, see Allen Buchanan, *Human Rights, Legitimacy, and the Use of Force* (Oxford: Oxford University Press, 2010), 54–58; Powers and Faden, *Structural Injustice*, 63–69, 132–141; Barbara Herman, *The Moral Habitat* (Oxford: Oxford University Press, 2021), 180–188, 207–216; and John Tasioulas, "The Moral Reality of Rights," in *Freedom from Poverty as a Human Right*, ed. Thomas Pogge (Oxford University Press, 2007), 75–101.

35. Tasioulas, "The Moral Reality of Rights," 94.

36. Herman, *The Moral Habitat*, 188.

37. O'Neill's arguments can be found in various places; for example, Onora O'Neill, "The Dark Side of Human Rights," *International Affairs* 81, no. 2 (2005): 427–439.

38. Beitz, *The Idea of Human Rights*, 128.

39. Henry S. Richardson, "Institutionally Divided Moral Responsibility," *Social Philosophy and Policy* 16, no. 2 (1999): 218–249.

40. Henry Shue, "Mediating Duties," *Ethics* 98, no. 4 (1988): 687–704.

41. Saladin Meckled-Garcia, "On the Very Idea of Cosmopolitan Justice: Constructivism and International Agency," *Journal of Political Philosophy* 16, no. 3 (2008): 245–271.

42. Andrew Altman and Christopher Heath Wellman, *A Liberal Theory of International Justice* (Oxford: Oxford University Press, 2009); Allen

NOTES 275

Buchanan, "Political Legitimacy and Democracy," *Ethics* 112, no. 4 (2002): 689–719.

43. Amartya Sen, "Elements of a Theory of Human Rights," *Philosophy & Public Affairs* 32, no. 4 (2004): 315–356.

44. Derek Parfit, *Reasons and Persons* (Oxford: Clarendon Press, 1984).

45. Leif Wenar, "Responsibility and Severe Poverty," in *Freedom from Poverty as a Human Right: Who Owes What to the Very Poor?*, ed. Thomas Pogge (Oxford: Oxford University Press, 2007).

46. Annette Baier, "Poisoning the Wells," in *Values at Risk*, ed. Douglas MacLean (Totowa, NJ: Rowman and Allanheld, 1986), 49.

47. H. L. A. Hart and Tony Honoré, *Causation in the Law*, 2nd ed. (Oxford: Clarendon Press, 1985).

48. Baier, "Poisoning the Wells," 64.

49. Tim Hayward, "On Prepositional Duties," *Ethics* 123, no. 2 (2013): 264–291.

Chapter 5

1. James K. Galbraith, *The Predator State* (New York: Free Press, 2008).

2. For more wide-ranging discussions of these and other issues of justice in the organization of global agricultural markets, see Madison Powers, "Food, Fairness, and Global Markets," in *Oxford Handbook of Food Ethics*, ed. Anne Barnhill, Tyler Doggett, and Mark B. Budolfson (New York: Oxford University Press, 2018), 367–398; Madison Powers, "Food and the Global Political Economy," *Ethics and International Affairs* 35, no. 1 (Spring, 2021): 99–117.

3. Sophia Murphy, David Burch, and Jennifer Clapp, *Cereal Secrets: The World's Largest Grain Traders and Global Agriculture: Oxfam Research Report* (Oxford: Oxfam International, 2012).

4. United States Department of Agriculture, *Packers and Stockyards Division: Annual Report 2018* (Washington, DC: USDA, 2018), https://www.ams.usda.gov/sites/default/files/media/PSDAnnualReport2018.pdf.

5. Koen De Backer and Sébastien Miroudot, "Mapping Global Value Chains," *OECD Trade Policy Papers, No. 159* (Paris: OECD Publishing, 2013), http://dx.doi.org/10.1787/5k3v1trgnbr4-en.

6. Thomas L. Sporleder and Michael A. Boland, "Exclusivity of Agrifood Supply Chains: Seven Fundamental Economic Characteristics," *International Food and Agribusiness Management Review* 14, no. 5 (2011): 27–51.

276 NOTES

7. James M. Macdonald and Penni Korb, "Agricultural Contracting Update: Contracts in 2008," *Economic Information Bulletin No. 72* (Washington, DC: Economic Research Service, US Department of Agriculture, 2011).

8. Macdonald and Korb, "Agricultural Contracting."

9. National Chicken Council, "Broiler Chicken Industry Key Facts 2019," https://www.nationalchickencouncil.org/about-the-industry/statistics/broiler-chicken-industry-key-facts/.

10. Gary Gereffi, *Global Value Chains and Development: Redefining the Contours of 21st Century Capitalism* (Cambridge: Cambridge University Press, 2018), 137–175.

11. Mark Wever et al., "Supply Chain-Wide Consequences of Transaction Risks and Their Contractual Solutions: Towards an Extended Transaction Cost Economics Framework," *Journal of Supply Chain Management* 48, no. 1 (2012): 73–91.

12. C. Robert Taylor and David A. Domina, *Restoring Economic Health to Contract Poultry Production* (Normal, AL: Report prepared for the Joint US Department of Justice and US Department of Agriculture/GIPSA Public Workshop on Competition Issues in the Poultry Industry, May 21, 2010), http://www.dominalaw.com/documents/Restoring-Economic-Health-to-Contract-Poultry-Production.pdf.

13. Stephen Martinez, "Vertical Coordination in the Pork and Broiler Industries: Implications for Pork and Chicken Products," *Agricultural Economic Report No. 777* (Washington, DC: Economic Research Service, US Department of Agriculture, 1999).

14. Douglas H. Constance, "The Southern Model of Broiler Production and Its Global Implications," *Culture and Agriculture* 30, no 1. (2008): 17–31.

15. Constance, "The Southern Model."

16. Larry L. Burmeister, "Lagoons, Litter and the Law: CAFO Regulation as Social Risk Politics," *Southern Rural Sociology* 18, no. 2 (2002): 56–87.

17. World Bank, *World Development Report 2008: Agriculture for Development* (Washington, DC: World Bank, 2007).

18. Martin Prowse, *Contract Farming in Developing Countries: A Review.* (Agence Francaise de Development, 2012), http://www.afd.fr/home/recher che/actualites-publications-rch?actuCtnId=77586; Marc F. Bellemare and Jeffrey R. Bloem, "Does Contract Farming Improve Welfare? A Review," *World Development* 112 (December 2018): 259–271, www.sciencedirect.com/science/article/abs/pii/S0305750X18303188?via%3Dihub.

NOTES 277

19. David Ricardo, *The Principles of Political Economy and Taxation* (1817; repr., London: J. M. Dent, 1973); and James Mill, *Elements of Political Economy* (London: C. & R. Baldwin, 1821).

20. World Bank, *World Development Report 2008*.

21. See International Labor Organization (ILO), *World Employment Report 2004-05: Employment, Productivity, and Poverty Reduction* (Geneva: ILO, 2005); and Per Pinstrup-Anderson and Derrill D. Watson II, *Food Policy for Developing Countries* (Ithaca, NY: Cornell University Press, 2011), 178–179.

22. Dani Rodrik, *The Globalization Paradox: Democracy and the Future of the World Economy* (New York: W. W. Norton and Company, 2011), 156.

23. Gereffi, *Global Value Chains*, 43–71.

24. Shantayanan Devarajan and Dani Rodrik, "Trade Liberalization in Developing Countries: Do Imperfect Competition and Scale Economies Matter?," *The American Economic Review* 79, no. 2 (1989): 283–287.

25. Rodrik, *The Globalization Paradox*, 139–142.

26. Rodrik, *The Globalization Paradox*, 50–55.

27. Rodrik, *The Globalization Paradox*, 55–61.

28. Rodrik, *The Globalization Paradox*, 139–142.

29. For explanations of why some countries experience sustained patterns of shared prosperity from global economic integration while others do not, see Gereffi, *Global Value Chains*, 1–39; and International Bank for Reconstruction and Development, *World Development Report: Trading for Development in the Age of Global Value Chains* (Washington, DC: World Bank Group, 2020), 66–101.

30. World Bank, "Protecting Land Rights Is Key to Large-Scale Land Acquisitions" (Washington, DC: World Bank, 2010), http://econ.worldb ank.org/WBSITE/EXTERNAL/EXTDEC/0,,contentMDK:22694293~pag ePK:64165401~piPK:64165026~theSitePK:469372,00.html

31. Beth Robertson and Per Pinstrup-Anderson, "Global Land Acquisition: Neo-Colonialism or Development Opportunity," *Food Security* 2, no. 3 (2010): 271–283.

32. P. Collier, *The Plundered Planet: Why We Must—and How We Can—Manage Nature for Global Prosperity* (Oxford: Oxford University Press, 2010).

33. Olivier De Schutter, "How Not to Think of Land-Grabbing: Three Critiques of Large-Scale Investments in Farmland," *Journal of Peasant Studies* 38, no. 2 (2011): 249–279; Richard Schiffman, "Hunger, Food

278 NOTES

Security, and the African Land Grab," *Ethics & International Affairs* 27, no. 3 (2013): 239–249.

34. United Nations, *Making the Law Work for Everyone (Vol. I), Report of the Commission on the Legal Empowerment of the Poor* (Rolling Meadows, IL: Toppan Printing Company America, Inc., 2008), http://www.unrol.org/article.aspx?article_id=26.

35. For a global databank of contract documents and details regarding acquisition, see "An Online Repository of Open Land Contracts," https://www.openlandcontracts.org/.

36. World Bank, *Development Report 2008*.

37. World Bank, *Development Report 2008*.

38. OECD-FAO, *Agricultural Outlook 2015*, https://doi.org/10.1787/19991142; World Food Programme, *2020: The Global Report on Food Crises* (Rome: World Food Programme, 2020).

39. Jason Hickel, *The Divide: Global Inequality from Conquest to Free Markets* (New York: W.W. Norton and Company, 2018).

40. William Easterly, *The Tyranny of Experts: Economists, Dictators, and the Forgotten Rights of the Poor* (NY: Basic Books, 2013).

41. Mark Blyth, *Austerity: The History of a Dangerous Idea* (Oxford: Oxford University Press, 2013); Ngaire Woods and Amrita Narlikar, "Global Governance and the Limits of Accountability: The WTO, the IMF, and the World Bank," *International Social Science Journal* 53 (2001): 569–583; International Financial Institution Advisory Commission (aka the Meltzer Commission), *The Report of the International Financial Institution Advisory Commission* (Washington, DC: Library of Congress. Congressional Research Service, 2001), http://www.policyarchive.org/browse-publishers/480; and Miriam Ronzoni, "The Global Order: A Case of Background Injustice? A Practice-Dependent Account," *Philosophy and Public Affairs* 37 no. 3 (Summer 2009): 229–256.

42. See Wolfgang Streeck, *How Will Capitalism End?* (London: Verso, 2017), 113–141; Robert Kuttner, *Can Democracy Survive Global Capitalism?* (New York: W.W. Norton and Company, 2018), 121–148.

43. James Buchanan, *Debt and Taxes, The Collected Works of James Buchanan*, vol. 2 (Indianapolis: Liberty Fund, 2000), 493–518. The 1993 Maastricht Treaty provided that current deficits of member states could not exceed 3% of their GDP, and overall sovereign debt was capped at 60% of GDP.

44. Katherina Pistor, *The Code of Capital: How the Law Creates Wealth and Inequality* (Princeton, NJ: Princeton University Press, 2019).

NOTES 279

45. For arguments that some proponents of market fundamentalist ideology had no intention of shrinking the state but instead, aimed to use it for their own preferred purposes, see Fred Block and Margaret R. Somers, *The Power of Market Fundamentalism: Karl Polanyi's Critique* (Cambridge, MA: Harvard University Press, 2014), 193–220.

46. Pistor, *The Code of Capital*.

47. Mariah Blake, "How Hillary Clinton's State Department Sold Fracking to the World," *Mother Jones* (September/October Issue, 2014), https://www.motherjones.com/politics/2014/09/hillary-clinton-fracking-shale-state-department-chevron/.

48. Michael Porter, "How Competitive Forces Shape Strategy," *Harvard Business Review* 57 (March–April, 1979): 137–145.

49. For example, when the Maastricht Treaty eliminated capital controls and guaranteed free movement of goods, services, and people throughout the European Union, member nations intensified their competition to attract capital by lowering wages, taxes, labor safeguards, and other kinds of regulations. See, e.g., Streeck, *How Will Capitalism End?*, 174–183.

50. Nicholas Shaxson, *The Finance Curse: How Global Finance Is Making Us All Poorer* (London: Penguin Random House, 2018), 38–49.

51. Peiley Lau, "The World Bank's Doing Business Rankings: Relinquishing Sovereignty for a Good Grade," https://www.oaklandinstitute.org/blog/world-bank%E2%80%99s-doing-business-rankings-relinquishing-sovereignty-good-grade.

52. World Bank, "Statement: World Bank Group to Discontinue Doing Business Report," https://www.worldbank.org/en/news/statement/2021/09/16/world-bank-group-to-discontinue-doing-business-report.

53. Jagdish Bhagwati, *Free Trade Today* (Princeton, NJ: Princeton University Press, 2003), 58.

54. Nina Bandelj and Elizabeth Sowers, *Economy and State: A Sociological Perspective* (Malden, MA: Polity Press, 2010), 187–188.

55. Streeck, *How Will Capitalism End?*, 174–183.

56. Emmanuel Saez and Gabriel Zucman, *The Triumph of Injustice: How the Rich Avoid Taxes and How to Make Them Pay* (New York: W. W. Norton and Company, 2019).

57. Shaxson, *The Finance Curse*, 63–66.

58. Ludvig Wier, Thomas Tørsløv, and Gabriel Zucman, "The Missing Profits of Nations," *Review of Economic Studies* (2022): 1–36, https://doi.org/10.1093/restud/.

280 NOTES

59. Jannick Damgaard, Thomas Elkjaer, and Niels Johannesen, "The Rise of Phantom Investments," *Finance and Development* 56, no. 3 (September 2019), https://www.imf.org/external/pubs/ft/fandd/2019/09/the-rise-of-phantom-FDI-in-tax-havens-damgaard.htm.

60. Global Alliance for Tax Justice, Public Services International, and the Tax Justice Network, "The State of Tax Justice 2021," November 2021, https://taxjustice.net/wp-content/uploads/2021/11/State_of_Tax_Justice_Repo rt_2021_ENGLISH.pdf

61. Brooke Harrington, *Capital Without Borders: Wealth Managers and the One Percent* (Cambridge, MA: Harvard University Press, 2016).

62. Dev Kar and Sarah Freitas, "Illicit Financial Flows from Developing Countries: 2001–2010," http://www.gfintegrity.org/report/illicit-financ ial-flows-from-developing-countries-2001-2010/. See also Philipp Genschell, "Globalization, Tax Competition and the Welfare State," *Politics and Society* 30, no. 3 (2002): 245–272; and Gabriel Zucman, *The Hidden Wealth of Nations* (Chicago: University of Chicago Press, 2015).

63. For example, see data provided by the Deputy Governor for Financial Stability, Bank of England, cited by Shaxson, *The Finance Curse*, 8.

64. For a case study illustrating these points in the pharmaceutical industry, see Susan K. Sell, "What COVID-19 Reveals About Twenty-First Century Capitalism: Adversity and Opportunity," *Development* 63 (2020): 150–156, https://doi.org/10.1057/s41301-020-00263-z.

65. Wolf Richter, "Risks Pile Up Quietly in the US Corporate Bond Market" (June 24, 2018), citing data provided by John Lonski, Chief Economist at Moody's Capital Markets Research, https://wolfstreet.com/2018/06/24/risks-pile-up-quietly-in-the-us-corporate-bond-market/.

66. William D. Cohan, "Opinion: Only the Fed Can Save Us," *New York Times*, August 19, 2019.

67. Richter, "Risks Pile Up."

68. Bank for International Statistics, "Semi-Annual Derivative Statistics, June 2017," Credit Suisse Global Wealth Report, 2016.

69. Financial Stability Board, "Global Monitoring Report on Non-Bank Financial Intermediation 2022," https://www.fsb.org/2022/12/global-mon itoring-report-on-non-bank-financial-intermediation-2022/.

70. Saez and Zucman, *Triumph of Injustice*, 76–79.

71. Mariana Mazzucato, "Financing Innovation: Creative Destruction vs. Destructive Creation," *Industrial and Corporate Change* 22, no. 4 (2013): 851–867; and Tim Hayward, *Global Justice and Finance* (Oxford: Oxford University Press, 2019), 54–70.

NOTES 281

72. Streeck, *How Will Capitalism End?*, 24.
73. Global Justice Now, "69 of the Richest 100 Entities on the Planet Are Corporations, Not Governments, Figures Show," October 17, 2018, https://www.globaljustice.org.uk/news/2018/oct/17/69-richest-100-entit ies-planet-are-corporations-not-governments-figures-show#.
74. Stefania Vitali, James B. Glattfelder, and Stefano Battiston, "The Network of Global Corporate Control," *PloS One* 6, no. 10 (2011): e25995, https://doi.org/10.1371/journal.pone.0025995.
75. Galbraith, *The Predator State*, 127.

Chapter 6

1. Intergovernmental Panel on Climate Change (IPCC), *Climate Change and Land: An IPCC Special Report on Climate Change, Desertification, Land Degradation, Sustainable Land Management, Food Security, and Greenhouse Gas Fluxes in Terrestrial Ecosystems, Summary for Policymakers* (IPCC, 2019), https://www.ipcc.ch/srccl/chapter/summ ary-for-policymakers/#:~:text=This%20Summary%20for%20Policymak ers%20(SPM,Action%20in%20the%20near%2Dterm.
2. Erle C. Ellis et al., "Anthropogenic Transformation of the Biomes, 1700 to 2000," *Global Ecology and Biogeography* 19 (2010): 589–606, https://doi.org/10.1111/j.1466-8238.2010.00540.x.
3. Brooke A. Williams et al., "Change in Terrestrial Human Footprint Drives Continued Loss of Intact Ecosystems," *One Earth* 3, no. 3 (2020): 371–382.
4. Intergovernmental Science-Policy Platform on Biodiversity and Ecosystem Services (IPBES), *The Global Assessment Report on Biodiversity and Ecosystem Services of the Intergovernmental Science-Policy Platform on Biodiversity and Ecosystem Services, Summary for Policymakers* (Bonn, Germany: IPBES secretariat, 2019), https://doi.org/10.5281/zen odo.3553579.
5. Food and Agriculture Organization (FAO), *State of Food Insecurity in the World 2009* (Rome: FAO, 2009).
6. Jonathan A. Foley, "Can We Feed the World and Sustain the Planet?" *Scientific American* (November 2011); Ellis et al., "Anthropogenic Transformation."
7. Food and Agriculture Organization (FAO), *The State of Food Insecurity in the World 2001* (Rome: FAO, 2002). The proposed FAO definitions became more expansive over the years, but the most encompassing def-initional refinements post-1996 were controversial and never formally

282 NOTES

endorsed by member states of the UN's Committee on Food Security. See Jessica Fanzo, "Ethical Issues for Human Nutrition in the Context of Global Food Security and Sustainable Development," *Global Food Security* 7 (2015): 15–23, https://doi.org/10.1016/j.gfs.2015.11.001.

8. The International Covenant on Economic, Social and Cultural Rights (ICESCR) of 1966, recognized "the right of everyone to an adequate standard of living for himself and his family, including adequate food . . . and to the continuous improvement of living conditions" (Article 11, para. 1) as well as "the fundamental right of everyone to be free from hunger" (Article 11, para. 2). For elaboration, see Committee on Economic, Social and Cultural Rights, "General Comment No. 12: The Right to Adequate Food, Art. 11" (E/C.12/1999/5 – May 12, 1999), https://unstats.un.org/sdgs/report/2016/goal-02/ht.

9. United Nations, *Sustainable Development Goals Report 2016*, https://unstats.un.org/sdgs/report/2016/Overview/.

10. UN, *SDGs Report* 2016.

11. E.g., FAO, *State of Food Insecurity 2009*; H. C. J. Godfray et al., "Food Security: The Challenge of Feeding 9 Billion People," *Science* 327 (2010): 812–818; Government Office for Science, *Foresight, 2011: The Future of Food and Farming: Challenges and Choices for Global Sustainability*. (London: Government Office for Science, United Kingdom, 2011); Royal Society of London, *Reaping the Benefits: Science and the Sustainable Intensification of Global Agriculture* (London: Royal Society, 2009).

12. Organisation for Economic Cooperation and Development (OECD), *Food Security: Challenges for the Food and Agricultural System* (Paris: OECD, 2013), 38, http://dx.doi.org/10.1787/9789264195363-en.

13. Michiel van Dijk et al., "A Meta-Analysis of Projected Global Food Demand and Population at Risk of Hunger for the Period 2010–2050," *Nature Food* 2 (2021): 494–501, https://doi.org/10.1038/s43016-021-00322-9.

14. Government Office for Science, *Foresight Report.*

15. United Nations, Department of Economic and Social Affairs, Population Division, "World Population Prospects 2019: Highlights" (ST/ESA/SER.A/423). (2019), https://population.un.org/wpp/Publications/Files/WPP2019_Highlights.pdf.

16. Anne Barnhill and Jessica Fanzo, "Nourishing Humanity Without Destroying the Planet," *Ethics and International Affairs* 35, no. 1 (2021): 69–81.

NOTES 283

17. Marco Springmann et al., "Options for Keeping the Food System Within Environmental Limits," *Nature* 562, no. 7728 (October 2018): 519–525, https://doi.org/10.1038/s41586-018-0594-0.

18. Jonathan A. Foley et al., "Global Consequences of Land Use," *Science* 309, no. 5734 (2005): 570–574, https://doi.org/10.1126/science.1111772.

19. Food and Agriculture Organization (FAO), *Status of the World's Soil Resources: Main Report* (Rome, Italy: FAO, 2015), http://www.fao.org/documents/card/en/c/c6814873-efc3-41db-b7d3-2081a10ede50/.

20. IPCC, *Climate Change and Land.*

21. United Nations Convention to Combat Desertification, "Contribution to the 2018 High Level Political Forum on Sustainable Development Submission from the UNCCD," April 27, 2018, https://sustainabledevelopment.un.org/content/documents/17997UNCCD_contribution_to_HLPF_2018_FINAL.pdf.

22. FAO, *Status of the World's Soil Resources.*

23. David Pimentel, "Soil Erosion: A Food and Environmental Threat," *Journal of the Environment, Development and Sustainability* 8 (2006): 119–137; United Nations Convention to Combat Desertification, *Global Land Outlook*, 1st ed. (Bonn, Germany, 2017), https://www.unccd.int/sites/default/files/documents/2017-09/GLO_Full_Report_low_res.pdf.

24. Pimentel, "Soil Erosion."

25. The estimate is provided by Rick Cruse, a professor of agronomy at Iowa State University and director of the Daily Erosion Project. Quoted by Tom Philpott, "Gully Washers," *Modern Farmer*, August 12, 2020, https://modernfarmer.com/2020/08/gully-washers/.

26. IPCC, *Climate Change and Land.*

27. Food and Agriculture Organization (FAO), *State of Knowledge of Soil Biodiversity: Status, Challenges and Potentialities, Summary for Policymakers* (Rome: FAO, 2020). See also D. L. Evans et al., "Soil Lifespans and How They Can Be Extended by Land Use and Management Change," *Environmental Research Letters* 15, no. 9 (2020): 0940b2, https://iopscience.iop.org/article/10.1088/1748-9326/aba2fd.

28. Intergovernmental Panel on Climate Change, *Climate Change 2022: Impacts, Adaptation, and Vulnerability.* Contribution of Working Group II to the Sixth Assessment Report of the Intergovernmental Panel on Climate Change (H. -O. Pörtner et al. eds. (Cambridge: Cambridge University Press, 2022), https://www.ipcc.ch/report/ar6/wg2/.

29. IPCC, *Climate Change and Land.*

30. UNCCD, *Global Land Outlook.*

284   NOTES

31. Montpellier Panel, "No Ordinary Matter: Conserving, Restoring and Enhancing Africa's Soils" (December 2014), https://ag4impact.org/wpcontent/uploads/2014/12/MP_0106_Soil_Report_LR1.pdf.
32. Government Office for Science, *Foresight*, 28.
33. Jason Clay, "Freeze the Footprint of Food," *Nature* 475 (2011): 287.
34. UNESCO, "Human Alteration of the Nitrogen Cycle: Threats, Benefits and Opportunities," *UNESCO-SCOPE Policy and Benefits* 4 (2007): 1–6.
35. Vaclav Smil, *Enriching the Earth: Fritz Haber, Carl Bosch, and the Transformation of World Food Production* (MIT Press, 2004); Jan Willem Erisman et al., "How a Century of Ammonia Synthesis Changed the World," *Nature Geoscience* 1, no. 10 (2008): 636–639, https://doi.org/10.1038/ngeo325.
36. Erisman et al., "A Century of Ammonia Synthesis."
37. Government Office for Science, *Foresight Report*, 15.
38. Jesse H. Ausubel, Iddo K. Wernick, and Paul E. Waggoner, "Peak Farmland and the Prospect for Land Sparing," *Population and Development Review* 38, Issue Suppl. s1 (2013): 221–242, February 2013, https://doi.org/10.1111/j.1728-4457.2013.00561.x.
39. Yunhu Gao and Andre Cabrera Serrenho, "Greenhouse Gas Emissions from Nitrogen Fertilizers Could Be Reduced by up to One-Fifth of Current Levels by 2050 with Combined Interventions," *Nature Food* 4 (2023): 170–178, doi:10.1038/s43016-023-00698-w.
40. Edwin D. Ongley, *Control of Water Pollution from Agriculture* (Rome: Food and Agriculture Organization of the United Nations, 1996).
41. Peter P. Motavalli, Keith W. Goyne, and Ranjith P. Udawatta. "Environmental Impacts of Enhanced Efficiency Nitrogen Fertilizers," *Plant Management Network*, July 30, 2008, http://www.plantmanagement network.org/pub/cm/symposium/enhanced/impacts/.
42. For estimates of crop absorption of one-third to one-half of the nitrogen applied to soil as fertilizer, see David Tilman, "The Greening of the Green Revolution," *Nature* 396 (November 19, 1998): 211–212. The slightly lower estimates are from UNESCO, *Human Alteration of the Nitrogen Cycle*.
43. Ongley, *Control of Water Pollution*; Jan Willem Erisman et al., "Consequences of Human Modification of the Global Nitrogen Cycle," *Philosophical Transactions of the Royal Society of London. Series B, Biological Sciences* 368, no. 1621 (May 27, 2013): 20130116, https://doi.org/10.1098/rstb.2013.0116.
44. Erica Goode, "Farmers Put Down the Plow for More Productive Soil," *New York Times*, March 9, 2015.

NOTES 285

45. For example, about one-third of current annual US nitrogen fertilizer used in maize agriculture is used to compensate for the long-term loss of soil fertility through erosion and organic matter loss. W. S. Jang et al., "The Hidden Costs of Land Degradation in US Maize Agriculture," *Earth's Future* 9 (2020): e2020EF001641, https://doi.org/10.1029/2020EF001641.

46. Donald Scavia et al., "Assessing and Addressing the Re-Eutrophication of Lake Erie: Central Basin Hypoxia," *Journal of Great Lakes Research* 40, no. 2 (2011): 226–246, https://doi.org/10.1016/j.jglr.2014.02.004.

47. Jeremy Hance, "Lethal Algae Blooms: An Ecosystem Out of Balance," *The Guardian*, January 4, 2020.

48. Gao and Serrenho, "Greenhouse Gas Emissions."

49. Government Office for Science, *Foresight Report*, 30–35.

50. IPCC, *Land and Climate*, chapter 4.

51. Aimable Uwizeye et al., "Nitrogen Emissions Along Global Livestock Supply Chains," *Nature Food* 1 (2020): 437–446, doi:10.1038/s43016-020-0113-y.

52. Hanjin Tian et al., "A Comprehensive Quantification of Global Nitrous Oxide Sources and Sinks," *Nature* 586 (2020): 248–256, https://www.nature.com/articles/s41586-020-2780-0.

53. Joseph Poore and Thomas Nemecek, "Reducing Food's Environmental Impacts Through Producers and Consumers," *Science* 360, no. 6392 (2018): 987–992, doi:10.1126/science.aaq0216.

54. Christopher Bren d'Amour et al., "Future Urban Land Expansion and Implications for Global Croplands," *Proceedings of the National Academies of Science* 114, no. 34 (August 22, 2017): 8939–8944, https://doi.org/10.1073/pnas.1606036114.

55. d'Amour et al., "Future Urban Land Expansion."

56. d'Amour et al., "Future Urban Land Expansion."

57. Bruce M. Campbell et al., "Agriculture Production as a Major Driver of the Earth System Exceeding Planetary Boundaries," *Ecology and Society* 22, no 4 (2017): 8, https://doi.org/10.5751/ES-09595-220408.

58. Springmann et al., "Options."

59. Uwizeye et al., "Nitrogen Emissions."

60. United Nations Environment Programme (UNEP), *Making Peace with Nature: A Scientific Blueprint to Tackle the Climate, Biodiversity and Pollution Emergencies* (Nairobi: UNEP, 2021), 23, 73, https://www.unep.org/resources/making-peace-nature.

61. NYDF Assessment Partners, "Taking Stock of National Climate Action for Forests. Goal 7 Progress Report," October 2021. www.forestdeclaration.org.

286 NOTES

62. Philip G. Curtis et al., "Classifying Drivers of Global Forest Loss," *Science* 361, no. 6407 (September 14, 2018): 1108–1111, https://doi.org/10.1126/science.aau3445.

63. Florence Pendrill et al., "Agricultural and Forestry Trade Drives Large Share of Tropical Deforestation Emissions," *Global Environmental Change* 56 (2019): 1–10; Noriko Hosonuma et al., "An Assessment of Deforestation and Forest Degradation Drivers in Developing Countries," *Environmental Research Letters* 7, no. 4 (2012): 044009.

64. For reporting based on government data, see Eduardo Simões, "Brazil Amazon Deforestation Jumped 85% in 2019 vs 2018: Government Data," *Reuters*, January 14, 2020, https://www.reuters.com/article/us-brazil-deforestation-idUKKBN1ZD2W0?edition-redirect=uk; Greenpeace, "Amazon Deforestation Reaches Highest Level in More Than a Decade," November 18, 2019, https://www.greenpeace.org/international/story/27133/amazon-deforestation-highest-rate-in-decade/.

65. Eric L. Bullock et al., "Satellite-Based Estimates Reveal Widespread Forest Degradation in the Amazon," *Global Change Biology* 26, no. 5 (2020): 2956–2969, https://doi.org/10.1111/gcb.15029.

66. For an explanation of the change in the boundary benchmark for forest conversion from its initial formulation in 2009 to the 2015 revision, see Campbell et al., "Agriculture Production."

67. Johan Rockström et al., "Planetary Boundaries: Separating Fact from Fiction. A Response to Montoya, et al.," *Trends in Ecology and Evolution* 33, no. 4 (April 1, 2018): 233–234, https://doi.org/10.1016/j.tree.2018.01.010.

68. Frank Biermann and Rakhyun E. Kim, "The Boundaries of the Planetary Boundary Framework: A Critical Appraisal of Approaches to Define a "Safe Operating Space" for Humanity," *Annual Review of Environmental Resources* 45 (2020):497–521, https://doi.org/10.1146/annurev-environ-012320-080337.

69. Campbell et al., "Agriculture Production as a Major Driver."

70. International Union for Conservation of Nature (IUCN) "Conservation Successes Overshadowed by More Species Declines: IUCN Red List Update," June 23, 2015, https://www.iucn.org/content/conservation-successes-overshadowed-more-species-declines-iucn-red-list-update.

71. Yiwen Zeng et al., "Environmental Destruction Not Avoided with the Sustainable Development Goals," *Nature Sustainability* 3 (2020): 795–798.

72. UNEP, *Making Peace*, 70.

73. Robert Watson, "Loss of Biodiversity Is Just as Catastrophic as Climate Change," *The Guardian*, May 6, 2019.

NOTES 287

74. Jennifer Clapp, *Food*, 3rd ed. (Cambridge: Polity, 2020), 56.
75. Food and Agriculture Organization (FAO), *The State of the World's Biodiversity for Food and Agriculture*, ed. J. Bélanger and D. Pilling. FAO Commission on Genetic Resources for Food and Agriculture Assessments (Rome: FAO, 2019), http://www.fao.org/3/CA3129EN/CA3129EN.pdf.
76. FAO, "What Is Happening to Agrobiodiversity?," http://www.fao.org/3/y5609e/y5609e02.htm
77. Food and Agriculture Organization (FAO), "Once Neglected, These Traditional Crops Are Our New Rising Stars," February 10, 2018, https://www.fao.org/fao-stories/article/en/c/1154584/.
78. FAO, *The State of the World's Biodiversity*.
79. FAO, *The State of the World's Biodiversity*.
80. IPBES, *Summary*.
81. E. O. Wilson, "My Wish to Build the Encyclopedia of Life," TED Talk, 2007, https://www.ted.com/talks/e_o_wilson_my_wish_build_the_e ncyclopedia_of_life/transcript.
82. UNEP, *Making Peace*, 62. See also Pendrill et al., "Agricultural and Forestry Trade." Pendrill and colleagues estimate that 70–80% of tropical deforestation is due to pasture expansion for beef or plantations mainly producing soy and other feed for livestock, or palm oil.
83. Greenpeace International, *Countdown to Extinction*, June 10, 2019, https://www.greenpeace.org/international/publication/22247/countd own-extinction-report-deforestation-commodities-soya-palm-oil/.
84. UNEP, *Making Peace*, 107.
85. Nguyen Tien Hoang and Keiichiro Kanemoto, "Mapping the Deforestation Footprint of Nations Reveals Growing Threat to Tropical Forests," *Nature Ecology and Evolution* 5 (2021): 8450953, https://doi.org/10.1038/s41559-021-01417-z.
86. Hoang and Kanemoto, "Mapping the Deforestation Footprint."
87. UNEP, *Making Peace*, 15.
88. UNEP, *Making Peace*, 15.
89. UNEP, *Making Peace*, 26.
90. Cécile A. J. Girardin et al., "Nature-Based Solutions Can Help Cool the Planet: If We Act Now," *Nature* 593 (May 13, 2021): 191–194.
91. E.g., Eric A. Coleman et al., "Limited Effects of Tree Planting on Forest Canopy Cover and Rural Livelihoods in Northern India," *Nature Sustainability* 4 (2021): 997–1004, https://doi.org/10.1038/s41893-021-00761-z.

288   NOTES

92. J. -F. Bastin et al., "The Global Tree Restoration Potential," *Science* 365, nos. 76–79 (2019), doi:10.1126/science.aax0848pmid:31273120.

93. Sky1.5 is one of three pathways analyzed first in its 2018 report and largely replicated in its 2020 update. See Royal Dutch Shell, "The Energy Transformation Scenarios: An Overview," https://www.shell.com/pro mos/energy-and-innovation/summary-report/_jcr_content.stream/ 1613991541540/f91916c4527649c220d980582a53095403809767/shell-energy-transformation-scenarios-overview.pdf. For the reference to Brazil, see Adam Vaughn, "Shell Boss Says Mass Reforestation Needed to Limit Temperature Rises to 1.5C," *The Guardian*, October 9, 2018.

94. Torbern Tagesson et al., "Recent Divergence in the Contributions of Tropical and Boreal Forests to the Terrestrial Carbon Sink," *Nature Ecology and Evolution* 4 (2020): 202–209, https://doi.org/10.1038/s41 559-019-1090-0.

95. Robert Heilmayr, Cristian Echeverría, and Eric F. Lambin, "Impacts of Chilean Forest Subsidies on Forest Cover, Carbon and Biodiversity," *Nature Sustainability* 3 (2020): 701–709. https://doi.org/10.1038/s41 893-020-0547-0.

96. Katharyn A. Duffy et al., "How Close Are We to the Temperature Tipping Point of the Terrestrial Biosphere?" *Science Advances* 7, no. 3 (January 13, 2021): eaay1052. doi:10.1126/sciadv.aay1052; Giuliano Maselli Locosselli et al., "Global Tree-Ring Analysis Reveals Rapid Decrease in Tropical Tree Longevity with Temperature," *Proceedings of the National Academies of Science* 117, no. 52 (December 29, 2020): 33358–33364, https://doi.org/10.1073/pnas.2003873117.

97. Paul I. Palmer et al., "Net Carbon Emissions from African Biosphere Dominate Pan-Tropical Atmospheric CO_2 Signal," *Nature Communications* 10 (2019): 3344, https://doi.org/10.1038/s41467-019-11097-w.

98. Bill Anderegg et al., "Risks to Mitigation Potential of Forests," *Science* 368, no. 6497 (June 19, 2020): eaaz7005, https://doi.org/10.1126/science. aaz7005.

99. Susan Cook-Patton et al., "Protect, Manage and Then Restore Lands for Climate Mitigation," *Nature Climate Change* 11 (2021): 1027–1034, https://doi.org/10.1038/s41558-021-01198-0.

100. High Level Panel of Experts (HLPE), *Biofuels and Food Security* (Rome: FAO, Committee on World Food Security, 2013).

101. Dr. Anne Larigauderie, executive secretary of the IPBES, made these observations in opening remarks at a 2018 UN biodiversity meeting in Egypt. Intergovernmental Science-Policy Platform on Biodiversity and Ecosystem Services (IPBES), "Climate Change/Biodiversity

NOTES   289

Loss: Inseparable Threats to Humanity That Must Be Addressed Together," Public Release: November 15, 2018, https://www.eurekalert.org/pub_releases/2018-11/tca-cc111518.php.

102. Chris Malins, *Biofuel to the Fire: The Impact of Continued Expansion of Palm and Soy Oil Demand Through Biofuel Policy* (Oslo, Norway: Rainforest Foundation Norway, March 10, 2020).

103. For the proposal to set aside half of the Earth for nature, see E. O. Wilson, *Half-Earth: Our Planet's Fight for Life* (New York: W.W. Norton, 2016). The commitment to set aside 30% by 2030—known as the 30 × 30 provision—was included in the 2022 Kunming-Montreal Global biodiversity framework adopted at the 15th Conference of Parties to the Convention on Biological Diversity, https://www.cbd.int/doc/c/e6d3/cd1d/daf663719a03902a9b116c34/cop-15-l-25-en.pdf.

104. Judith Schleicher et al., "Protecting Half of the Planet Could Directly Affect Over One Billion People," *Nature Sustainability* 2 (2019): 1094–1096, https://doi.org/10.1038/s41893-019-0423-y.

105. Johan Rockström J. et al., "Planetary Boundaries: Exploring the Safe Operating Space for Humanity." *Ecology and Society* 14, no. 2 (2009): art 32, http://www.ecologyandsociety.org/vol14/iss2/art32/.

106. Kari-Oca 2 Declaration, https://www.ienearth.org/kari-oca-2-declaration/.

107. "Indigenous Peoples in a Changing World of Work," *Indigenous Navigator*, May 2021, https://indigenousnavigator.org/sites/indigenousnavigator.org/files/media/document/Indigenous%20peoples%20in%20a%20changing%20world%20of%20work%20-%20wcms_792208.pdf.

108. Food and Agricultural Organization (FAO) and FAO Regional Office for Latin America and the Caribbean (FILAC), *Forest Governance by Indigenous and Tribal People. An Opportunity for Climate Action in Latin America and the Caribbean* (Santiago: FAO, 2021), https://doi.org/10.4060/cb2953en.

109. La Via Campesina, "The 2022 Geneva Declaration," June 28, 2022, https://viacampesina.org/en/geneva-end-wto-build-international-trade-based-on-peasants-rights-and-food-sovereignty/.

Chapter 7

1. Junguo Liu et al., "Water Scarcity Assessments in the Past, Present, and Future," *Earth's Future* 5 (2017): 545–559, https://doi.org/10.1002/2016 EF00051.

290 NOTES

2. UN-Water, *Summary Progress Update 2021: SDG 6—Water and Sanitation for All* (Geneva, Switzerland: UN-Water, 2021), https://www.unwater.org/publications/summary-progress-update-2021-sdg-6-water-and-sanitation-for-all/.

3. UNESCO World Water Assessment Programme, *UN World Water Development Report 2021: Valuing Water* (Paris: UNESCO, 2020), 8, https://www.unesco.org/reports/wwdr/2021/en.

4. Mesfin M. Mekonnen and Arjen Y. Hoekstra, "Four Billion People Facing Severe Water Scarcity," *Science Advances* 2, no. 2 (February 12, 2016): e1500323, https://doi.org/10.1126/sciadv.1500323.

5. Peter Burek et al., *Water Futures and Solution—Fast Track Initiative (Final Report).* IIASA Working Paper (IIASA, Laxenburg, Austria: WP-16-006, 2016), http://pure.iiasa.ac.at/id/eprint/13008/.

6. 2030 Water Resources Group, "Charting Our Water Future: Economic Frameworks to Inform Decisionmaking," https://www.mckinsey.com/client_service/sustainability/latest_thinking/~/media/A7CB542C7FA24CD191964C7952EA2D81.ashx.

7. Robert I. McDonald et al., "Water on an Urban Planet: Urbanization and the Reach of Urban Water Infrastructure," *Global Environmental Change* 27 (2014): 96–105, https://doi.org/10.1016/j.gloenvcha.2014.04.022.

8. United Nations Environment Programme (UNEP), *Options for Decoupling Economic Growth from Water Use and Water Pollution. Report of the International Resource Panel Working Group on Sustainable Water Management* (Paris: UNEP, 2016), https://www.resourcepanel.org/reports/options-decoupling-economic-growth-water-use-and-water-pollution.

9. See P. C. D. Milly et al., "Stationarity Is Dead: Whither Water Management?" *Science* 319 (February 1, 2008): 573–574.

10. Richard Damania et al., *Uncharted Waters: The New Economics of Water Scarcity and Variability* (Washington, DC: World Bank, 2017), https://doi.org/10.1596/978-1-4648-1179-1.

11. Julie Padowski and Steven Gorelick, "Global Analysis of Urban Surface Water Supply Vulnerability," *Environmental Research Letters* 9, no. 10 (2014): 104004.

12. Romain Hugonnet et al., "Accelerated Global Glacier Mass Loss in the Early Twenty-First Century," *Nature* 592 (2021): 726–731, https://doi.org/10.1038/s41586-021-03436-z.

13. J. M. Maurer, J. M. Schaefer, S. Rupper, and A. Corley, "Acceleration of Ice Loss Across the Himalayas over the Past 40 Years," *Science Advances*

NOTES 291

5, no. 6 (June 19, 2019): eaav7266, https://doi.org/10.1036/1097-8542. BR0702191.

14. J. M. Shea et al., "Modelling Glacier Change in the Everest Region, Nepal Himalaya," *The Cryosphere* 9 (2015): 1105–1128, https://doi.org/10.5194/tc-9-1105-2015.

15. Yao Tandong et al., "Asian Water Tower Change and Its Impacts," *Bulletin of the Chinese Academy of Science* 34 (2019): 1203–1209, doi:10.16418/j.issn.1000-3045.2019.11.003. [English translation].

16. W. W. Immerzeel et al., "Importance and Vulnerability of the World's Water Towers," *Nature* 577 (2020): 364–369, https://doi.org/10.1038/s41586-019-1822-y.

17. P. C. D. Milly and K. A. Dunne, "Colorado River Flow Dwindles as Warming-Driven Loss of Reflective Snow Energizes Evaporation," *Science* 13: 367, no. 6483 (2020): 1252–1255, doi:10.1126/science.aay9187.

18. Justin S. Mankin et al., "Mid-Latitude Freshwater Availability Reduced by Projected Vegetation Responses to Climate Change," *Nature Geoscience* 12 (2019): 983–988, https://doi.org/10.1038/s41561-019-0480-x.

19. Tom Gleeson and Brian Richter, "How Much Groundwater Can We Pump and Protect Environmental Flow Through Time? Presumptive Standards for Conjunctive Management of Aquifers and Rivers," *River Research Applied* 34 (2018): 83–92, https://doi.org/10.1002/rra.3185.

20. Alexandra S. Richey et al., "Quantifying Renewable Groundwater Stress with GRACE," *Water Resources Research* 51 (2015): 5217–5238, https://doi.org/10.1002/2015WR017349.

21. United Nations Environment Programme, *Global Environment Outlook: Environment for Development (GEO-4)* (Valletta, Malta: Progress Press, 2007).

22. Richey et al., "Quantifying Renewable Groundwater."

23. Carle Dalin et al., "Groundwater Depletion Embedded in International Food Trade," *Nature* 543 (2017): 700–704, https://doi.org/10.1038/natu re21403.

24. FAO, *The State of Food and Agriculture 2020: Overcoming Water Challenges in Agriculture* (Rome: FAO, 2020), https://www.fao.org/documents/card/en/c/cb1447en.

25. FAO, *The State of Food and Agriculture 2020*.

26. World Bank, "Deep Wells and Prudence: Towards Pragmatic Action for Addressing Groundwater Overexploitation in India," 2012, https://documents1.worldbank.org/curated/en/272661468267911138/pdf/516760ESW0P0951round0Water129101110.pdf.

292 NOTES

27. National Institute for Transforming India (NITI), "Composite Water Management Index (CWMI)," 2018, http://www.niti.gov.in/writereadd ata/files/document_publication/2018-05-18-Water-index-Report_v S6B.pdf.

28. *The Economist*, "Groundwater Is Helping to Feed the World, but It Is Dangerously Depleted," February 28, 2019, https://www.economist.com/special-report/2019/02/28/groundwater-is-helping-to-feed-the-world-but-it-is-dangerously-depleted.

29. Nathan Halverson, "California Is Sinking Faster Than Ever, Thanks to Massive Overpumping of Water," *Grist* (June 10, 2015), https://grist.org/climate-energy/california-is-sinking-faster-than-ever-thanks-to-mass ive-overpumping-of-water/?utm_campaign=socialflow&utm_source= facebook&utm_medium=update.

30. *The Economist*, "Groundwater."

31. Kenneth Belitz, Miranda S. Fram, and Tyler D. Johnson, "Metrics for Assessing the Quality of Groundwater Used for Public Supply, CA, USA: Equivalent-Population and Area," *Environmental Science and Technology* 49, no. 14 (2015): 8330–8338, https://doi.org/10.1021/acs.est.5b00265.

32. Grant Ferguson and Tom Gleeson, "Vulnerability of Coastal Aquifers to Groundwater Use and Climate Change," *Nature Climate Change* 2 (2012): 342; and Ebru Kirezci et al., "Projections of Global-Scale Extreme Sea Levels and Resulting Episodic Coastal Flooding over the 21st Century," *Scientific Reports* 10 (2020): 11629, https://doi.org/10.1038/s41 598-020-67736-6.

33. Robert J. Nicholls et al., "A Global Analysis of Subsidence, Relative Sea-Level Change and Coastal Flood Exposure," *Nature Climate Change* 11 (2021): 338–342, https://doi.org/10.1038/s41558-021-00993-z.

34. David L. Feldman, *Water Politics* (Cambridge: Polity, 2017), 23–24, 54–56.

35. Global Water Partnership (GWP), *Integrated Water Resources Management* (Stockholm, Sweden: Global Water Partnership, 2000), 22.

36. Malin Falkenmark, "The Greatest Water Problem: The Inability to Link Environmental Security, Water Security and Food Security," *International Journal of Water Resources Development* 17, no. 4 (2001): 539–554.

37. Robert Glennon, *Unquenchable: America's Water Crisis and What to Do About It* (Washington, DC: Island Press, 2009), 183–193, https://doi.org/10.1038/s41586-019-1594-4.

38. Charles J. Vörösmarty et al., "Global Threats to Human Water Security and River Biodiversity," *Nature* 467 (2010): 555–561, https://doi.org/10.1038/nature09440.

NOTES   293

39. World Bank Group, *High and Dry: Climate Change, Water, and the Economy* (Washington, DC: World Bank, 2016), https://openknowledge.worldbank.org/handle/10986/23665.

40. UN-Water, "Summary Progress Update 2021—SDG 6—Water and Sanitation for All," Version: 1 March 2021. Geneva, Switzerland, 2021, https://www.unwater.org/publications/summary-progress-update-2021-sdg-6-water-and-sanitation-all.

41. UN-Water, "Summary Progress Update 2021."

42. WHO/UNICEF Joint Monitoring Program for Water Supply, Sanitation and Hygiene (JMP), "Progress on Household Drinking Water, Sanitation and Hygiene 2000–2020," https://data.unicef.org/resources/progress-on-household-drinking-water-sanitation-and-hygiene-2000-2020/.

43. United Nations World Water Assessment Programme, *The United Nations World Water Development Report 2017: Wastewater, The Untapped Resource* (Paris: UNESCO, 2017).

44. Stephen J. Hoffman, *Planet Water: Investing in the World's Most Valuable Resource* (Hoboken, NJ: John Wiley and Sons, 2009), 91–154.

45. UN-Water, "Summary Progress Update 2021," 8.

46. UN-Water, "Summary Progress Update 2021."

47. Luis A. Andres et al., *Doing More with Less: Smarter Subsidies for Water Supply and Sanitation* (Washington, DC: World Bank, 2019), https://openknowledge.worldbank.org/handle/10986/32277.

48. United Nations Development Program (UNDP), "Human Development Report 2006: Beyond Scarcity: Power, Poverty, and the Global Water Crisis," 2006, 2, http://hdr.undp.org/en/reports/global/hdr2006/chapters/.

49. Megan Konar et al., "The Water Footprint of Staple Crop Trade Under Climate Change and Policy Scenarios," *Environmental Research Letters* 11 (2016): 035006; Neal T. Graham et al., "Future Changes in the Trading of Virtual Water," *Nature Communications* 11(2020): 3632, https://doi.org/10.1038/s41467-020-17400-4.

50. UNEP, *Options for Decoupling.*

51. UN-Water, "Summary Progress Update," 9

52. Arjen Y. Hoekstra and Ashok K. Chapagain, "Water Footprints of Nations: Water Use by People as a Function of Their Consumption Pattern," *Water Resource Management* 21 (2007): 35–48, https://doi.org/10.1007/s11269-006-9039-x; Arjen Y. Hoekstra and Mesfin M. Mekonnen, "The Water Footprint of Humanity," *Proceedings of the National Academies of Sciences* 109, no. 9 (February 28, 2012): 3232–3237, https://doi.org/10.1073/pnas.1109936109.

294 NOTES

53. Water Footprint Network, "National Water Footprint, 2023," https://wat erfootprint.org/en/water-footprint/national-water-footprint/.
54. Francis Gassert, "One-Quarter of World's Agriculture Grows in Highly Water-Stressed Areas," (October, 2013), https://www.wri.org/insights/ one-quarter-worlds-agriculture-grows-highly-water-stressed-areas.
55. Gassert, "One-Quarter."
56. For a discussion of strengths, weaknesses, and versions of the dependency thesis, see François Bourguignon, "Inequality and Globalization: How the Rich Get Richer as the Poor Catch Up," *Foreign Affairs* 95, no. 1 (2016): 11–15.
57. Paolo D'Odorico et al., "Global Virtual Water Trade and the Hydrological Cycle: Patterns, Drivers, and Socio-Environmental Impacts," *Environmental Research Letters* 14 (2019): 053001.
58. Carle Dalin et al., "Groundwater Depletion Embedded in International Food Trade," *Nature* 543 (2017): 700–704.
59. Dalin et al., "Groundwater Depletion."
60. Omid Khazani and Nabih Bulos, "As Water Table Lowers, Tehran and Much of Iran Are Slowly Sinking," *Los Angeles Times*, August 2, 2021, https://www.latimes.com/world-nation/story/2021-08-02/lower-water-table-climate-change-tehran-iran-sinking.
61. World Resources Institute, "Water Risk Atlas," https://www.wri.org/ aqueduct.
62. Matthew Rodell, Isabella Velicogna, and J. S. Famiglietti, "Satellite-Based Estimates of Groundwater Depletion in India," *Nature* 460 (2009): 999–1002, https://doi.org/10.1038/nature08238.
63. World Wildlife Fund, *Living Waters: Conserving the Source of Life*, 2002, 10.
64. Arjen Y. Hoekstra, *The Water Footprint of Consumer Society*, 2nd ed. (London and New York: Routledge/Earthscan, 2020), 94.
65. Yuan Liu et al., "Contributions of Climatic and Crop Varietal Changes to Crop Production in the North China Plain, Since 1980s," *Global Change and Biology* 16 (2010): 2287–2299, 10.1111/j.1365-2486.2009.02077.x; Xu Zhao et al., "Physical and Virtual Water Transfers for Regional Water Stress Alleviation in China," *Proceedings of the National Academies of Sciences* 112 (2015): 1031–1035.
66. Werner Aeschbach-Hertig and Tom Gleeson, "Regional Strategies for the Accelerating Global Problem of Groundwater Depletion," *Nature Geoscience* 5 (2012): 853–861, 10.1038/Ngeo1617.
67. Yong Jiang, "China's Water Scarcity," *Journal of Environmental Management* 90 (2009): 3185–3196; Taisheng Du et al., "China's Food Security Is

Threatened by the Unsustainable Use of Water Resources in North and Northwest China," *Food and Energy Security* 3, no. 1 (2014): 7–18, https://doi.org/10.1002/fes3.40; and Liqiang Ge et al., "Evaluation of China's Water Footprint," *Water Resource Management* 25 (2011): 2633–2647.

68. China Water Risk, "North China Plain Groundwater: >70% Unfit for Human Touch," February 26, 2013, https://www.chinawaterrisk.org/about/.

69. Nadya Ivanova, "Toxic Water: Across Much of China, Huge Harvests Irrigated with Industrial and Agricultural Runoff," 2013, https://www.circleofblue.org/2013/world/toxic-water-across-much-of-china-huge-harvests-irrigated-with-industrial-and-agricultural-runoff/. For attempts to quantify quality-based water scarcity from all sources (surface water and groundwater) in China, see Ting Ma et al., "Pollution Exacerbates China's Water Scarcity and Its Regional Inequality," *Nature Communications* 11 (2020): 650, https://doi.org/10.1038/s41467-020-14532-5.

70. Molly A. Maupin et al., "Estimated Use of Water in the United States in 2010: U.S. Geological Survey Circular 1405," 2014, https://pubs.usgs.gov/circ/1405/#:~:text=Water%20use%20in%20the%20United,lowest%20level%20since%20before%201970.

71. Virginia L. McGuire, "Water-Level Changes in the High Plains Aquifer, Predevelopment to 2009, 2007–2008, and 2008–2009, and Change in Water Storage, Predevelopment to 2009," U.S. Geological Survey Scientific Investigations Report 2011-5089 (U.S. Geological Survey, Reston, VA. 2011), https://pubs.usgs.gov/sir/2011/5089/pdf/SIR2011-5089.pdf.

72. Matthew R. Sanderson and R. Scott Frey, "Structural Impediments to Sustainable Groundwater Management in the High Plains Aquifer of Western Kansas," *Agriculture and Human Values* 32 (2015): 401–417, https://doi.org/10.1007/s10460-014-9567-6.

73. United States Department of Homeland Security (DHS) Office of Cyber and Infrastructure Analysis, "Analysis of High Plains Resource Risk and Economic Impacts," August 2015, https://rrbwp.nebraska.gov/Reference/OCIA%20-%20Analysis%20of%20High%20Plains%20Resource%20Risk%20and%20Economic%20Impacts%20%282%29.pdf.

74. David R. Steward et al., "Tapping Unsustainable Groundwater Stores for Agricultural Production in the High Plains Aquifer of Kansas, Projections to 2110," *Proceedings of the National Academies of Sciences* 110, no. 37 (September 2013): E3477–86–E3486, https://doi.org/10.1073/pnas.1220351110.

296 NOTES

75. Matthew R. Sanderson and Vivian Hughes, "Race to the Bottom (of the Well): Groundwater in an Agricultural Production Treadmill," *Social Problems* 66, no. 3 (August 2019): 392–410, https://doi.org/10.1093/soc pro/spy011.

76. Caroline Winter, "Nestlé Makes Billions Bottling Water It Pays Nearly Nothing For," *Bloomberg Businessweek*, September 21, 2017, https://www.bloomberg.com/news/features/2017-09-21/nestl-makes-billions-bottl ing-water-it-pays-nearly-nothing-for. See also Alex Brown, "Lawmakers Open Groundwater Fight Against Bottled Water Companies," Pew Trusts. org, February 12, 2020, https://www.pewtrusts.org/en/research-and-analysis/blogs/stateline/2020/02/12/lawmakers-open-groundwater-fight-against-bottled-water-companies.

77. Maria Cristina Rulli, Antonio Saviori, and Paulo D'Odorico, "Global Land And Water Grabbing," *Proceedings of the National Academies of Sciences* 110 (2013): 892–897, https://doi.org/10.1073/pnas.1213163110.

78. Jampel Dell'Angelo, Paulo D'Odorico, and Maria Cristina Rulli, "The Neglected Costs of Water Peace," *Wiley Interdisciplinary Reviews: Water* (2018): 5e1316, https://doi.org/10.1002/wat2.1316.

79. For an inventory of watershed effects see, Thomas Winter et al., "Ground Water and Surface Water: A Single Resource 9-14," U.S. Geological Survey Circular #1139, 1998, https://pubs.usgs.gov/circ/circl139/pdf/circl139. pdf; United States Government Accountability Office, "Gao-09-610, Bottled Water: FDA Safety and Consumer Protections Are Often Less Stringent Than Comparable EPA Protections for Tap Water," 2009, https://www.gao.gov/assets/a291471.html.

80. For a survey of permissive legal regimes that facilitate excessive appro- priation, see Food and Agriculture Organization (FAO), *Modern Water Rights: Theory and Practice* (Rome: Food and Agriculture Organization of the United Nations, 2006), https://www.fao.org/publications/card/en/c/ a3201b76-6082-5c25-b4e5-66c854cbd43b/..

81. FAO, *Modern Water Rights*.

82. Alasdair Cohen and Isha Ray, "The Global Risks of Increasing Reliance on Bottled Water," *Nature Sustainability* 1 (2018): 327–329, https://doi.org/ 10.1038/s41893-018-0098-9. See also David Hall and Emanuele Lobina, "Conflicts, Companies, Human Rights and Water: A Critical Review of Local Corporate Practices and Global Corporate Initiatives." A report for Public Services International (PSI) for the 6th World Water Forum at Marseille, March 2012, https://www.world-psi.org/sites/default/files/ documents/research/psiru_conflicts_human_rights_and_water.pdf.

NOTES 297

83. Peter H. Gleick, *Bottled and Sold: The Story Behind Our Obsession with Bottled Water* (Washington, DC: Island Press, 2010); Ryan Felton, "Should We Break Our Bottled Water Habit?," Consumerreports.org, October 9, 2019, https://www.consumerreports.org/bottled-water/sho uld-we-break-our-bottled-water-habit/.

84. For US trends, see Craig Anthony (Tony) Arnold, "Water Privatization Trends in the United States: Human Rights, National Security, and Public Stewardship," *William and Mary Environmental Law and Policy Review* 33 (2009), 785–849. For parallel trends globally, see Peter H. and Gleick et al., *The New Economy of Water: The Risks and Benefits of Globalization and Privatization of Fresh Water* (Oakland, CA: Pacific Institute Studies in Development, Environment and Security, 2002).

85. International Finance Corporation (IFC), *Expanding Access to Clean Water* (Washington, DC: World Bank, 2021), https://www.ifc.org/wps/wcm/connect/industry_ext_content/ifc_external_corporate_site/ppp/resources/ifcs+position+on+water+ppps.

86. International Bank for Reconstruction and Development, *Water Resources Management: A World Bank Policy Paper* (Washington, DC: World Bank, 1993), 9–10, https://documents1.worldbank.org/cura ted/en/940261468325788815/pdf/multi-page.pdf.

87. World Bank, "Water Resources Management," 14.

88. World Bank, "Water Resources Management," 9, 14–15, 30.

89. World Bank, "Water Resources Management," 12–13.

90. Organizations established to further the privatization agenda include the 2030 Water Resources Group. Membership includes the World Bank, the World Economic Forum, and major water corporations, including Nestle, Coca-Cola, and Veolia. https://www.2030wrg.org/. The Global Infrastructure Initiative was created by member nations of the Group of 20 (G20) to create investment environments that are more conducive to major foreign investors and to assist in connecting governments with financiers. See http://www.globalinfrastructureinitiative.com/.

91. Arnold, "Water Privatization Trends," 793–797.

92. E.g., Maria Jose Romero, *"What Lies Beneath?": A Critical Assessment of PPPs and Their Impact on Sustainable Development* (Brussels, Belgium: European Network on Debt and Development, 2015), http://eurodad.org/files/pdf/559e6c832c087.pdf; Nancy Alexander, *The Emerging Multi-Polar World Order* (Washington, DC: Heinrich Böll Stiftung, December 2014), http://us.boell.org/2014/12/03/emerg ing-multi-polar-world-order; Saul Estrin and Adeline Pelletier,

298 NOTES

"Privatization in Developing Countries: What Are the Lessons of Recent Experience?" *The World Bank Research Observer* 33, no. 1 (February 2018): 65–102, https://doi.org/10.1093/wbro/lkx007.

93. Antonio Estache, Sergio Perelman, and Lourdes Trujillo, "Infrastructure Performance and Reform in Developing and Transition Economies: Evidence from a Survey of Productivity Measures," World Bank Policy Research Working Paper 3514, 2005, https://openknowle dge.worldbank.org/bitstream/handle/10986/8844/wps3514.pdf?seque nce=1.

94. Accounts of the circumstances in the Cochabamba case are numerous. I draw upon the summary in Arnold, "Water Privatization Trends," 798.

95. Food and Water Watch, "Public-Private Partnerships: Issues and Difficulties with Private Water Service, 2010," https://foodandwaterwa tch.org/wp-content/uploads/2021/03/Public-Private-Water-Service-FS-Apr-2010.pdf.

96. Philippe Marin, *Public-Private Partnerships for Urban Water Utilities: A Review of Experiences in Developing Countries*. Trends and Policy Options, no. 8 (Washington, DC: World Bank, 2009), https:// openknowledge.worldbank.org/handle/10986/2703. For discussion of key findings, see Corporate Accountability International, "The Truth About Public-Private Partnerships," https://www.corporateaccountabil ity.org/resources/truth-public-private-partnerships/.

97. Cochabamba Declaration, December 8, 2000, https://www.iatp.org/ sites/default/files/Cochabamba_Declaration_The.htm.

98. For a survey of the global remunicipalization trend, see Satoko Kishimoto, Lavinia Steinfort, and Olivier Petitjean, "The Future Is Public: Towards Democratic Ownership of Public Services," 2019, https://futureispublic.org/wp-content/uploads/2019/11/TNI_the-fut ure-is-public_online.pdf.

99. Food and Water Watch, "Public-Private Partnerships."

100. See Edward Glaeser and James Poterba, "Economic Perspectives on Infrastructure Investment," July 14, 2021, https://www.economicstrate gygroup.org/wp-content/uploads/2021/07/GlaeserPoterba_071421. pdf; Auditor General of Ontario, Infrastructure Ontario: Alternative Financing and Procurement, 2014, https://www.auditor.on.ca/en/cont ent/annualreports/arreports/en14/305en14.pdf.

101. See, e.g., European Court of Auditors, "Special Report 09/2018: Public Private Partnerships in the EU: Widespread Shortcomings and Limited Benefits," 2018, https://www.eca.europa.eu/Lists/ECADocuments/SR18

NOTES 299

_09/SR_PPP_EN.pdf; United Kingdom, National Audit Office, PF1 and PF2, "Report by the Comptroller and Auditor General," 2018), para. 1.19.
102. Gleick, "The New Economy of Water," 37–38.
103. Arnold, "Water Privatization Trends," 803–831.
104. National Research Council, "Privatization of Water Services in the United States: An Assessment of Issues and Experience" (2002), 87, 102–103, https://nap.nationalacademies.org/catalog/10135/privatization-of-water-services-in-the-united-states-an-assessment.
105. Zygmunt J. B. Plater, "Environmental Law and Three Economies: Navigating a Sprawling Field of Study, Practice, and Societal Governance in Which Everything is Connected to Everything Else," *Harvard Environmental Law Review* 23 (1999): 366.
106. Madison Powers, "Water, Justice, and Public Health," in *Oxford Handbook of Public Health Ethics*, ed. Jeffrey Kahn, Nancy Kass, and Anna Mastroianni (New York: Oxford University Press, 2019), 556–570; Chiara Cordelli, *The Privatized State* (Princeton and Oxford: Princeton University Press, 2020).
107. Léo Heller, *The Human Rights to Water and Sanitation* (Cambridge: Cambridge University Press, 2022), 124.
108. World Bank, *The Costs of Meeting the 2030 Sustainable Development Goal Targets on Drinking Water, Sanitation, and Hygiene* (Washington, DC.: World Bank, 2016), http://www.worldbank.org/en/topic/water/publication/the-costs-of-meeting-the-2030-sustainable-development-goal-targets-on-drinking-water-sanitation-and-hygiene.
109. United Nations Conference on Trade and Development, *World Investment Report 2014: Investing in the SDGs: An Action Plan* (Geneva: United Nations, 2014), http://unctad.org/en/PublicationsLibrary/wir2014_en.pdf.
110. World Bank, The Public-Private Legal Resource Center (PPP IRC), "Government Objectives: Benefits and Risks of PPPs," https://ppp.worldbank.org/public-private-partnership/overview/ppp-objectives, 2015. For discussion of risks, see The Bretton Woods Project, "Throwing Evidence to the Wind? The World Bank Continues Pushing PPPs," *The Bretton Woods Observer: A Quarterly Critical Review of Developments at the World Bank and IMF*, August 28, 2015.
111. World Bank PPPIRC, "Government Objectives: Benefits and Risks."
112. Joseph Stiglitz, *Making Globalization Work* (New York: W. W. Norton, 2007), 211–244.
113. Peter Dietsch, *Catching Capital: The Ethics of Tax Competition* (New York: Oxford University Press, 2015).

300 NOTES

114. For PPPs in the Bank's current portfolio, see World Bank, "Private Participation in Infrastructure (PPI)" database, https://ppi.worldbank. org/data. For a statement of the Bank's pro-privatization stance, see World Bank, "From Billions to Trillions: Transforming Development Finance—Post-2015 Financing for Development: Multilateral Development Finance," April 2, 2015, http://siteresources.worldbank. org/DEVCOMMINT/Documentation/23659446/DC2015-   0002(E) FinancingforDevelopment.pdf.

Chapter 8

1. Immanuel Wallerstein, "The Next Big Turn," in *Does Capitalism Have a Future?*, ed. Immanuel Wallerstein et al. (New York: Oxford University Press, 2013), 4.
2. UNFCCC, "Nationally Determined Contributions Under the Paris Agreement. Synthesis Report by the Secretariat," October 26, 2022, https://unfccc.int/sites/default/files/resource/cma2022_04.pdf.
3. United Nations Environment Program (UNEP), *Emissions Gap Report 2022: The Closing Window – Climate Crisis Calls for Rapid Transformation of Societies*, https://www.unep.org/resources/emissions-gap-report-2022.
4. UNEP, *Emissions Gap Report 2022*, xxii.
5. Will Steffen et al., "The Trajectory of the Anthropocene: The Great Acceleration," *Anthropocene Review* 2, no. 1 (2015): 81–98.
6. Tim Gore, *Confronting Carbon Inequality* (London: Oxfam and the Stockholm Environment Institute, September 21, 2020), https://oxfami library.openrepository.com/bitstream/handle/10546/621052/mb-conf ronting-carbon-inequality-210920-en.pdf.
7. Benedikt Bruckner et al., "Impacts of Poverty Alleviation on National and Global Carbon Emissions," *Nature Sustainability* 5 (2022): 311–320, doi:10.1038/s41893-021-00842-z.
8. Madison Powers, "Individual Responsibility in the Anthropocene," in *Applying Nonideal Theory to Bioethics: Living and Dying in a Nonideal World*, ed. Elizabeth Victor and Laura Guidry-Grimes (New York: Springer Publishing, 2021), 145–168.
9. Walter Sinnott-Armstrong, "It's Not My Fault: Global Warming and Individual Obligations," in *Perspectives on Climate Change*, ed. Walter Sinnott-Armstrong and Richard Howarth (Oxford: Elsevier, 2005), 285–307.

NOTES 301

10. Julia Nefsky, "Consequentialism and the Problem of Collective Harm: A Reply to Kagan," *Philosophy and Public Affairs* 39 (2011): 364–395.
11. Naomi Oreskes and Erik M. Conway, *Merchants of Doubt: How a Handful of Scientists Obscured the Truth on Issues from Tobacco Smoke to Global Warming* (New York: Bloomsbury Press, 2011).
12. John Barry, *Rethinking Green Politics: Nature, Virtue, and Progress* (Thousand Oaks, CA: Sage Publications, 1999), 72.
13. Climate Change Committee, *Progress in Reducing Emissions: 2021 Report to Parliament* (London: House of Lords Library, June 2021).
14. International Energy Agency (IEA), *World Energy Outlook 2021* (Paris: IEA, 2021), 158–162.
15. Organisation for Economic Co-operation and Development, *Climate Finance Provided and Mobilised by Developed Countries: Aggregate Trends Updated with 2019 Data* (Paris: OECD, 2021).
16. Jocelyn Timperley, "The Broken $100-Billion Promise of Climate Finance: And How to Fix It," *Nature* 598 (2021): 400–402, *https://doi.org/10.1038/d41586-021-02846-3*.
17. Tracy Carty, Jan Kowalzig, and Bertram Zagema, *Climate Finance Shadow Report 2020* (London: Oxfam, 2020).
18. Independent Expert Group on Climate Finance, *Delivering on the $100 Billion Climate Finance Commitment and Transforming Climate Finance* (Independent Expert Group on Climate Finance, New York: United Nations, 2020).
19. Independent High-Level Expert Group on Climate Finance, *Finance for Climate Action: Scaling up Investment for Climate and Development*, November 2022, https://www.lse.ac.uk/granthaminstitute/wp-content/uploads/2022/11/IHLEG-Finance-for-Climate-Action.pdf.
20. International Energy Agency, *Net Zero by 2050: A Roadmap for the Global Energy Sector* (Paris: IEA, 2021).
21. Organization for Economic Co-operation and Development (OECD), "Net ODA" (2023), https://data.oecd.org/oda/net-oda.htm.
22. Philip Hoxie, Stephanie Mercier, and Vincent H. Smith, "The Cost of Cargo Preference for International Food Aid Programs," *AEI Economic Perspectives*, March 2020, https://www.aei.org/wp-content/uploads/2020/03/The-Cost-of-Cargo-Preference-for-International-Food-Aid-Progr ams.pdf?x91208.
23. Dambisa Moyo, *Dead Aid* (New York: Farrar, Strauss, and Giroux, 2009), 115.

302 NOTES

24. Steven Pinker, *Enlightenment Now: The Case for Reason, Science, Humanism, and Progress* (New York: Penguin Books, 2018).

25. Karl Ritter, "Explainer: Why Quitting Coal Is So Hard," AP News, November 13, 2021, https://apnews.com/article/climate-business-glasgow-europe-environment-and-nature-a456c5684eabb05b85cda4e17cad3938.

26. IEA, *World Energy Outlook 2021*, 333–337.

27. Thomas Wiedmann et al., "Scientists' Warning on Affluence," *Nature Communications* 11 (2020): 3107, https://doi.org/10.1038/s41467-020-16941-y.

28. Jennifer Hillman and David Sacks, "Blog Post, Making Sense of China's Pledge to Stop Building Coal-Fired Power Plants Abroad," October 4, 2021, https://www.cfr.org/blog/making-sense-chinas-pledge-stop-building-coal-fired-power-plants-abroad.

29. Lorenzo Rosa et al., "The Water Footprint of Carbon Capture and Storage Technologies," *Renewable and Sustainable Energy Reviews* 138 (2021): 110511.

30. Hans Nicholas Jong, "Emissions and Deforestation Set to Spike Under Indonesia's Biomass Transition," *Mongabay Series* (September 21, 2022), https://news.mongabay.com/2022/09/emissions-and-deforestation-set-to-spike-under-indonesias-biomasstransition/?utm_campaign=Cropped&utm_content=20221005&utm_medium=email&utm_source=Revue%20Land.

31. William Rex et al., *Supporting Hydropower: An Overview of the World Bank Group's Engagement* (Washington, DC: World Bank Group, 2014).

32. Christiane Zarfl et al., "A Global Boom in Hydropower Dam Construction," *Aquatic Sciences* 77 (2015): 161–170.

33. Rosetta C. Blackman et al., "Mapping Biodiversity Hotspots of Fish Communities in Subtropical Streams Through Environmental DNA," *Scientific Reports* 11 (2021): 10375, https://doi.org/10.1038/s41598-021-89942-6.

34. International Rivers, "Environmental Impacts of Dams," (2023), https://archive.internationalrivers.org/environmental-impacts-of-dams.

35. Günther Grill et al., "An Index-Based Framework for Assessing Patterns and Trends in River Fragmentation and Flow Regulation by Global Dams at Multiple Scales," *Environmental Research Letters* 10 (2015): 015001.

36. Hannah Beech, "'Our River Was Like a God': How Dams and China's Might Imperil the Mekong," *New York Times*, October 12, 2019.

37. Beech, "Our River."

NOTES 303

38. Emilio F. Moran et al., "Sustainable Hydropower in the 21st Century," *Proceedings of the National Academy of Sciences* 115, no. 47 (Nov 2018): 11891–11898; doi:10.1073/pnas.180942611.

39. Chris A. Boulton, Timothy M. Lenton, and Niklas Boers, "Pronounced Loss of Amazon Rainforest Resilience Since the Early 2000s," *Nature Climate Change* 12 (2022): 271–278, https://doi.org/10.1038/s41 558-022-01287-8.

40. Matthew P. McCartney et al., "The Water Resource Implications of Changing Climate in the Volta River Basin, IWMI Research Report 146" (Colombo, Sri Lanka: International Water Management Institute, 2012), doi:10.5337/2012.219.

41. Peilei Fan et al., "Recently Constructed Hydropower Dams Were Associated with Reduced Economic Production, Population, and Greenness in Nearby Areas," *Proceedings of the National Academy of Sciences* 119, no. 8 (2022): e2108038119, https://doi.org/10.1073/pnas.210 8038119.

42. Jamie Morgan, "Electric Vehicles: The Future We Made and the Problem of Unmaking It," *Cambridge Journal of Economics* 44, no. 4 (July 2020): 953–977,https://doi.org/10.1093/cje/beaa022.

43. Thea Riofrancos et al., *Achieving Zero Emissions with More Mobility and Less Mining* (Davis, CA: Climate and Community Project, UC Davis, January 2023), http://www. climateandcommunity.org/ more-mobility-less-mining.

44. Laurie Parsons et al., *Disaster Trade: The Hidden Footprint of UK Production Overseas* (London: Royal Holloway, University of London, 2021), https://www.disastertrade.org/publications.

45. Kenneth Pomeranz, *The Great Divergence: China, Europe, and the Making of the Modern World* (Princeton, New Jersey: Princeton University Press, 2000).

46. Tim Parrique et al., *Decoupling Debunked: Evidence and Arguments Against Green Growth as a Sole Strategy for Sustainability* (Brussels: European Environmental Bureau, 2019), https://eeb.org/library/decoupling-debunked/.

47. Doris Fuchs et al., "Power: The Missing Element in Sustainable Consumption and Absolute Reductions Research and Action," *Journal of Cleaner Production* 132 (2016): 298–307.

48. Servaas Storm and Enno Schröder, "Economic Growth and Carbon Emissions: The Road to 'Hothouse Earth' Is Paved with Good Intentions,"

304 NOTES

International Journal of Political Economy 49, no. 2 (2020): 153–173, doi:10.1080/08911916.2020.1778866.

49. Stephen Stapczynski, Akshat Rathi, and Godfrey Marawanyika, "How to Sell 'Carbon Neutral' Fossil Fuel That Doesn't Exist," *Bloomberg Green*, August 11, 2021, https://www.bloomberg.com/news/features/2021-08-11/the-fictitious-world-of-carbon-neutral-fossil-fuel.

50. Chris Mooney et al., "Countries' Climate Pledges Built on Flawed Data, Post Investigation Finds," *Washington Post*, November 7, 2021, https://www.washingtonpost.com/climate-environment/interactive/2021/gre enhouse-gas-emissions-pledges-data/.

51. Intergovernmental Panel on Climate Change, *Climate Change 2022: Mitigation of Climate Change. Contribution of Working Group III to the Sixth Assessment Report of the Intergovernmental Panel on Climate Change*, ed. P. R. Shukla et al. (Cambridge: Cambridge University Press, 2022), doi:10.1017/9781009157926.

52. For a classic discussion of path dependency, see Douglas North, *Institutions, Institutional Change, and Economic Performance* (Cambridge: Cambridge University Press, 1990). For a discussion of path dependency in environmental policies, see John S. Dryzek and Jonathan Pickering, *The Politics of the Anthropocene* (Oxford: Oxford University Press, 2019), 27–57.

53. Unearthed/Greenpeace, "Thousands of Tonnes of Banned Pesticides Shipped to Poorer Countries from British and European Factories," 2020, https://unearthed.greenpeace.org/2020/09/10/banned-pesticides-eu-exp ort-poor-countries/.

54. Gabrielle Hecht, "The African Anthropocene," *Aeon*, February 2018, https://aeon.co/essays/if-we-talk-about-hurting-our-planet-who-exac tly-is-the-we.

55. Roland Geyer, Jenna R. Jambeck, and Kara Lavender, "Production, Use, and Fate of All Plastics Ever Made," *Science Advances* 3, no. 7 (July 19, 2017), doi:10.1126/sciadv.1700782.

56. International Energy Agency, *The Future of Petrochemicals: Towards a More Sustainable Chemical Industry* (Paris: IEA, 2018), https://www.iea. org/reports/the-future-of-petrochemicals.

57. Matthew Macleod et al., "The Global Threat from Plastic Pollution," *Science* 373, no. 6650 (July 2, 2021): 61–65, doi:10.1126/science.abg5433.

58. Kyla Tienhaara and Lorenzo Cotula, "Raising the Cost of Climate Action? Investor-State Dispute Settlement and Compensation for Stranded Fossil Fuel Assets," International Institute for Environment and Development, October 2020, https://pubs.iied.org/sites/default/files/pdfs/migrate/ 17660IIED.pdf.

NOTES 305

59. Tienhaara and Cotula, "Raising the Cost of Climate Action?"
60. Global Justice Now, "Corporate Courts vs the Climate," September 16, 2021, https://www.globaljustice.org.uk/resource/corporate-courts-vs-the-climate-briefing/.
61. Simon L. Lewis and Mark A. Maslin, *The Human Planet: How We Created the Anthropocene* (New Haven, CT: Yale University Press, 2018), 383.
62. Clifford Krauss, "As Western Oil Giants Cut Production, State-Owned Companies Step Up," *New York Times*, October 14, 2021.
63. Oliver Belcher et al., "Hidden Carbon Costs of the 'Everywhere War': Logistics, Geopolitical Ecology, and the Carbon Boot-Print of the US Military," *Transactions of the Institute of British Geographers* 45 (2020): 65–80, https://doi.org/10.1111/tran.12319; Neta C. Crawford, "Pentagon Fuel Use, Climate Change, and the Costs of War," November 2019, https://watson.brown.edu/costsofwar/files/cow/imce/papers/Penta gon%20Fuel%20Use%2C%20Climate%20Change%20and%20the%20Co sts%20of%20War%20Revised%20November%202019%20Crawford.pdf.
64. Bill McKibben, "The Pentagon's Outsized Part in the Climate Fight," *New York Review of Books*, June 27, 2019, https://www.nybooks.com/daily/2019/06/27/the-pentagons-outsized-part-in-the-climate-fight/.
65. Belcher et al., "Hidden Carbon Costs."
66. Olivier Bois von Kursk et al., "Navigating Energy Transitions: Mapping the Road to 1.5°C," International Institute for Sustainable Development, October 2022, https://www.iisd.org/publications/report/navigating-ene rgy-transitions.
67. James Gustave Speth, *They Knew: The Federal Government's Fifty-Year Role in Causing the Climate Crisis* (Cambridge, MA: MIT Press, 2021), 144.
68. Richard Heinberg, "Is the Energy Transition Taking Off – or Hitting a Wall?," Independent Media Institute, October 4, 2022, https://independen tmediainstitute.org/is-the-energy-transition-taking-off-or-hitting-a-wall/.
69. Business & Human Rights Resource Centre & Indigenous Peoples' Rights International (IPRI), "An Appeal to the UNFCCC and State Parties at COP27," 2022, https://media.business-humanrights.org/media/docume nts/Appeal_COP27_final_12_10_2022.pdf.

Chapter 9

1. Anand Giridharadas, *Winners Take All: The Elite Charade of Changing the World* (New York: Alfred A Knopf, 2018).

306 NOTES

2. Christina Milesi et al., "A Strategy for Mapping and Modeling the Ecological Effects of US Lawns," (2005), https://www.isprs.org/proceedings/XXXVI/8-W27/milesi.pdf.

3. Adam Smith, *The Wealth of Nations*, ed. Edwin Cannan (New York: Modern Library, 2000), 771.

4. Quoted in Fred Magdoff and John Bellamy Foster, "Approaching Socialism," *Monthly Review* 57, no. 3 (2005): 19–61.

5. Adolph A. Berle, *Power Without Property: A New Development in American Political Economy* (New York: Harcourt, Brace, and World, 1959), 98.

6. Frederick Douglass, West India Emancipation," speech delivered at Canandaigua, New York, August 4, 1857. In *The Life and Writings of Frederick Douglass*, ed. Philip S. Foner, vol. 2 (New York: International Publishers, 1950), 437.

7. Eric D. Weitz, *A World Divided: The Global Struggle for Human Rights in the Age of Nation-States* (Princeton and Oxford: Princeton University Press, 2019).

8. UNESCO, "Expert Meeting on Human Rights, Basic Needs, and the Establishment of a New International Economic Order," Paris, June 19–23, 1978, UN Doc. SS78/Conf. 630/12.

9. Ranier Forst, "The Justification of Human Rights and the Basic Right to Justification: A Reflexive Approach," *Ethics* 120, no. 4 (2010): 711–740.

10. Yael Tamir, *Why Nationalism* (Princeton: Princeton University Press, 2019).

11. Joe Turner and Dan Bailey, "'Ecobordering': Casting Immigration Control as Environmental Protection," *Environmental Politics* 31, no. 1 (2021): 1–22, https://doi.org/10.1080/09644016.2021.1916197.

12. For a discussion of Friedrich List's well-known views on the threshold question, see Eric Hobsbawm, Nations and Nationalism (Cambridge: Cambridge University Press, 1990), 3–31.

13. C. A. Bayley, *Remaking the Modern World 1900–2015: Global Connections and Comparisons* (Hoboken, NJ: Wiley Blackwell, 2018), 284–286.

14. Worldwide Fund for Nature, *Living Planet Report 2016* (Gland, Switzerland: WWF, 2016), 74–81.

15. Peter Mair, *Ruling the Void: The Hollowing of Western Democracy* (London: Verso, 2013), 103.

16. Francois Jarrige and Thomas Le Roux, *The Contamination of the Earth: A History of Pollutions in the Industrial Age*, trans. Janice Egan and Michael Egan (Cambridge, MA: MIT Press, 2020), 33–38, 63–86, and 144–176.

Index

For the benefit of digital users, indexed terms that span two pages (e.g., 52–53) may, on occasion, appear on only one of those pages.

2030 Water Resources Group, 184

Acemoglu, Daron, 88
Agenda 2030, 23
agriculture
  commodity trap and, 122–23
  contract model of production
    in, 117–21
  deforestation and, 126–27, 168,
    169, 173–74, 179, 180–81
  global land grab and, 125
  greenhouse gas emissions from,
    153, 160–67
  Haber-Bosch process and, 157
  high-risk commodities and, 12,
    150–51, 173–74, 178, 179
  intensification of, 150, 155–56,
    157, 158, 160, 162, 163
  Southern Model of, 120
  subsidies for, 134, 200–1, 221–22,
    225, 252–53
  supply chain management in,
    116–21, 127–28, 147, 163
  water pollution and, 158–60,
    191, 199
  in water-stressed regions, 197,
    198–201
Aichi Biodiversity Targets, 170
Alston, Philip, 85–86
Aristotle, 32, 33

Bali Principles of Climate Justice,
  82, 260

Beitz, Charles, 100, 102
beneficence
  imperfect duties of, 103–5
Berle, A.A., 254
Berlin, Isaiah, 54–55
biodiversity
  Aichi Biodiversity Targets
    and, 170
  biosphere integrity and, 1–2, 167,
    170–71, 230–31
  crop diversity in relation
    to, 171–72
  dams, habitat destruction
    and, 232
  genetic diversity as a component
    of, 170, 171–72
  habitat loss and, 169–70, 232
  high-risk commodities,
    deforestation, and, 12, 150–51,
    173–74, 178, 179
  planetary boundary for, 170–71
  pollinators and, 172
  Red list and, 170
  species loss and, 170, 171–72
  zoonotic disease and, 171
biofuels, 177–78
biogeochemical cycles
  nitrogen and
    phosphorous, 165–66
  nitrogen fertilizer as disruptor of,
    116, 165–66
  planetary boundary for,
    165, 166–67

308 INDEX

Boulding, Kenneth, 36
Brundtland Report, 18–20
Buffett, Warren, 134–35

capitalism
 financialization and, 140
 future of, 8, 15, 30, 31–32, 36–37,
  46–47, 227, 229–30, 253, 261
 logic of, 7, 25–29, 33–34, 36–37, 38
 neoliberal conception of,
  51, 60–61
climate change
 agriculture's contribution to, 154–
  55, 158, 160–65, 168
 carbon footprint and, 163, 164,
  204, 218, 220, 235, 244
 carbon offsets and, 235–37
 carbon sinks, sequestration, and
  storage, 161, 167–68, 174, 175–
  77, 178, 230–31, 235–37
 coal and, 227–29, 241, 242–43
 Conference of Parties (COP) and,
  222, 223–24, 245
 consequences for agriculture, 116,
  155, 164, 172
 consumption and, 218–22,
  226, 229–30
 dams, hydropower, and, 231–33
 deforestation and, 108, 167–
  69, 175–77
 emissions gap and, 216
 individual harms from, 105, 106
 livestock and, 161–62
 nature-based solutions
  and, 175–79
 oil and gas production and, 125,
  176, 239–40, 241–42, 243–
  44, 245
 Paris Climate Agreement and,
  216, 223–24, 235–36, 244
 planetary boundaries and, 2,
  96, 150, 165, 168–69, 170–71,
  179, 219

 relative sea level rise and, 188
 solar alternatives and, 227–28, 245
 water and, 185, 186–87, 188–89,
  215, 230–31
comparative advantage
 conceptions of, 122
 commodity trap and, 122–23
consumption
 global GDP and, 218, 226
 merchants of doubt and, 220
 unequal patterns of, 42–43, 44,
  173–74, 184, 195, 196–97,
  218, 235
 See also ecological
  (environmental) burdens of
  consumption
corporations, multinational
 investor-state dispute settlement
  provisions and, 242–43
 natural resource curse and, 125
 use of market power and political
  influence by, 4–5, 22–23, 69,
  86–87, 92, 103, 124–25, 126–28,
  131, 132, 135, 137–40, 143–44,
  147, 173, 179–80, 208, 212,
  241–42, 250–51

decoupling
 decarbonization and, 40, 234, 235
 dematerialization and, 23, 40–41,
  234, 235
 environmental Kuznet's curve
  and, 39–40
 water footprint reduction and, 13,
  23, 194–95, 235
democracy
 accountability and, 10–11, 25, 37–
  38, 65–66, 72–73, 84, 93, 115,
  130–32, 211–13, 214–15, 251,
  255–56, 259
 market fundamentalism and, 54,
  58–59, 62, 212
 privatization and, 211–13, 214–15

INDEX 309

Doha Declaration on Financing
for Development, 224
domination and unequal power,
1–71, 72–73
doughnut economics, 37–38, 41–42
Douglass, Fredrick, 254
duties
assignment of, 97–98, 99–102, 107
dynamic conception of, 98–99
to future generations, 110–11, 130
imperfect, 103–5
indeterminacy of, 97–98, 103–4
perfect, 97–98, 103–5
portfolio of, 100–1
pre-institutional existence
of, 99–101
secondary, 99–100, 101–2,
106, 109–10
specification of, 75, 99, 101
timeless conception of, 97–98

ecological (environmental) burdens
of consumption, 4, 41, 43, 44,
46–47, 91, 115–16, 125, 127–28,
173–74, 179, 195–96, 204, 221,
227, 234–35, 236, 251, 252, 253,
257, 259
ecologically destructive market
practices, 11, 12, 94, 108, 115,
140, 150–51, 249, 252–53, 257,
259, 261
ecological futures, control over, 1, 74,
80–81, 249, 259
ecological relief, 234–35, 236
Ecomodernism, 38
economic growth, 6–7, 16, 20–21, 28,
34, 36, 37, 38, 40–42
economic (socioeconomic)
inequality, 43–47, 83, 85–86,
127–28, 139–40, 193, 214, 247
efficiency, 40, 62–64, 129, 191–92,
194–96, 200, 205–6, 207–8,
213, 215

egalitarian(ism), 6, 51, 82–83, 84
emissions
African quality diesel and, 238–39
agricultural, 153, 160–67
from automobiles, 228, 233–
34, 239–40
biofuels and, 177–78
carbon capture and storage and,
38, 230–31
Emissions Gap Report on, 216
Energy Charter Treaty and
stranded assets due to control
of, 242
fossil fuel subsidies and, 223
fracking and, 133, 239–40, 241–42
green new deal and reduction of,
21, 37, 226
greenwashing and, 236
hard-to-abate, 237
hydropower or hydroelectric
power and, 185, 231–33
from livestock, 161–62
from military, 244–45
nature-based climate solutions
and, 175–77
nitrous oxide (N2O) as a
contributor to, 161–62
offshoring of, 234–35
Paris Agreement, 216, 223–24,
235–36, 244
plastic and petrochemicals and the
future of, 239–40
sunk costs problem and, 227–
28, 245–46
technological innovation and
reduction of, 38, 226–27, 230,
245–46, 259–60
whack-a-mole problem and
reduction of, 230, 233–34

environmental health risks, 1, 9, 55,
74, 80, 86–87, 113, 126
environmental Kuznet's curve, 39–40

310 INDEX

environmental load displacement, 234–35, 237–38
exploitation, 25, 70, 71–72, 114–15, 125

Faden, Ruth, 92
false hopes, examples of, 217–30
false starts, examples of, 230–37
financial sector
  collateralized loan obligations (CLOs) and, 142–43
  derivatives and, 144
  highly leveraged asset markets and, 143–44
  influence of, 94, 140, 141, 146–47
  junk bonds, 143
  shadow banking system and, 142, 145–47
  speculative investments and, 11, 86–87, 94, 115, 116, 141, 143, 144, 145–46, 249
  tax havens, tax competition, and preservation of, 35, 138–40, 144–46, 214, 251
food security, 11, 126, 127, 151–53, 162, 163, 198, 200–1, 233, 237, 252–53
Food and Agriculture Organization (FAO), 151–52, 153–54, 171–72
foreign direct investment
  in agricultural production facilities, 124–25
  for land acquisition, 137
  regulatory arbitrage and, 137–38
  tax havens and, 139
  virtual water and, 202
forests
  afforestation and, 175–77
  agricultural production in tropical, 168, 169, 173–74
  definition of deforestation and, 167

  deforestation footprints of consumption and, 173–74
  habitat destruction and fragmentation of, 170
  high-risk commodities from, 12, 150–51, 173–74, 178, 179
  planetary boundary for land use changes and, 168–69
  protection by indigenous peoples, 180
  rights of forest dwellers and, 108, 178–79, 180–81
Foster, John Bellamy, 28
freedom
  associated with efficiency aims, 63–64
  domination and, 67–69, 70–71, 72–73
  exploitation and, 68, 70
  fairness and, 64–65
  market fundamentalism and, 52–53, 66–73
  multi-dimensional conception of, 67, 68
  non-interference conception of, 9, 66–67
  social freedom and social exclusion and, 69–73
  threats to individual liberty and, 52, 53–54, 56–57
Friedman, Milton, 52, 53–54, 59, 60–61, 63
Fundamental Law of Welfare Economics, 62–63
future (or distant) generations, 105, 110–13, 130

Galbraith, James K., 147
Geneva Declaration, 179–81, 260
Gilpin, Robert, 22–23
global land grab, 125
global political economy, definition of, 22–23

INDEX   311

global warming. *See* climate
change
gross domestic product (GDP),
34–36, 39–40, 41–42, 123–24,
125–26, 131, 156–57, 195, 218,
226, 233
group harm, 105, 108, 110

Hayek, Friedrich, 52–54, 59–60, 66,
135–36, 137
Hayward, Tim, 96
Haber-Bosch process, 157
Heller, Leo, 212–13
high-risk commodities, 12, 150–51,
173–74, 178, 179
humanitarian assistance, 75, 76, 90–
91, 179–80, 251
human progress, 7, 30, 31, 32–33,
226–27, 261
human rights
basic needs and, 1, 8, 9, 11, 74, 78,
80, 130, 147, 212–13, 249
dual-purpose or high-priority, 1,
4–5, 9, 74–75, 78–79, 80–81,
84, 87, 89, 91, 113, 114–15, 249,
253, 260
duties to future (or distant)
generations and, 105, 110–13
duties to protect as a central aspect
of, 1, 5–6, 9–10, 72–73, 74,
75, 82–83, 86–87, 89, 94, 97,
101–2, 103, 104–5, 106, 109–10,
113, 249–50
dynamic conception of, 98–99
as enforceable, 4–5, 77, 80–81,
110–12, 249, 250, 254
group harm and, 105, 108, 110
Indigenous perspectives on,
43–44, 81–82, 93, 108, 167–68,
178–81, 246–47, 260
inequality and, 6, 82–84, 85–87
institutional enforcement of, 77,
89, 93–94, 102, 249–50

"morality of the depths"
and, 76–77
naturalistic and natural law
conception of, 97–98, 100
normative distinctiveness of, 74–
75, 110–11
positive and negative rights or
duties and, 99–100
power relations and, 5, 9–10,
14–15, 48, 74, 84, 86–87, 90–92,
93–94, 102, 114–15, 249, 250–
51, 253–55
structural insecurity or structural
vulnerability of, 86, 89, 91, 114
sustainability and, 81, 82, 89, 91,
149–50, 260
targeted approach to, 1, 5, 9, 74–2,
82, 84–85, 92–93, 113, 250
threats to, 3–4, 5–6, 33–34, 76–77,
87, 92, 94, 97, 98–99, 102, 109–
10, 112–13, 114–15, 175, 182,
194, 256–57
unique moral responsibility
of states for, 5–6, 22, 102,
103, 110
well-being or welfare as rationale
for, 1, 9, 10, 65, 74, 75, 78–80,
81–82, 84, 89, 96

Indigenous Peoples' Rights
International (IPRI), 246–
47, 260
integrated water resource
management (IWRM),
190, 210–11
intergenerational justice,
105, 110–13
Intergovernmental Panel on Climate
Change (IPCC), 154–55,
161, 237
Intergovernmental Platform on
Biodiversity and Ecosystem
Services (IPBES), 170–71

312 INDEX

International Federation for Human Rights, 247
International Monetary Fund (IMF), 22–23, 49, 103, 121–22, 128–30, 139, 207, 213–14, 225–26
International Union for Conservation of Nature (IUCN), 17–18, 170

Jackson, Tim, 36–37

Kari-Oca 2 Declaration, 179–80, 260

Laborde, Cecile, 67, 68
Lanchester, John, 257–58
land
agricultural uses of, 151–52, 153–56, 163–64, 168, 179
areas affected by humans, 149
climate change impact on, 149–55, 161
climatically unsuitable, 154–55
degradation, 149, 151–52, 153–54, 155–56, 161, 167–68, 174
desertification, 149, 155, 156, 161
dispossession from, 125, 180–81
in dryland regions of Africa and Asia, 155, 156
food security and, 151–53
forest conversion, 163, 173
global acquisition of, 125
heavily ploughed, 154
intensive agricultural uses of, 154–55
land footprint of agriculture, 151–52, 155–56, 157, 162, 166–67
large-scale monocropping agriculture and, 173
planetary boundary for land use changes, 168–69

for production of livestock animals, 153, 158, 161–62, 166–67, 173
rule of law and property rights in, 125, 126
urbanization and, 164
See also soil degradation, erosion, and nutrient loss
La Via Campesina, 180–81
Limits to Growth, The, 20–21
Locke, John, 100

Magdoff, Fred, 28
Malthus, Thomas, 20–21, 226–27
Marshall, Alfred, 30
markets
anti-competitive practices and, 115–16, 135
bilateral trade agreements and, 131, 132, 135, 242–43
commodity trap in global, 122–23
deregulated and preferentially regulated, 50, 51, 128–29, 132, 135, 137, 259
export-driven (export-led) production in global, 121–23, 124, 126–27, 179, 229
extractive practices or institutions and, 35, 86–87, 88, 89, 109–10, 125, 167–68, 179, 202, 247, 249
geographically concentrated agriculture and, 120
for global commodities, 12, 115–16, 117, 121–23, 127, 147, 150–51, 169, 173, 179, 196–97, 200
global value chains and organization of, 115–16, 122–23
"just in time" production in global, 118

INDEX 313

market power and market
concentration, 65–66, 69, 71–
72, 114, 115–21, 124, 127–29,
135, 250, 258–59
oligopoly, 116–17, 119–20
oligopsony, 117
predatory practices or activities, 1,
3–5, 9–11, 46–47, 48, 51–52, 62,
73, 74, 87–89, 94–95, 108, 110,
113, 114, 140, 147, 179–80, 209,
215, 248, 249, 251, 257, 259, 261
regulatory arbitrage and, 135,
136–38, 145–46
rent-seeking and, 116, 128, 132–
33, 135
self-regulating (or self-correcting),
49–50, 59, 60–62, 70–71
tax competition and, 139–40, 214
market fundamentalism
austerity and, 51, 128–32, 135–36
"debt brake" and, 131
deregulation and, 50, 128–29, 132,
135–36, 137
European Union and, 64–65
"excesses of democracy" as a
complaint of, 212
fairness arguments and, 64–66
Mont Pelerin Society and, 53–54
neoliberalism and, 8, 49–50
opposition to state intervention in
markets and, 50–51, 54
opposition to social welfare
policies and, 48–51, 54
opposition to economic and social
rights by, 50, 79
rationales for, 52–66
social stability arguments and,
64, 65–66
trade (or economic) liberalization
and, 50, 51, 225
Marx, Karl (or Marxist, Marxism),
25–26, 27, 32, 119
Mill, John Stuart, 102, 122

Miller, David, 78
Moyn, Samuel, 82–83, 85–86

nationalism
anti-immigrant politics, 257–58
ecological survivalism, 257–58
economic, 224, 225–26, 257–58
national self-determination, 255–56
natural resource curse, 125
Neoclassical economics, 49, 62–
64, 65
neoliberalism
definitional debates, 49–50
Mont Pelerin Society and, 53–54
policy recommendations of, 8,
50–52, 128–29
relation to market
fundamentalism, 8, 49–50
See also market fundamentalism
New International Economic
Order, 255
Nickel, James, 78

O'Connor, James, 27
oil and gas
fracking and, 133, 239–
40, 241–42
petrochemicals and, 239–40
state-owned companies, 243–44
O'Neill, Onora, 99–100
Organisation for Economic
Cooperation and Development
(OECD), 34, 39, 139–40, 225

Pareto efficiency, 63, 64
Parfit, Derek, 105
Paris Climate Agreement, 216, 223–
24, 235–36, 244
path dependencies, examples
of, 238–46
planetary boundaries
for biogeochemical processes, 1–2,
11–12, 150, 158, 165, 166–67

314 INDEX

planetary boundaries (*cont.*)
  for biosphere integrity, 1–2, 170–71, 230–31
  for climate system, 2–3, 11–12, 150, 165, 179 (*see also* climate change)
  core boundaries and, 2, 170–71
  Earth system resilience and, 2, 127
  for freshwater, 1–3
  for land use changes, 168–69
  for nitrogen and phosphorus, 11–12, 116, 150, 165–66
  safe operating space and, 2, 26–27, 37–38, 80, 165
  transgression of, 2, 28, 166, 168–69, 170–71
Plato, 31–32
pleonexia, 32
pollution
  from extractive industries, 45, 86–87, 109–10, 202, 233–34
  from nitrogen fertilizer, 158–60, 166–67
  from poultry and livestock facilities, 120, 153
  in sacrifice zones, 71–72, 91, 252
  from toxic dumping or export products, 40–41, 91, 238–39
  water management and, 190, 191, 193
Porter, Michael, 134–35

Rawls, John, 57, 65–66
Raworth, Kate, 37–38
Raz, Joseph, 92
rebound effect, 40, 195, 228–29, 237–38
Red list, 170
resource(s)
  capitalism and depletion of, 28
  constraints imposed by limited, 20–21
  decoupling and, 13, 23, 40–41, 194–231, 234, 235

ecological debt and, 43–44
ecological footprint and, 42–43
export-driven (export-led)
  policies and, 121–23, 124, 126–27, 179, 229
  human rights and, 86–87, 91, 109–10, 114–15
  investment and allocation decisions and, 8, 29, 37–38, 211, 252
  material footprint and, 40–41
  natural resource curse and extraction of, 125
  state sovereignty and control over, 94–95, 129–30, 179–80, 255
  substitution policies, 40
  unsustainability definitions and depletion of, 21, 23, 24–25, 80, 88, 149–50
  See also water scarcity
rights. *See* human rights
Rio Declaration on Environment and Development, 18–19, 81
Robinson, James A., 88
Rockstrom, Johan, 179
Rodrik, Dani, 123

sacrifice zones, 45, 71–72, 91, 252
Sen, Amartya, 104
shadow banking system, 142, 145–47
Shelton, Dinah, 86–87
Shue, Henry, 76–77, 92
Smil, Vaclav, 30
Smith, Adam, 253
social exclusion, 71–73
soil degradation, erosion, and nutrient loss, 1–2, 39–40, 116, 120, 125–26, 127–28, 153–58, 159–60, 161, 172, 177, 180–81, 186, 191, 219, 232
states
  as agents of injustice, 253, 256–58

INDEX 315

colonialism, colonial rule, and, 25, 83, 198–99, 255, 258–59
institutional and regulative capacity of, 5–6, 22, 101, 102, 103, 132, 140, 147
national self-determination arguments for, 255–56
See also human rights responsibilities of
Streeck, Wolfgang, 146
stranded assets, 14, 119, 241, 243, 245–46
supply chain management, 116–21, 127–28, 147, 163
sustainability
affluence and its impact on, 42–44, 45, 90, 91, 122–23, 124, 125, 126–28, 147–48, 153, 164–65, 178, 195, 196, 203–4, 217–18, 219–20, 221, 225–26, 229–30, 235, 236, 246, 250–51, 252–54, 258, 259, 261–62
biofatalism and, 31
conceptions of, 17–25
decoupling and, 13, 23, 40–41, 194–95, 234, 235
doughnut economics as a pathway to, 37–38, 41–42
economic growth as an obstacle to, 34–42
influence of inequality on, 42–46
Limits to Growth, The and, 20–21
"logic of capitalism" and, 25–30
Malthus, Thomas and, 20–21, 226–27
no-growth or de-growth alternatives for, 36–37, 39
psychological explanations of impediments to, 30–34
Sustainable Development Goals (SDGs), targets, and, 18–19, 152, 183, 192–93, 194, 203–4, 213

unsustainability, definition of, 24–25, 80, 88, 149–50
unsustainable water use, 183–84, 186–87
See also planetary boundaries

Tasioulas, John, 98–99
Tawney, R. H., 54–55
technological innovation
diffusion of, 240
market-driven, 38, 226–29
path dependency as an impediment to, 14, 238–46
planned obsolescence and, 239
sunk costs as an impediment to, 227–28, 245–46
rebound effect and, 40, 195, 228–29, 237–38
treadmill effect, 160

United Nations Convention to Combat Desertification (UNCCD), 156
United Nations Declaration on the Rights of Indigenous Peoples (UNDRIP), 181
United Nations Environmental Program (UNEP), 167–68, 174, 216, 219
United Nations Framework Convention on Climate Change (UNFCCC), 222–23, 246–47
unsustainability, definition of, 24–25, 80, 88, 149–50
UN-Water, 183

Veblen, Thorstein, 44–45
vertical integration, 118–19

Washington Consensus, 49, 50
water privatization
Cochabamba Declaration on, 208

316 INDEX

water privatization (*cont.*)
    contract provisions and, 205,
        209, 210–12
    democratic decision-making and,
        211–13, 214–15
    effects on consumers and the poor,
        206, 207–10, 212–13
    efficiency of, 207–8, 211, 213–14
    environmental implications
        of, 210–11
    full cost recovery and, 206,
        207, 209–10
    infrastructure deficit argument
        and, 213–14
    municipal finance, debt, and, 129,
        144–45, 205–6, 207, 209
    public-private partnerships
        (PPP)and, 205, 209, 210–11,
        212, 213–14
    remunicipalization and, 208–
        9, 211
    special purpose vehicles (SPVs)
        and, 144–45
    World Bank policies and, 205–7
water scarcity
    agriculture as a contributing cause
        of, 184, 191, 193, 197
    aquifer recharge rates and, 186–
        87, 191
    bottled water and, 202, 203–4
    decoupling and management of,
        194–95, 235
    definitions of, 183–84
    extractive industries and, 202–4
    glacier-fed rivers and, 185–86
    groundwater depletion and, 186–
        89, 197, 198, 199–200
    legal frameworks governing,
        203, 204
    human rights and, 182, 191–92,
        194, 196–97, 204–5, 212–13, 215

impact of urbanization and
    economic growth on, 184, 190
industrial waste and, 193
integrated water resource
    management (IWRM)and,
    190, 210–11
Mar del Plata conference and, 184
physical scarcity as a contributor
    to, 182, 184–85
planetary boundaries and, 1–3
regional variations in, 183–84,
    185, 186–87
sanitation, treatment, and,
    182, 192–94
subsidence, groundwater
    extraction, and, 188
subsidies and, 193
surface water and, 185–86
Sustainable Development Goal
    (SDG) 6, targets, and, 183, 192–
    93, 194, 203–4, 213
virtual water trade and, 196–
    97, 202
water footprint and, 195–97, 199,
    230–31, 235
water-intensive agricultural
    production, 198–201
World Bank and, 187, 191, 193,
    205–6, 207–8, 213–14
See also water privatization
Watson, Robert, 170–71
wealth
    concentration of, 25, 57–58, 65–66,
        88, 89, 90–91, 123–24, 135, 138–
        40, 147, 250–52, 257
    essential services and
        concentration of, 214, 252
    philanthropies and control of,
        90–91, 251
    political power from possession
        of, 57–58, 65–66, 88, 89, 251

INDEX 317

tax havens, tax competition, and preservation of, 35, 138–40, 144–46, 214, 251

World Bank
agriculture and development, 121–22
Doing Business Report, 137
export-led growth, 121–22, 125–26
privatization, 128–29, 205–6, 207–8, 213–14
structural adjustment policies, 128–32
water policies and analysis, 187, 191, 193, 205–6, 207–8, 213–14

World Commission on Environment and Development, 18

World Trade Organization (WTO), 130–31, 258

zoonotic disease, 171